PAUL RADIN

Primitive Religion

ITS NATURE AND ORIGIN

DOVER PUBLICATIONS, INC.

NEW YORK

International Standard Book Number: 0-486-20393-X
Library of Congress Catalog Card Number: 57-4452

Manufactured in the United States of America
Dover Publications, Inc.
180 Varick Street
New York, N. Y. 10014

To Doris

New Preface

I am reprinting *Primitive Religion* without making any alterations in the text apart from one minor correction. In part this is due to circumstances beyond my control, in part it is due to the fact that, despite a number of formulations which I made in my book that today I find too sharp and too uncompromising, I have not altered my viewpoint to any marked degree. On the whole my presentation of the religious beliefs and experiences of primitive peoples has stood the test of time amazingly well.

Perhaps it might be well to restate what I had in view in my book. It was first of all a protest against the manner in which these religions had been described by the majority of anthropologists, missionaries, administrators and students of comparative religion. Secondly, it was an attempt to examine carefully three specific aspects of these religions: the nature of the religious experience itself, the varying degree to which individuals possessed it, and, lastly, the role played by social-economic forces and the extent to which the latter fashioned and directed the basic expressions religion had assumed in the aboriginal world.

Lowie in his well-known work *Primitive Religion* (New York, 1924) was the first to properly emphasize the importance of the religious experience, at least of one type of such experience, but neither he nor anyone else had recognized the part played by the social-economic factor. This neglect was not accidental. Apparently most students of the subject felt, in contradistinction to what admittedly held true for the great historic religions, namely, that they could not be divorced from the vicissitudes of the economic order in which they were embedded and that religion was frequently secondarily utilized for distinctly nonreligious purposes, that this did not occur in the aboriginal world. Even so distinguished an anthropologist and economist as Raymond Firth (*Primitive Economics of the New Zealand Maori*, London, 1929) felt it had no place there. It was to demonstrate that primitive peoples differed only in degree from our own religions in this respect, and that as a matter of fact far cruder and more direct secondary utilizations of religion can be found there than in the historic faiths, that I stressed the economic factor so strongly, particularly in the chapter of my book entitled *The Economic Determinants*. Yet, allowing for over-statements, I do not think that I unduly exaggerated it. I at no time regarded it as determining, in any primary sense, the actual nature of the basic religious beliefs. What I contended was that the economic factor was always present and very frequently determined the direction which the religious expression took and profoundly influenced the formulations made. I doubt whether anyone today would seriously disagree with me on this point.

The stressing of the role of the economic factor was, of course, only one part of the viewpoint I was expounding. As important, if indeed not much more so, was my attempt to define more precisely the psychophysical make-up of those individuals whom we must regard as specifically responsible for the major reformulation and reorganization of the religious beliefs. Here it was particularly important to be certain of the accuracy and the authenticity of the data used. Wherever I could, consequently, I utilized only information given by native informants in their own language or contained in rituals and myths. It cannot be too definitely emphasized that what we must have is a record which tells us what participants in native cultures have themselves said, the generalizations they themselves have made and the speculations in which they themselves have indulged. There exists no substitute for this. No descriptions by even the most perceptive and the most well-informed observers can adequately take its place. Where we are perforce compelled to use such descriptions, and we often are, they must be critically scrutinized and examined and only then accepted when they are properly documented. Even then, for many aspects of our subject, it is best to remain sceptical, for it is almost impossible for a European observer, no matter how objective he tries to be, not to introduce emphases and interpretations which come from his own culture and which are expressions of his own personality. This holds, of course, for me as much as it does for other outside observers.

As to the validity of my own generalizations the reader must judge for himself. I hope I have always made it clear when I was generalizing or indulging in speculations and that I have kept both distinct from those made by native informants.

Lugano, 1956   PAUL RADIN

Preface

The following work is an attempt to describe, in brief compass, the religion and the religious experience of aboriginal peoples. While concrete facts have, I hope, never been neglected, they have been made subsidiary to my main purpose, that of presenting the religions encountered in simple societies, in such manner that the reader will be in a position to understand the individuals and the forces that have been at work in fashioning the basic expressions which religion has there assumed. I have throughout sought to interpret religion in terms of human personalities and not in terms of generalized men and women who are made to serve as a kind of academic cement for vague ideas and still vaguer emotions. For that reason, in spite of my best endeavours, I have derived little help from the works of those of my predecessors who insisted upon emphasizing what they termed the psychological side of religion. These scholars, I cannot but feel, have been playing what might be called a form of intellectual golf, using conceptual pellets to which they have given such names as *supernatural power, awe-inspiring, mystical thrill;* a game, moreover, that seems to have been played in an ideological heaven where, at the end of each day, they find themselves effectively and decisively bunkered. Their method has led to the treatment of religion as if it were completely divorced both from life and from the vicissitudes of the economic order in which each religion is so intimately embedded, and it has contributed, in no small degree, toward making the study of religion an artificial and subjective contemplation of verbalized facts and hypostasized events.

Throughout this book I have chosen my material only from first-hand descriptions and have, wherever possible, used information given in the words of native informants or presented by scholars who knew intimately the culture and the language of the people they were depicting. This procedure has not been prompted by pedantry but by the simple desire to have my presentation and my interpretations rest on as accurate a basis of fact as was possible. For the same reason I have deemed it best to quote the pertinent facts at substantial length instead of contenting myself with short and often meaningless excerpts. In the present condition of acute ignorance which prevails among lay readers with regard to aboriginal religions, the first duty of the scholar is to them.

It is difficult to know whom I have to thank first and to whom I am most indebted for many of the ideas and interpretations here advanced. For more than twenty-five years I have been fairly consistently occupied with the subject of religion, particularly aboriginal religion. During that time I probably have dipped into every book and monograph, large or small, that has appeared. I naturally do not remember all of them or the extent to which I have borrowed or even plagiarized from them, but to forestall any claims of undue originality that may be falsely attributed to me, I hereby humbly and sincerely acknowledge their inspiration, large and small, and surrender all rights to priority. To one source of inspiration, however, I do wish to acknowledge a deep and abiding debt of gratitude, to the Winnebago Indians, who enabled me to obtain an accurate and complete account of their religion and whose influence has been paramount in shaping my notions of aboriginal religions.

—PAUL RADIN

Contents

PRIMITIVE RELIGION

Its Nature and Origin

1

The Nature and Substance of Religion

TO describe the nature of religion is extremely difficult. Obviously it means different things to different people. We may safely insist, however, that it consists of two parts: the first an easily definable, if not precisely specific feeling; and the second certain specific acts, customs, beliefs, and conceptions associated with this feeling. The belief most inextricably connected with the specific feeling is a belief in spirits outside of man, conceived of as more powerful than man and as controlling all those elements in life upon which he lays most stress. On the one hand these two components may be regarded as always having been associated and thus as forming an inseparable and indissoluble whole; on the other, one of them may be regarded as having preceded the other in time.

The customs and beliefs play an important role among all individuals. The specific feeling, on the contrary, varies in degree with each person. The less intense it is, the greater the relief with which the customs and beliefs stand out and the stricter the punctilious adherence to them. The converse is not true, however, for the greatest intensity of feeling may accompany the observance of the customs without any decrease in their importance.

Yet beliefs and customs do not as such contain any religious ingredient. They belong to that large body of strictly folkloristic elements toward which the individual and the group assume an attitude of passive acceptance. They are embedded in a mechanism devised by man for determining and evaluating the interrelationship between him and the external world. What makes certain of them part of the religious unit is their connexion with the specific feeling. The degree in which this feeling exists does not matter nor does it matter whether this feeling is held by every member of the group.

This feeling itself is not a simple unit. Its physiological indications are specific acts which we are accustomed to regard as the external signs of mental and emotional concentration, such as folding the hands, reclining the head, kneeling, and closing the eyes. Psychologically, on the other hand, it is characterized by a far more than normal sensitiveness to specific beliefs, customs, and conceptions, manifesting itself in a thrill, a feeling of exhilaration, exaltation, awe, and in a marked tendency to become absorbed in internal sensations. Negatively one finds an abeyance of interest in external impressions. The condition itself, we may surmise, differs little from such states as intense æsthetic enjoyment or even the joy of living, for example. What distinguishes it from them is the nature of the subject matter calling it forth.

Naturally enough, the specific feeling is not often encountered in a pure form among primitive peoples. It is rare enough among ourselves. From the nature of the folkloristic background with which it has been always specifically associated among primitive men, it has become assimilated to their other emotions as well. This composite feeling may, in the case of certain individuals, frequently dwarf other feelings. With the vast majority of men and women, however, it is only one among others, rising at times to a predominant position yet more frequently becoming almost completely obliterated. Often indeed it is artificial, in the extreme, to attempt a separation.

The other component we have already described. It is the belief, invariably found associated with the specific feeling, in spirits outside of man, to whom are ascribed powers greater than his and who are depicted as in control of everything on which man lays most stress. This, from now on, we shall call the religious feeling. The spirits thus predicated have at all times been identified with the physical and the social-economic background. The specific quality of the religious feeling is thus conditioned by that background. It is the emotional correlate of the struggle for existence in an insecure physical and social environment.

This struggle for existence must not be interpreted too narrowly. It had, particularly in the early phases of man's history, a spiritual as well as a biological side. The spiritual side was concerned with the battle of that reflective consciousness which is the especial earmark of the human as opposed to the animal mind, with the physical make-up he has in common with his animal ancestors. This mentality has expressed itself most clearly in what might be called the social precipitates of fear. Among all peoples these have clustered around three things: first, the physiological facts of birth, puberty, disease, and death; second, the contact of man with the external world and the forces of nature; and third, the collision of man with man.

The manifold customs and beliefs connected with these three elemental forces represent what I have called the social precipitates of fear. Those associated with birth, puberty, disease, and death have conceivably maintained their original form most tenaciously. Physiological facts do, after all, remain unchanged.

It is not surprising then that religion has, at all times, been overwhelmed with such specific precipitates. By themselves, they in no sense partake of the religious, nor would they ever have led to the development of religion as such. And this holds not only for these particular beliefs but for the other elements in religion as well. None of them, as such, contain a religious element and yet they are always found associated with religious feeling. How is this to be explained?

There is, broadly speaking, only one possible explanation, and that is to regard religion as one of the most important and distinctive means for maintaining life-values. As these vary, so will the religious unit vary. Religion is thus not a phenomenon apart and distinct from mundane life nor is it a philosophical inquiry into the nature of being and becoming. It only emphasizes and preserves those values accepted by the majority of a group at a given time. It is this close connexion with the whole life of man that we find so characteristically developed among all primitive cultures and in the early phases of our own civilization. Only when other means of emphasizing and maintaining the life-values are in the ascendant, does religion become divorced from the whole corporate life of the community. "The history of humanity" is, as M. Reinach has very correctly observed, "the history of a progressive laicization."

In the midst of the multiplicity of life-values three stand out most prominently and tenaciously—the desire for success, for happiness, and for long life. Similarly, from among the heterogeneous mass of beliefs, the one which stands out most definitely is the belief in spirits who bestow on man success, happiness, and long life. At the basis of primitive religion there thus lies a specific problem: the nature of the relation of these spirits to the life-values of man. It is well to bear this clearly in mind, for most theorists and theologians have assumed just the reverse. And it is also well to remember that this association is secondary, that it does not flow from the nature of the spirits as originally conceived.

Yet all we have just said does not help us to answer the one question in religion which so many regard as paramount. What is it that originally led man to postulate the supernatural? The reader will, I hope, pardon me if, in answering it, I digress somewhat from my main theme.

To understand the beginnings of religion we must try to visualize as accurately as we can the conditions under which man lived at the dawn of civilization. Manifestly he lived in a variable and essentially inimical physical environment and possessed a most inadequate technological preparation for defending himself against this environment. His mentality was still overwhelmingly dominated by definitely animal characteristics although the life-values themselves—the desire for success, for happiness, and for long life—were naturally already present. His methods of food production were of the simplest kind—the gathering of grubs and berries and the most elementary type of fishing and hunting. He had no fixed dwellings, living in caves or natural shelters. No economic security could have existed, and we cannot go far wrong in assuming that, where economic security does not exist, emotional insecurity and its correlates, the sense of powerlessness and the feeling of insignificance, are bound to develop.

With fear man was born. Of that there can be little doubt. But this fear did not exist in a vacuum. Rather it was the fear inspired by a specific economic situation. All this naturally led to a disorientation and disintegration of the ego. The mental correlate for such a condition is subjectivism, and subjectivism means the dominance of magic and of the most elementary forms of coercive rites. If the psychoanalysts wish to call this narcissism, there can be no legitimate objection.

Expressed in strictly psychological terms the original postulation of the supernatural was thus simply one aspect of the learning process, one stage of man's attempt to adjust the perceiving ego to the things outside himself, that is, to the external world. This attempt did not begin with man. It is clearly rooted in his animal nature and has, from the very beginning, been expressed in three generalized formulae. According to the first one, the ego and the objective world interact coercively; according to the second, man coerces the objective world, and, according to the third, the objective world coerces man. With the coming of man there appeared for the first time a differential evaluation of the ego and the external world. That evaluation which ascribed the coercive power to man alone or to the coercive interaction of the ego and the object found its characteristic expression in magic and compulsive rites and observances; that which ascribed this coercive power to the object found its characteristic expression in the religious activity.

We can arrange this hypothetical evolution, from magic to religion, in four stages:

1. The completely coercive and unmediated. Here the relation between the ego and the objective world is almost in the nature of a tropism.

2. The incompletely coercive and unmediated. Here a measure of volition is imputed to the object.

3. The reciprocally coercive. Here volition is imputed to both the ego and the object.

4. The non-coercive. Here the ego is regarded as being in conscious subjection to the object.

In other words, we are dealing here with a progressive disentanglement of the ego from an infantile subjectivism; the freeing of man, as Freud has correctly observed, from the compulsive power of thought. But this freeing of man from his compulsive irrational anchorage did not take place in that intellectual vacuum with which psychologists so frequently operate, but in a material world where man was engaged in a strenuous struggle for existence. From the very first appearance of man, consequently, there must have begun that economic utilization of religion which has always remained its fundamental characteristic. In fact it is the never-ceasing impact of this doubly real social-economic struggle which has specifically brought about the freeing of man's activities from the compulsive power of thought.

But we have digressed far from our original question. Let us return to it now and, from our new vantage point, ask again: Why did man originally postulate the supernatural?

The correlate of economic insecurity, we have seen, is psychical insecurity and disorientation with all its attendant fears, with all its full feeling of helplessness, of powerlessness, and of insignificance. It is but natural for the psyche, under such circumstances, to take refuge in compensation fantasies. And since the only subject matter existing in that primal dawn of civilization was the conscious struggle of man against his physical and economic environment, and his unconscious struggle against his animal-mental equipment as stimulated by his reflective consciousness, the main goal and objective of all his strivings was the canalization of his fears and feelings and the validation of his compensation dreams. Thus they became immediately transfigured, and there emerged those strictly religious concepts so suggestively discussed by the well-known German theologian Rudolf Otto in his work called *Das Heilige*.[1] Being a theologian and a mystic he naturally misunderstood the true nature of these concepts and of their genesis.

From fear, according to Otto, came awe, the terrible, the feeling of being overpowered and overwhelmed, crystallizing into what he calls the *tremendum* and the *majestas;* out of the sense of helplessness, of powerlessness, of insignificance, came that *creature-feeling* so well described in the Old Testament, and out of the compensation fantasies arose, finally, the concept of that *completely other* which is rooted in the familiar and which is yet entirely new. From the compulsion implied in coercion there developed eventually that willing sense of subjection which is implied in *fascination*. All the ingredients are here from which the supernatural arose. Merged and interpenetrated with what is always primary, the implications of living and the economic struggle for existence in an inimical physical environment, they gave us primitive religion.

Man thus postulated the supernatural in order primarily to validate his workaday reality. But not every man felt the need for it to the same degree, a fact that can be easily demonstrated by examining the differences in the definitions of the supernatural and the formulations of the relationship between the ego and the supernatural postulated as existing. It is of fundamental importance to understand this if we wish correctly or fruitfully to analyse primitive religion.

If religious feeling is to be characterized as a far more than normal sensitiveness to certain customs, beliefs, and superstitions, it is fairly clear that no individual can remain in this state continuously. In some individuals, however, it can be called up easily. These are the truly religious people. They have always been few in number. From these to the essentially unreligious individual the gradations are numerous. If these gradations are arranged in the order of their religious intensity, we have three types: the truly

---

[1] All bibliographical references will be found in the appendix, p. 307 *et seq.*

religious, the intermittently religious, and the indifferently religious. The intermittently religious really fall into two groups—those who may be weakly religious at almost any moment; and those who may be strongly religious at certain moments, such as at temperamental upheavals and crises.

In the intermittently and indifferently religious groups are included by far the large majority of people, but since so many extra-religious factors enter into their religious consciousness, they are actually the most poorly adapted for the study of religion. To understand religion and its developments we must study those individuals who possess the religious feeling in a marked degree. Much of the confusion that exists in so many analyses of primitive religion is due to the fact that, in so far as these analyses were based on the study of distinct individuals, the individuals selected belonged to the class of intermittently religious or, at best, the abnormally religious. The only way of avoiding confusion is to start with the markedly religious individual and then study the expressions of religion among the intermittently and indifferently religious with reference to him.

Yet it is not enough to postulate this division of people into three religious groups; we must also try to discover when the religious feeling is called forth. Now quite apart from the degree of religious susceptibility a given person may possess, it may legitimately be asserted that the members of all three groups show a pronounced religious feeling at certain crises of life, and that these crises are intimately connected with all the important social-economic life-values of the tribe—puberty, sickness, death, famine, etc. The frequent appearance, on such occasions, of temperamental disturbances is unquestionably a great aid in heightening this religious feeling. Whatever be the cause, however, it is during individual and tribal crises that the majority of men and women are possessed of what, in spite of other ingredients, must be designated as a true religious feeling.

It is at crises that the majority of men obtain their purest religious thrill, because it is only at such times that they are prone to permit inward feelings to dominate. Yet more than that: it is only at crises that the majority of men obtain a religious feeling at all. In the case of the markedly religious man the situation is quite different. His specific susceptibility permits him to obtain a religious thrill on innumerable occasions, and since with each thrill are associated certain beliefs and attitudes, he sees the entire content of life from a religious viewpoint. For him the function of religion is always that of emphasizing and maintaining the life-values of man, life-values which are determined by his traditional background and which are always primary. Such is his formulation. And this formulation is taught to the intermittently and indifferently religious, who accept it unhesitatingly as far as they comprehend it. Assuredly they rarely see life entirely from a religious standpoint. There are occasions, however, in the corporate life of a community—such as at a ceremony or a ritual—where a religious feeling is, at times, diffused over the whole content of life. Certainly even the intermittently and indifferently religious who participate in these activities must partake somehow of this feeling. At a ceremony many of the conditions favourable to the calling forth of a religious thrill are given—the presence of truly religious people, acts and customs associated with religious feeling, a conscious detachment from the outer world, and, lastly, the important fact that an individual has been taught to expect a religious feeling at such times.

Summing up, it may be said that all people are spontaneously religious at crises, that the markedly religious people are spontaneously religious on numerous other occasions as well, and that the intermittently and indifferently religious are secondarily religious on occasions not connected with crises at all.

With this difference in religious intensity has always gone a marked difference in the interest manifested in strictly religious phenomena and theories. The non-religious man is simply not articulate in such matters and leaves their definition and formulation entirely to the religiously articulate members of his group. The failure to recognize this has led many ethnological theorists unwittingly into numerous misrepresentations of primitive thought and religion. It lies at the basis of the fundamental error running through one of the major theoretical discussions of primitive mentality written in the last fifty years, the well-known work of M. Lévy-Bruhl, *Les Fonctions mentales dans les sociétés inférieures*. Had M. Lévy-Bruhl recognized the presence of these different types of individuals, I feel confident that he would never have postulated either a *prelogical mentality* or *mystical participation* as the outstanding traits of all primitive thinking and that he would never have been led into the strange error of denying the existence, among primitive groups, of individuals who think as logically as do some of us and who are found alongside of others as irrational as are so many of us. For M. Lévy-Bruhl all primitive thought is really a form of experience lying somewhere between magic and the earliest appearance of religion. What he has really done is to identify all primitive thinking with what is really the very earliest stage of thought, one in which the ego and the external world are regarded as continually constraining each other and where the individual is, in the most unrelieved Freudian fashion, regarded as still completely under the domination of the compulsive power of thought. But such a condition can have applied, at best, only to the very earliest period of man's history. Among no primitive peoples of today is such thinking found, and where certain approximations to it are encountered, they are found among individuals who represent the characteristically non-religious attitude of mind which we have just discussed.

Let me give an illustration. This will show better than any general psychological discussion how these two contrasting types of mind, the religious and the essentially non-religious, approach the concept of the supernatural, particularly the concept of supernatural power which, under the general name of *mana*, has played such a great role in all recent theories of primitive religion. Codrington defined *mana* as "a force altogether distinct from physical power which acts in all kinds of ways for good and evil and which it is of the greatest advantage to possess and control." [2] Subsequent European students of the subject described it differently. Indeed there were certain contradictions in Codrington's own account. The differences between these various authors are of two kinds, one group emphasizing the essentially impersonal aspect of the *mana* concept, the other the personal; one stressing the idealistic-mystical, the other the materialistic-magical side.

We cannot simply dismiss this conflict of opinion as due to a difference in the approach and temperament of the investigators. Manifestly there must have been something in the data themselves that led to this division of opinion.

In all discussions concerning primitive religion it is always best to begin the inquiry with the actual statements of natives and not with the generalizations and syntheses of European observers no matter how correct they may seem. The moment we observe this elementary caution we discover that the informants themselves fall into two groups. An old Maori interviewed in 1921 by Beattie[3] manifestly regarded *mana* as, in no sense, supernatural power *per se*, but rather as something localized in a specific object or at best as personal magnetism. He apparently could not conceive of it in any other manner. The gods differ from man only in the fact that their *mana* can never be overwhelmed or destroyed. Man's can. This particular Maori is thus an excellent example of the religious thinker and formulator, to be contrasted with those Maori who could conceive of *mana* only as supernatural power and who stressed its predominantly magical side, thus representing the non-religious and matter-of-fact individuals. To such a class also belonged the Fiji Islander who told an investigator that "a thing has *mana* when it works; it has no *mana* when it does not work."

Occasionally one is fortunate enough to have a native himself present the two viewpoints. To a Dakota priest we are indebted for the following statement of the priest-thinker's interpretation:

> *Ton* is the power to do supernatural things. All the gods have *ton*. When the people say *ton*, they mean something that comes from a living thing, such as the birth of anything or the discharge from a wound or a sore or the growth from a seed.[4]

And surely it was no religious man who, among the Maori, insisted that gods die unless there are priests to keep them alive, or who permitted one Maori deity to say to another: "When men no longer believe in us, we are dead." But it was a Maori religious thinker and formulator of no low order who described the god *Io-te-pukenga* as "the source of all thought, reflection, memories; of all things planned by him to possess form, growth, life, thought, strength. There is nothing outside his jurisdiction. All things are his." Similarly it was only the religious thinker among the Dakota who could say that

> The *sicun* is an immaterial god whose substance is never visible. It is the potency of mankind and the emitted potency of the gods. Considered relative to mankind, it is many, but apart from mankind it is one.

No further evidence then is needed to demonstrate the existence of two general types of temperament among primitive peoples, that of the priest-thinker and that of the layman; the one only secondarily identified with action, the other primarily so; the one interested in the analysis of the religious phenomena, the other in their effect. To the former *mana* was the generalized essence of a deity residing in an object or in man; to the latter it was magical potency, that which worked, had activity, was an effect.

2

The Role of the Religious Formulator

FOR a proper understanding of primitive religion, it is necessary to know not only why man postulated the supernatural and what purpose it fulfilled but also what individuals in a given society formulated it and the extent to which this formulation differed from man to man. That only a very small number of individuals in any group are interested in making an analysis of religious phenomena and that an even smaller number are qualified to do so, is patent. This is true in our own cultures and holds true to a much greater degree among primitive peoples. Although the number of religious thinkers and co-ordinators is relatively smaller in primitive societies than among ourselves, they nevertheless play an infinitely more important role. Not that their influence as such is greater. It is in fact smaller. But religion among primitive people is concerned with the maintenance of life-values and, since no other means of stressing and maintaining them exist there, it permeates every phase of existence. For this reason the task of the formulator and definer becomes larger, more varied, and more significant.

The predication, among primitive peoples, of religion as essential to success, happiness, and long life or as necessary for meeting and overcoming the crises of life, whether they be strictly biological or economic in character, cannot simply be taken as a self-evident proposition. It must on the contrary be regarded as embodying the theory and interpretation of the specifically religious man and formulator. It inheres neither in the nature of the religious feeling nor is it implicit in the belief in spirits. The degree to which this predication will be regarded as satisfactory and efficacious depends upon the closeness of the relation of the religious unit to the life-values of the members of a given group. Only among the complex civilizations of Africa, Polynesia, and the Americas were these formulators either numerous enough, or did they feel themselves strong enough, to elaborate a consistent theory according to which the spirits were to be venerated for their own sake, or according to which hymns and prayers were to be intoned to them in thankfulness for having created man and the world in which he lived. Among the vast majority of tribes this was not the case, and the strength of religion lay in its being rooted in the everyday life and demands of the community.

This theory is clearly and succinctly set forth in the following exhortation of a Winnebago Indian which I quote in some detail because it is the best description of the interpenetration of every phase of life with religion that I know [1] :

My son, when you grow up, see that you are of some benefit to your fellowmen. There is only one way in which you can aid them and that is by fasting. Our grandfather, the Fire, he who at all times stands in the centre of our dwelling, sends forth many kinds of blessings. Be sure that you make an attempt to obtain his.

Remember to have our grandfathers, the war-chiefs, the spirits who control war, bless you. See that they have compassion upon you. Then, some day, as you travel along the road of life, you will know what to do and encounter no obstacles. Without effort you will then be able to gain the prize you desire. The honour will be yours to glory in. If reverently you fast and thirst yourself to death, then these war-blessings will be bestowed upon you. Yet not without constant effort are these blessings procurable. If you do not possess one of the spirits from whom to obtain this strength and power, you will be of no consequence socially and those around you will show you little respect.

Some day in life you will find yourself travelling along a road filled with obstacles and then you will wish you had fasted.

Try to be a leader of men. Yet not with the blessings of one, not with the blessings of twenty spirits, can you go on the warpath. For that the blessings of all spirits are necessary.

If you cannot obtain war-blessings, fast at least for position in life. If you fast then when you marry you will get along well. You will not have to worry about your having children and your life will be a happy one. Fast for the food you are to receive.

If you are blessed by the spirits and if you then blow your breath upon people who are ill, they will become well. Thus will you help your fellowmen.

Everyone must take care of himself in life and must try to obtain such knowledge as will enable him to live in comfort and happiness. Try therefore to learn about the things you will need. If you know them, then as you travel along in life, you will not have to go to the expense of buying them from others, but you will have your own medicines. If you act in this way and if, in addition, you fast properly, you will never be caught off guard in life.

So shall you travel on your journey through life, along the virtuous road taken by all your fellowmen and your actions and behaviour will never become the butt of your neighbour's sarcasm.

Help yourself as you go along the road of life. The earth has many narrow passages scattered over it. If you have something with which to strengthen yourself, then when you get to these narrow turns you will be able to pass through them safely and your fellowmen will respect you.

This same subordination of religion to the specific needs of man is encountered everywhere. Even in so complex a civilization as that of the semi-Bantu Iyala of northern Nigeria, a priest has no hesitation in reducing the function of the supreme god Awwaw to that of satisfying the particular wants of the moment.

Let rain fall. Make our yams grow big and let us get food [he prays.[2] And then he adds]: We then kill a goat and fowl, leave the blood and feathers and eat the rest with beer. We are not sacrificing at all to Awwaw this year, since rain has fallen early.

Here manifestly the religious man has adjusted himself so completely to the viewpoint of his non-religious fellow-tribesmen that he is practically at one with them. From this to the concepts of some of the more sophisticated Maori, the West African and Dakota priests, not to mention, of course, the ancient Mexicans and Peruvians, the gradations are numerous.

Wherever economic conditions permitted, a priesthood of some kind developed whose purposes were always of a twofold nature. The first purpose was so to elaborate and manipulate the religious beliefs that they would strengthen the authority of the elders, in this manner also strengthening their own, for they generally belonged to the same age group. The second purpose was the attainment and enhancement of the priests' economic security. Thus freed from the urgent requirements of having to spend the greater part of their lives in the pursuit of food for themselves, the shaman, medicine-man, or priest found himself, in contradistinction to the other members of his group, provided in varying degree with the leisure necessary for the analysis and synthesis of the religious phenomena. And where the economic order was such that the wealth and power of the community was actually concentrated in their hands, in West Africa, for instance, there an aristocracy could develop which at times expressed itself in abstract thinking of a high order. Among the Yoruba, for example, we encounter the following hymn with its highly ethical concern, at least theoretically, for the slave and the orphan:

I

The sun shines and sends its burning rays down upon us,
The moon rises in its glory.
Rain will come and again the sun will shine.
And over it all passes the eye of God.
Nothing is hidden from him.
Whether you be in your home, whether you be on the water,
Whether you rest in the shade of a tree in the open,
Here is your master.

II

Did you think that because you were more powerful than some poor
  orphan,
You could covet his wealth and deceive him,
Saying to yourself, "I cannot be seen"?
So then remember that you are always in the presence of God.
Not today, not today, not today!
But some day he will give you your just reward
For thinking in your heart
That you have but cheated a slave, an orphan.

Similarly, among the Maori, where a most rigid caste system
prevailed, the thinker-priests of the upper caste elaborated a
theology of the most transcendental kind clustering around the
worship of a deity named Io who is completely unknown to the
lower caste and the plebeians. This Io is endowed with a series
of names of a highly abstract and abstruse nature. He is Io-the-
omnierudite, Io-the-unseen-face, Io-the-everlasting, Io-the-immu-
table, Io-the-parentless, Io-who-renders-not-to-man-that-which-he-
withholds. He is the origin of all things and he has retained for
himself the spirit and the life and the form. There is nothing outside or beyond him, and with him is the power of life, of death,
and of godship.

Different in their way but still specifically representing a special
class were the priests of the Dakota. The social-economic order in
which they flourished was a democracy where wealth and prestige
belonged to the custodians of the rituals who, at the same time,
were the acknowledged warriors. These priests formed close fraternities in which they developed an esoteric theology and an
amazing analysis of the subjective requirements for a true religious
experience. One of the priests soliloquizes:

All classes of people know that when human power fails, they must
look to a higher power for the fulfilment of their desires. There are

many ways in which the request for help from this higher power can be made. This depends on the person. Some like to be quiet and others want to do everything in public. Some like to be alone, away from the crowd, to meditate upon many things. In order to secure a fulfilment of his desire a man must qualify himself to make his request. Lack of preparation would mean failure to secure a response to his petition. Therefore when a man makes up his mind to ask a favour of *Wakan tanka* he makes due preparation. It is not fitting that a man should suddenly go out and make a request of *Wakan tanka*.

When a man shuts his eyes, he sees a great deal. He then enters his own mind, and things become clear to him, but objects passing before his eyes would distract him. For that reason a dreamer makes known his request through what he sees when his eyes are closed. He resolves to seek seclusion on the top of a butte or other high place. When at last he goes there he closes his eyes, and his mind is upon *Wakan tanka* and his work.

No man can succeed in life alone, and he cannot get the help he wants from men.[3]

Yet in spite of the power even such priests wielded, nowhere do we find that glorification of a deity for its own sake which is so characteristic of the later Hebrew religion and the religions based upon it. Such conceptions would have been regarded as totally anti-social. Even in Peru, where the Inca was conceived as the direct descendant of the sun-god and where priest-poet could exclaim:

O Creator! O conquering Uiracocha, ever present Uiracocha!
Thou who art in the ends of the earth without equal!
Thou who gavest life and valour to man . . .

even here, there is no lengthy stressing of his greatness or an ecstatic extolling of his goodness but, instead, the hymn concludes with the simple request for life:

Grant this with long life
And accept this sacrifice,
O Creator!

The role of the religious formulator, with regard both to his own special group and to the community at large, was thus to interpret and manipulate the psychological correlates of the economic-social realities. Stated more concretely, his task was to define and elaborate both his own viewpoint and that of the matter-of-fact man. Essentially he was a "materialist," interested in the objective world, as opposed to the non-religious man, who was an inconsistent "idealist," in spite of his marked pragmatism or possibly by very virtue of it.

This seems to be precisely the reverse of what held and still holds for the theologians and the religious speculators of the great historic faiths, who are all idealists and mystics. But these, it must be remembered, are completely removed from the strife of life. They are in fact kept individuals. They possess no temporal authority and are simply adjuncts of this temporal power, lending their abilities to strengthening and extending it. Among primitive peoples, however, the situation was quite different. Wherever centralized authority developed, this was in the hands of the medicine-man or priest. If, consequently, his philosophical viewpoint was largely that of the materialist, this was not so much the reflection of any inherent mental trait as the reflection of his status and political power. Where there is little trace of a centralized authority, there we encounter no true priests, and religious phenomena remain essentially unanalysed and unorganized. Magic and simple coercive rites rule supreme.

The degree of objectivity attained by a given religious thinker in a primitive community, in the main, therefore reflects the degree of centralized authority it possesses. Since this varies in a most bewildering fashion from tribe to tribe, no consistent standard of objectivity prevails, nor does the analysis and synthesis of the religious formulator obtain general acceptance.

Bearing all this in mind we can now turn specifically to a description of the formulator's task. We begin with the knowledge that the definitions and formulations are dictated by the formulator's economic status and political power and by the large body of beliefs, customs, and rites which have, from time immemorial, clustered around the life-values of man and the physiological crises of life. How this task was effected, and the precise manner in which the religious thinker revaluated and reinterpreted the folkloristic background, emerge most clearly when the two viewpoints, the religious and non-religious, are contrasted.

In so vast a subject we can touch on only a few points. I shall accordingly confine myself to a discussion of magic and magical rites, the conception of spirits and deities, and the nature of their relation to man. Our remarks will apply, of course, equally to other aspects of religion such as the interpretations of disease and death, the doctrine of the soul, and the belief in immortality. But before we take up the thread of our analysis again, it is highly important to indicate briefly the nature of the association of the folkloristic background to the various aspects of man's life, personal and communal.

Magic has always been regarded as self-evident among primitive peoples, and elaborate arguments have been advanced to explain it. The legitimate objection to most of these explanations is that they are generally in a vacuum, that they almost always centre around the general problem of the purposes to be served by magic, and that they customarily end by effectively detaching the content of magic from the individuals who actually practise it. To prevent this we shall begin by asking a simple question. Who in primitive societies benefits most materially from the performance of magical rites? The answer is simple and decisive—the medicine-man, the shaman, and the priest. He is paid doubly for his services, first by receiving gifts either in the form of money or its equivalent and, secondly, by acquiring power. It is to his interest to invest as much of the daily life of a group as he possibly can with magical implications and rites. This does not mean that societies do not exist where every man is, so to speak, his own magician. They do; but they are few in number.

Our first question necessitates a second. Can we, without further analysis, calmly assume that fear is the primordial emotion with which man began? The answer must be definitely in the affirmative, but not in the sense claimed by most ethnological theorists. They think of fear in a generic fashion, as something inherited from our animal forebears. They are all fond of treating it as an instinct. They consequently speak of a fear of the dark, of a fear of the unknown, of a fear of the strange. But, psychology aside, what does the documentary evidence we now possess for primitive cultures in the form of prayers, myths, and autobiographies tell us about the nature of this primary fear? The answer is clear. Primitive man is afraid of one thing, of the uncertainties of the struggle of life. And we can be fairly certain that this fear of life is not the last remnant of the trauma of birth as some psychoanalysts contend. On the contrary, it is a very literal fear of the battle for existence under the difficult economic conditions that prevail in simple societies. The more uncertain is the food supply, the less man is technologically prepared, the greater naturally will be the feeling of insecurity and the more intense, consequently, will be the fear. That is why, in the very simple cultures, the world is regarded as more consistently infested with evil spirits and ill-willed ghosts than in the more complex. The fear of the struggle for life, however, is always there. A priest may phrase it symbolically as the narrow passages of life, as among the Winnebago, or resignedly, as the Fijian poem has it—

> Death is easy:
> Of what use is life?
> To die is rest ——

yet it is fear in the only concrete sense in which this means anything for the vast majority of men and women, namely, the dread of hunger and of economic insecurity.

Looking at it from this angle, we may well doubt whether the great physiological crises of life—birth, puberty, death—are more inherently the object of fear than are *per se* disease, pregnancy, or the sight of blood. Nor is it by any means self-evident that a man will be obsessed with the fear that a food animal will not appear at the appropriate time or that the grain will not mature or that the sun will not shine. Indeed the vast majority of individuals in a primitive group are quite averse to the phrasing of a problem in this negative manner. If, nevertheless, we do find it stated in this fashion, it is but natural to ask to whose interest it is to do so. Who, concretely speaking, would gain by it? The answer is: those credited with possessing the power to allay these doubts and fears. And so we again return to the medicine-men and the priests.

Whether there be such a thing as primordial fear or not is consequently immaterial. What is material is whether any evidence exists to link up the utilization of this primordial fear with the means and methods of obtaining food, with the achievement of personal and social values and aspirations, and with the physiological crises of life. That evidence is overwhelming. And since it is equally clear that there exists no reason for regarding such a linkage as inherent in the nature of any one of the constituent elements involved, we must assume it to be secondary in origin and that it has been established largely by those who have most to gain thereby. This does not mean that the religious man *per se* originated the connexion or that there are not, at the same time, certain social precipitates of fear which obviously antedate his activity.

We must visualize the situation then somewhat as follows. The religious formulator, at first unconsciously if you will, capitalized on the sense of insecurity of the ordinary man. This task was rendered all the more urgent, first, because the medicine-men and shamans themselves shared in this insecurity and, secondly, because of the very emotional-intellectual susceptibility which we have credited them with possessing. To judge from our data, this capitalization took the form of so interpreting the obstacles to success in the struggle for food, for happiness, and for long life, that they would appear greater than they really were. Possibly these obstacles may have actually seemed so to their highly sensitive and imaginative minds. But we must not forget that it was to their interest to do so.

In other words, the religious formulator developed the theory that everything of value, even everything unchangeable and predictable about man and the world around him, was surrounded and immersed in danger, that these dangers could be overcome only in a specific fashion and according to a prescription devised and perfected by him. This prescription stated, in addition, that the linkage and interpenetration of every aspect of life with the folkloristic background, and particularly with those magical practices which seem almost in the nature of compulsive neuroses, had existed from the beginning of man's appearance on earth. It was not argued that a specially qualified individual was needed to perform magical rites. This was, in fact, open to everyone. Yet it is clear that, if magic was to become part of the religious formulation, it had either to be transformed into something different from its original nature or employed in a different manner. This consequently became the first major task of the religious formulator.

The analysis of the struggle of the early religious thinker to displace or reinterpret magic abundantly demonstrates the correctness of the viewpoint that magic has everywhere preceded religion. It can be proved in other ways as well. Only where the thinker's position, however, was moderately secure and only under special economic-social conditions were his religious formulations ever generally accepted and not hopelessly distorted by the infiltrations and implications of the practices of magic.

The role of the religious formulator with respect to magic, as well as in other aspects of the folkloristic background, was thus concerned primarily with the freeing of a given act or rite from its compulsive and purely mechanical character. All magic, as we have seen, consists in the coercion of an object so that it will comply with the wishes and desires of the performer. The magical attitude is in its very nature so completely subjective that every act, every utterance and thought, of the individual attains an independent reality and becomes, in its turn, an object. But the moment it is, as it were, detached from him, it becomes inimical and dangerous. The purpose of every magical procedure is consequently to prevent the object, after it has once been brought under coercion, from acquiring independence. Only in this way can it be prevented from becoming dangerous and does it operate to a person's advantage.

When, consequently, M. Reinach in his felicitous manner, contends that, "thanks to magic, man takes the offensive against the objective world," what he is really thinking of is not so much magic as the role it has been given by the religious formulator.

In the analysis we have given above there are two premises: first, that primitive man has, from the very beginning, been able to distinguish in his thinking between himself and the outside world; and, second, that he does not assume the outside world as such to be inimical to him. It only becomes so secondarily when it clashes with the attainment of a strictly subjective goal. The first premise has never been seriously questioned except by M. Lévy-Bruhl and some of the psychoanalysts. We must, of course, not forget that the outside world of the matter-of-fact individual in primitive society is not a static world. It is being continually enlarged and altered by the projections of the thoughts and emotions of his waking and his sleeping state. That these are subjective in origin does not interfere with their becoming *bona fide* objects and of their being considered such. No mystical participation and no prelogical mentality need be or should be predicated. The justification for the second premise will become increasingly clearer to the reader as we proceed.

The task of the formulator thus becomes clear. He must—this cannot be stressed enough—free the magical act from its compulsive character. This task takes on two general forms: one which may be called its socialization, and the other, a transference of the coercive power from the subject to the object. In both cases there is a definite development away from an extreme type of subjectivism to some form of objectivism. It is because disease and death could not very well be attributed to any intrinsic desire of the ego for the self-infliction of pain or for self-destruction and had to be charged to some outside agency, that the first indications of objective thinking are to be found in the theories connected with their causation. The psychoanalysts of the Freudian school who have given considerable attention to the origin and growth of magic and religious beliefs wish apparently to push the analysis of thought still further back. To them the fear of disease and death simply constitutes one form of their favourite castration theme. But here, as in other instances where they are reconstructing the history of man, it is utterly impossible to accept their type of demonstration, quite apart from the doubts one may have concerning the accuracy of their data.

This socialization of cravings and goals originally highly individualistic is accomplished by objectivizing the attitude of the performer of a given magical rite and by the injection into his attitude of certain personal ethical qualifications, as well as by the insistence that the successful outcome of a rite subserve the good of the group and not simply the needs of a particular individual. In other words, the attitude toward the object to be coerced as well as the function the magical procedure is to subserve must become socialized. It is not strange, accordingly, that where the influence of the religious thinker is great, specific subjective requirements have been worked out for the approach to the magical and supernatural. The whole situation becomes objectivized—the psychical attitude of the participant, the contents of his mind, the end to be attained, and the function to be served by the coercion. These requirements are naturally not numerous in magic. If they were, magic would cease to be magic.

To illustrate the points we have just made, let me give a few examples.

Among the Maori, as among the vast majority of primitive peoples, a charm is recited over the corpse of a child in order to dispatch the soul to spiritland. The belief generally current in the simpler societies with regard to the relationship between the dead and the living is unequivocal. None should exist. Hence their funeral rites are always concerned with attempts at assuring the dead a quick, safe, and immediate passage to the next world and at preventing the ghost after death from hovering around the scenes endeared to him, any longer than can be helped. This is the primary purpose of the Maori charm. But the actual words seem to bear witness to something else, to introduce a new note. They run as follows:

Farewell, O my child! Do not grieve; do not weep; do not love; do not yearn for your parent left by you in the world. Go thou for ever. Farewell for ever.

Here manifestly both a clarification and a rationalization have taken place. We find not merely a message of farewell to the dead child but a statement of the specific conditions that would interfere with the immediate and permanent separation of the deceased from his family. And it should be specifically noted that although, this being a charm, the performer must be well aware of the fact that an object is to be coerced, and although the dangers attendant upon failure to coerce it successfully are well known, there is a clear appreciation of why the object should not want to be coerced. The fact that the object is a human being in no sense invalidates such an interpretation.

Now it is this new note, we insist, which indicates that the religious formulator has been at work. A fundamentally similar transformation was made by religious thinkers among other peoples as well, thus, for instance, among the Ojibwa of the eastern United States and Canada. Although we are dealing in the latter case with the reinterpretation of a myth and not specifically with a magical rite, it is quite pertinent in this connexion.

When, among the Ojibwa, an individual dies, it is believed that he still remains as sentient a being as when he was alive. His death has simply barred him from communicating with the living in a manner that they can recognize. His soul, still fully conscious and still possessed of all human longings and desires, travels to the land of the dead until it comes to a huge strawberry. If he partakes of it, then his return to the land of the living, alive, is for ever impossible. If he refuses, there is still the possibility of his returning. As far as the living are concerned, he possesses all the normal human desires and he is, accordingly, still a potential danger. As he flits along to his final destination he is suddenly seized from behind, and the Skeleton-Woman of the Land of the Dead breaks open his skull, takes out his brains, and substitutes for them a piece of moss. This completes his transformation from a sentient to a non-sentient being and frees him from his attachment to the world of men. What is so characteristic here is this, that, although the real objective remains the permanent dispatching of the soul of the deceased to the next world for the good of the community, most of the solicitude and sympathy expressed seems to be for the dead man.

In those tribes where there are no specially recognized medicine-men, as among the Kiwai Papuans of British New Guinea, for instance, no such concern for the dead is felt. The dead man is helped in no way. As in so many tribes, the spirits are believed, after death, to linger near their former home reluctant to leave the scenes endeared to them, and desirous of seeing their relatives before parting for ever. But, in contradistinction to the Ojibwa, the Kiwai keep their doors barred and, throwing food to the ghosts, cry: "Go back; do not come; you belong to the dead; it is not good for you to come." [4] Here we have the unrelieved folkloristic background unsystematized and uninterpreted.

The influence of the priest on the magical practices connected with the food supply is perhaps smallest even where his power is definitely marked. Yet there too it can frequently be detected. Among the Winnebago Indians, for instance, there exists a rite called "concentration of the mind" which is employed before hunting bears. The designation is manifestly due to the religious thinker. The rite itself is a typical example of coercion taking the usual form of a symbolical enticing of the animal through gifts of food. However, its efficacy does not depend simply upon the hunter's concentrating his mind upon the bear; the bear, too, must in some manner signify his awareness of what is taking place. This is indicated by having a streak of flame dart from the fireplace toward the gifts. The mind of the bear consents, in this manner, to having its possessor killed the next day. Here again we have an illustration of the primary function of the religious thinker, namely, to mitigate the rigorousness of the coercion exercised by the ego upon the object and a granting to the object of both independence and a measure of free will.

From the reinterpretation of magic let us now turn to the revaluations and reassessments which the religious formulator has introduced into the concept of the nature of the spirits and deities, as well as their relation to man.

For the religious as for the non-religious individual in primitive communities, the spirits and deities have no meaning except in their relation to the life-values and economic realities of man. The earliest and most persistent interpretation of this relationship is, we have seen, the magical-coercive. According to this view the spirit or deity is simply an object temporarily or permanently associated with the supernatural power to be coerced. If we can trust Landtman [5], among the Kiwai we find such a condition in all its purity. There, so it is contended, not only the conception of spiritual beings differs from one group or even individual to another but the magical practices vary still more. The natives will practise one rite as long as it seems to be of some avail and change to another when it fails them. The attitude of the Kiwai toward these spiritual beings thus represents coercion in its crudest form.

But even where the tribes concerned have highly developed civilizations, like that of the Maori or those of West and East Africa, coercion of the spirits is by no means infrequent. While the explanation of the character it has assumed in these cultures is of a highly special economic order, yet it does hold true that, even in the most highly organized societies, magical coercion plays a great role in religion. That is, of course, to be expected in view of its economic importance and the nature of its utilization.

The task of the religious formulator is consequently far more complex in these more highly organized societies than when he is dealing simply with the reorganization and revaluation of the folkloristic background. It is likewise more contradictory. As a thinker, for instance, he is impelled to transform coercion into willing consent; yet, as one who has most to gain by accentuating the difficulties of the approach to the spirits and the gaining of their help, he must insist on attention to minutiæ which play right into the hands of the very magical practices he wishes to displace. As a theologian he must give the deities real definiteness and separate them, as far as he can, from the turmoil of life; as a medicine-man or priest whose power depends upon the ordinary man he must, on the contrary, emphasize their closeness to this average man by indicating their relationship to his food supply and his life-values. Finally, to satisfy his own artistic-intellectual temperament he must elaborate the attitudes of humility, reverence, other-worldliness, and willing subjection to divine control. Yet these are apt to lead him to a subjectivism which, precisely among those primitive societies where the medicine-man or priest is politically dominant, is regarded as definitely antisocial. Thus the further he separates himself from the mass of people, the greater becomes the danger of the development of hostility toward him, a hostility latent, of course, in his whole position from the very beginning because he is an individual whose economic security depends only in part on his own exertions to secure food. Nor must we forget that he has many competitors with whom he is always in passive or active conflict.

Against this hostility threatening him from all directions he must secure himself by establishing some compromise with the attitudes, beliefs, and magical practices of the people. That, under these circumstances, his formulations and clarifications should not have attained a high degree of consistency and are rarely completely purged of older accretions is easily understandable. Given the economic milieu of all but a very few primitive societies, the conditions at best were distinctly unfavourable to the development of that particular type of leisure so essential for the emergence of consistent and well-integrated systems of thought, religious or other.

Allowing then for all these cross-purposes and cross-currents, let us examine the work of the religious formulator concretely. The ordinary conception of the relationship of a man to a spirit who dispenses happiness, long life, and success is, we have seen, one of coercion, just as it is toward an object in no way connected with the supernatural. In the evolution of religious thought this is the first point the thinker-priest attacks. He must at first proceed carefully and not too rapidly. The spirits and deities are, accordingly, represented as aware of the coercion and they are given an opportunity of either submitting to or avoiding it. An incident in a Winnebago myth illustrates this attitude neatly.

In this myth, the older buffalo-spirits are represented as cautioning the younger ones against approaching that part of the heavens through which the fumes from the tobacco offerings made by human beings ascend from the earth, for if they once inhale them they must appear on earth as real buffaloes to be shot by men. They have no choice but to stay away for, being young, they have not developed that resistance to the hypnotic effects of tobacco which the older spirits presumably possess.

In another Winnebago myth which bears evidence of marked reinterpretation the rationalization has gone a few steps farther. Earthmaker, the supreme creator of the Winnebago, is depicted as taking pity on the human race because, having created it last, all the gifts he possessed had already been distributed to the various spirits.

Thereupon [so runs the account] he created a herb which had a pleasant odour and which all the spirits immediately desired. But to them he said: "To all of you I have already given something valuable. You are all fond of this herb, is it not so? I am myself." Then he took some of the leaves, mashed them up, and, filling a pipe, smoked. The odour was pleasant to inhale. All the spirits craved for it and so he gave each one a puff and said: "Whatever, from now on, the human beings ask of me and for which they offer tobacco, that I will not be able to refuse. I myself will not be in control of this herb and since, of all these I have created, the human beings alone are poor, if they offer us a pipeful and make some request, we shall always grant it."

Here we have the coercive-magical relationship between the worshipper and the deity almost completely transformed into a conscious consent of the deity to accept an offering. Of the older conception of a magical constraint only the irresistibility of the tobacco fumes remains.

All the stages in the evolution from an uncontaminated magical formula and rite to a full-fledged contract between two willing agents can be discovered in this tribe; indeed, even a later stage, in which the worshipper is made to realize that even the fumes of tobacco have no intoxicating effect upon the deity and that a worshipper must approach him humbly and be pure in heart.

This is impressed upon the worshipper with pitiless rigour in a fasting experience recounted in one of their rituals. Here the spirits, angered at the presumption of a suppliant for power, send one deceptive messenger after another to him until he finally realizes what is required of him.[6]

At first [so the text runs] he thought he would fast once more just to spite the spirits who were deceiving him. But now he rubbed charcoal on his face and wept bitterly. In both hands he held tobacco and, facing the direction from which the night-spirits came, he stood weeping. Indeed he put himself in the most abject condition. To its very depths did his heart ache.

A final stage in the evolution of the concept of a deity is exhibited by a prayer taken from the same ritual. There we shall find illustrated terror, awe, humility, and the subordination of one's personal desires and hopes to the good of the group. It runs as follows:

Long ago our ancestors asked the spirits to bless them with life so that they might be happy. Here we are sitting around a fireplace and the spirits are extending life not only to our host and his band but to everyone. . . . And here am I, a person of no importance, permitted nevertheless to impersonate a spirit to whom offerings are to be made. Indeed I have been asked to impersonate one of the bravest of all the spirits, that one who is in control of the power of killing an enemy outright. On one side of his body this spirit controls life and on the other death. The worshippers are about to offer him a white dog, white feathers, and tobacco, all of them objects pleasing to Disease-Giver, and they will ask him for war power and for life. He is indeed a fear-inspiring spirit . . . and of all those that exist his is the name that one must not utter lightly. If then I pronounce his name and speak about this spirit whom, at the request of our host, I am impersonating, grant that I may not thereby be weakened!

Of this particular spirit, Disease-Giver, it is believed that no one knows which side he will present to the suppliant, his death-dealing or his life-giving. Here, of course, the suppliant asks that he direct his death-dealing gift toward the enemy. Surely this is a conception of the deity that must be regarded as a very late priestly transformation.

These Winnebago examples may be taken as typical of the general role played by the religious formulator everywhere. Naturally, economic, social, and political conditions alter the precise form his activity will take among different tribes. The Winnebago, for instance, are hunters and fishermen, with whom agriculture, while practised, is secondary. The disparity between the views of the religious thinker and the layman is, as a rule, not so very great there. In Africa, however, where complex types of society based on agriculture and on stock-raising exist and where a most intricate system of commodity exchange prevails, the disparity between the views of the religious thinker and the mass of people is, at times, unbridgeable. Populations are larger and society is markedly stratified. Moreover, since the security and power which priests can obtain are considerable, competition is intense and results in a race between them for the favour of the ordinary man. This means that their dialectical abilities are turned away from some of the problems with which a Winnebago thinker, for instance, would concern himself.

The average African priest is interested primarily in elaborating the magico-folkloristic background which, here in Africa, is closely intertwined with the worship of ancestors. To do this he must dispense with the theory of a simple coercion of the deity. He has in fact nothing to gain thereby and everything to lose. His theory is simple: relatives, living and dead, can best be approached through gifts. If coercion is out of the question, they can still be threatened and they must be made to keep their promise. It must also be remembered that the average man in these civilizations is economically fairly well secure; not easily satisfied and not easily duped. All these factors contributed to the stress's being laid by the priests not on the elaboration of the nature of the deity or the subjective qualifications of the suppliants but on the minutiæ of sacrifice and the role of the priest as an intermediary between two uncertain clients. Everything else was, so to speak, open. Only a somewhat sceptical and realistic solution was, accordingly, workable. Take, for instance, this prayer of the Shilluk of the Sudan [7] in connexion with the treatment of a sick person:

I implore thee, thou God. How are the people kept by thee all days! And thou walkest in the midst of the high grass and I walk with thee. . . . There is no one above thee, thou God. Thou becamest the grandfather of Nyikango; it is thou, Nyikango, who walkest with God. . . . If a famine comes is it not given by thee? So as this cow stands here, is it not thus: if she dies does her blood not go to thee? Thou God, to whom shall we pray, if it is not to thee? . . .

And then follow the details of the sacrifice. A cow is to be speared and the contents of her stomach taken out and thrown on the body of the sick person. One ear of the cow is to be cut off, cut into strips, tied together, and then attached to the leg of the patient. The right foreleg of the cow is also to be cut off, at once cooked and given to the people to taste. Then a broth of it is to be made and poured on the ground. It is the property of the god.

Manifestly here there is no danger that the average man will ever be lost sight of. Naturally, likewise, where the rewards for the priests were so ample, the competition among them would be tremendous, and so would be the specialization of their functions. In this general turmoil the god himself becomes of almost no importance. In the following example from the Dian of the Upper Volta of the Gold Coast of Africa [8] he is practically displaced as a force, in spite of all the pious phraseology. This example also affords us an idea of the somewhat perilous position of the priest in the face of a querulous public:

After the field is sown and no grain grows because no rain has fallen, the people of the village repair to the house of the earth-priest and say to him: "How comes it that no rain has fallen and yet you remain silent?" And the priest replies: "It is true. Do you now go away and return at dawn tomorrow. Catch a chicken and offer it to the rain-maker so that he may induce the rain to come." The next day the earth-priest himself carries a white or black chicken to the rain-maker, telling him: "Take this and call the rain lest we do not eat this year." The man answers: "God is strong; he can do everything; I nothing. Go then and be patient for two or three days. If the rain comes, then that will prove that I have done my utmost. If it does not come, that does not mean that it is my fault. If it falls, every master of a household in the village must bring me a chicken. If not, send a child to me so that I can give him the chicken already presented, for that means God has refused to grant his favour. Then you should go to another rain-maker so that he, in turn, may try his luck."

Here no one is willing to take a definite position, neither the priest nor the rain-maker nor, for that matter, the god. The people and the economic situation are in complete control and, with them, the magico-folkloristic background and the direct pragmatic viewpoint of the non-religious man.

But that, under favourable circumstances such as the existence of an aristocratic priestly class, some time would be devoted to religious philosophic speculation, the poem quoted on pages 18–9 amply attests. To this poem let me add the following Ewe discourse on God and the world:

When night or day approaches do we know what is going to happen to us on either occasion? But whether we are in a stream or whether it is night, we are everywhere still in the world. That is why we say that God is the world. Everything in the world is the creation of God: the fish in the water, men, good and evil, God has sent them all. The world is stronger than everything else and that is why we say that the world is God. You only know what you can know today, not that which is to take place in the future. God alone knows what will take place tomorrow. Mankind will never be able to comprehend God completely and that is why we say the world is God. No one can know everything that happens in the world.[9]

This same preoccupation with the refinement and systematization of the magico-folkloristic background found so characteristically developed in Africa is encountered in many other parts of the world, in fact, wherever a stratified society exists and an elaborate system of exchange of goods takes place. It is prevalent throughout Melanesia and Polynesia and can be legitimately regarded as an incipient form of modern commodity-fetishism. Throughout this area, and the same holds true essentially for Africa, it is not only the naturally religious individuals who strive for the lucrative position of priest. The non-religious individuals also compete and they bring with them the attitude of mind of such people, a fact reflected in the restrictions imposed on the speculative-creative activities of the religious formulator. This restriction is still further emphasized where a true caste society develops, as in parts of Melanesia and throughout Polynesia, for there the dominant caste employs the magico-folkloristic background to maintain its own control and to keep the commoners in subjection. Only a member of the ruling caste, for instance, is given the opportunity to become a religious systematizer, and his formulations naturally would be in the interests of his own group. To introduce any suggestion of freedom of choice is emphatically not in its interest. Instead of transforming the coercive nature of the magical rites such a thinker, on the contrary, stresses and magnifies it. That he, at the same time, also systematizes the spells and elaborates the rites a hundredfold is, of course, true, but this does not loosen his hold on the machinery of worship, for it remains completely in the hands of his own group. Herein lies the explanation for the tremendous significance attached to spells and incantations throughout this region. It represents the utilization of the most archaic forms of the magical rite by a special caste for the purpose of preserving its own position and securing the emoluments that flow from it—power, wealth, and security.

Dr. Malinowski [10] has described those spells well and demonstrated the intricate and amazing manner in which an elaborate economic system can be tied up with them. He has also indicated, in masterly fashion, the various factors that enter, for instance, into the building of a sea-going canoe; how a series of workers—first the owner, then the expert or experts, then a certain group of special helpers, and finally the whole community—participate, and he has pointed out the different systems of magic used during the various stages of the construction. Unfortunately he has failed utterly to explain why in a society so highly organized as that of the Trobriand Islanders we find no suggestions of a religious development higher than that of systematized spells and why the only synthesis of which the religious thinker was capable consisted in the elaboration of a theory of magic. Why should a viewpoint and an approach universally characteristic of societies organized on the simplest economic basis be the dominant trait of one possessing agriculture, stratified classes, and a system of exchange of unusual intricacy? In all such cases it is obligatory for an investigator to ask himself the simple question: who profits by this system and by such a theory? We have attempted an analysis above.

There is no need for additional examples here. I have tried to

show in this chapter the various ways in which the religious formulator impresses his personality and thought upon the folkloristic
background of his group. The larger questions, his influence upon
the development of deities from spirits, the elaboration of the
evidence for the existence of the supernatural and of the more
precise definitions of its nature, all these must be relegated to
future chapters.

3

The Economic Determinants

ALL students of ethnology are agreed that religion permeates every phase of primitive culture. To admit this, however, is really to say that the struggle for existence permeates every phase of life there. From the very nature of the case such a struggle must be conceived as largely economically conditioned. This fact has always been recognized theoretically. In practice, unfortunately, it has frequently been forgotten, due in large measure to the decay of native civilizations today but in some degree also to the popularity, during the last twenty-five years, of a pseudo-psychological approach. The travellers and missionaries of the seventeenth, eighteenth, and early nineteenth centuries had always been aware of it. In fact no great insight or vast accumulation of information was required to recognize the role of the economic determinants in the simpler civilizations and the specific and intimate connexion there of the method of food production with every phase of the struggle for wealth and power. This struggle took place in the less advanced cultures between individuals and between social and ceremonial units of various kinds, while in the more complex societies it developed between fairly well-delineated classes.

Let me state at the outset that I am fully aware of the danger that lurks in any over-emphasis of the economic side of religion and magic; I know how easy it is to minimize the importance of their actual content and of the multiple and often independent aspects religion and magic have taken on. I do wish to stress, however, that no correct understanding of the fluctuations either in their content or in their form is possible unless this interrelationship with the economic forces is fully recognized. Religious beliefs and attitudes were assuredly not created either by methods of food production or by some mechanism of exchange. But they did grow up together with them, and it was the economic system that made certain constituents and certain forms of religion relevant at one period and others relevant at another. It is well at all times to remember this fact. But more than this. The elaborations and superstructures religion has developed in its own right, whether they have ever become socially relevant or not, also constitute an essential part of its study and they will be given their due place.

Let us start with the beginning. Whatever may have been the mode of production in early palæolithic times, today there exists no tribe whose economic life is based on only one method of obtaining food. Not a few peoples exist today, it is true, whose economy is basically that of food-gatherers, but a certain amount of fishing and hunting is always practised even among these. The social and political organization of such tribes is generally of the simplest and most undifferentiated type and their technological equipment is on an equally low level. This is not to deny, of course, that a considerable degree of organization has taken place in the political-economic sphere.

It is not surprising then to find that, in such societies, the religious conceptions are completely dominated by magic and coercive rites, that no traces of religious leadership are encountered, and that no real attempts have been made at any but the most imperative co-ordination and reinterpretation of the folkloristic background. Nevertheless we have a right to anticipate that the shamans or medicine-men will even under these conditions indulge in some type of speculation concerning those problems that loom so large in religion proper, and that some attempt will be made to co-ordinate and evaluate the multifarious and inchoate folkloristic background.

In order to visualize the magico-religious milieu in which people with such a culture live, it is best to give a concrete instance. For the food-gathering societies one such example must suffice. I shall take the Yokuts of south central California because an unusually competent and illuminating description of this aspect of their life exists.[1] The one feature they possess which is not typical of this level of society is the existence of a fixed unit of exchange.

The most striking feature of Yokuts culture from the religious viewpoint is the fear inspired by the shamans. This is not due to any unusual power that they possess, for they have little, but to the alliance between them and the chief of the tribe. The latter controls or, at least, once controlled all the sources of income. These were, relatively speaking, fairly extensive considering the simple nature of the wealth-producing agencies. He had a monopoly on the trade of certain coveted objects, such as eagle-down, and the control of the rituals; he shared in the payments received by the local shamans and received money gifts from all visiting practitioners.

To understand fully the power of the shamans we should remember that all the organizational gifts they possessed went into the elaboration of the relations between them and the chief of the tribe. These two worked hand in glove, the chief increasing his sources of wealth by his alliance with the shamans and the latter gaining the protection of the chief, a protection sorely needed, for great risks attended the exercise of their profession.

How the two, the chief and the shaman, worked together, is admirably described by a native:

If a man, especially a rich one, did not join in a dance, the chief and his doctors would plan to make this man or some member of his family sick. . . . The doctor then sees to it that he is called in to make the cure. He makes several successive attempts to cure his victim, each time being paid for his services. He withholds his cure until he has financially broken the man and got him in debt. If he then cures the patient, he sucks the shot out and shows it to the bystanders, saying that the nigot [spirit] or a spring [spirit] has made him ill. On the other hand he may let the person die, in which case the family must perforce join in the mourning ceremony.

The money which the shaman has collected as fees in the case, he divides with the chief. Should the victim's relatives seek vengeance, for which they must obtain the chief's permission, the chief refuses his sanction on the ground of insufficient evidence. Has not the doctor shown that the nigot [spirit] had caused the illness?[2]

Thus the dread of the shaman hangs over the ordinary individual. That this dread is the outcome of the alliance between the chief and the shamans the example quoted above clearly demonstrates. The belief in spirits, or, for that matter, in magical rites and formulae, becomes of secondary consequence, a fact clearly shown by the looseness of the relation predicated between the individual and the supernatural powers. The gifts from such a supernatural power may, for instance, be accepted or rejected; the spirit may be sought specifically or he may, in other instances, come to a person voluntarily. Theoretically any individual can obtain his gift. Actually the number was drastically limited by the coterie of shamans protected by the power of the chief. The explanation for this limitation was naturally given in the terms of the shaman. It was, for instance, contended that the difficulties of establishing a successful relationship with the supernatural—fasting, praying in an isolated spot, taking a tobacco emetic, basking in the sun—all these were too troublesome, and the danger of making mistakes which might subsequently incur the ill will of the supernatural beings too great, for the generality of mankind to attempt them. Furthermore the shaman did not have to possess any temperamental qualifications. What he had to possess was the protection of the system. This the people at large seem to have recognized clearly, and it is this that explains the intensity of their opposition to him and of their hatred. Had it been exclusively supernatural power with which the ordinary man credited the shamans, it is somewhat difficult to see why the emphasis should have been placed so entirely on the evil side of their activities.

Where the belief in evil supernatural powers exists or uncertainty as to what such powers might do prevails, one would, on the supposition of most theorists, expect a general atmosphere of per-

petual fear and dread. All academic discussions of primitive religion in fact begin with it. And yet this is least developed among
the simplest tribes. Fear is clearly present but, as our example
shows, it is the fear arising out of economic insecurity and the
terror due to the machinations of individuals who manipulate
this insecurity in the interests of a well-known type of exploitation.

Since conditions comparable to those found among the Yokuts
are encountered in practically all tribes whose economy is based
mainly upon food-gathering, and since such an economy must
have preceded the hunting-fishing, agricultural, and pastoral
economies, it is intrinsically likely that those theorists are wrong
who assume that religion began as an articulation of the terror
felt by unanchored people before the unknown, a terror expressed
in the predication of spirits conceived of as inherently indifferent
or inimical. An example like the Yokuts, to which others might be
added, indicates that, on the contrary, it is only after the simple
methods of food production and their social concomitants have
changed that a real fear of the supernatural emerges. Seen in such
a connexion, the universal dread of the ghosts of the deceased and
the widespread occurrence of ancestor worship take on an entirely
different perspective. The possibility then arises that these need
not necessarily be interpreted simply as social crystallizations of
the fear inspired by certain dead individuals because they possess
magical and occult powers, but that they may represent a fear that
flows from their connexion with economic systems that, even in
the earliest societies, bore down heavily on the vast majority of
men and women.

Though witchcraft and magic are admittedly the salient traits
of the so-called religious life of the very simple cultures, we know
very well not only that they flourish in the more complex societies
but that they often attain an unheard-of development there. Many
students of ethnology have in fact assumed this to be the characteristic note of all primitive cultures. Even a competent scholar
like Firth, when making a specific study of the economics of so

highly integrated a civilization as that of the Maori of New Zealand, can think of the employment, in every phase of their industry, of magical spells and formulae, only as part of an irrational belief cradled in illusory power, and he falls back on meaningless psychological interpretations to explain it. We are to be satisfied with the statement that irrational belief helps the Maori to concentrate their faculties upon the work in hand and that it provides a useful element in organization. Mr. Firth, employing a time-honoured psychological interpretation, insists that this same belief shields the Maori "from the gnawing of doubt and fear in the face of the unknown, giving him confidence and assurance to face those forces the effect of which in reality he can neither foresee nor control. Resting his faith on his magic, he is filled with conviction that his labour will in due time yield its fruits." [3]

A much more realistic picture of the true significance of magic and witchcraft has recently been given by two students of African society, E. E. Evans-Pritchard and S. F. Nadel.[4] Here their full economic import emerges in startling fashion. Evans-Pritchard, on the basis of his study of the Zande of the Anglo-Egyptian Sudan, points out, first, that all members of the noble class and the rich and powerful among the commoners are immune from accusations; secondly, that the elaborate hierarchy of oracles of the Zande have as their chief object that of revealing witches; and, thirdly, that the chief's power is based upon the extent to which he can control the oracles.

Among the Nupe of West Africa the economic significance of witchcraft is equally marked. The head of the best-organized order of witches is there the official head of all the women in town. She supervises the market, organizes the common work of the women, and arbitrates their quarrels. She alone, of all the witches, is known and visible, recognized by the town authorities and by the king of Nupe. According to the official theory which Mr. Nadel summarizes, she makes use of her great powers of witchcraft for good purposes only. Because she is at one and the same time both the head of the women in the imaginary night-world of witchcraft and of the women in the real workaday world, she is also regarded as particularly qualified for still another type of work, that of ferreting out witches and fighting their secret antisocial activities.

This elaborate native theory has apparently been developed to explain the fact that the king or chief appoints her and that he generally selects a convicted or repentant witch, who is easily supervised and who is sufficiently trustworthy to be entrusted with so responsible a position. The advantages that accrue to the king by such an arrangement are obvious. By having complete control of the head of this "secret service" he keeps power within his own hands and can, at the same time, pretend to his fellowmen that he has gained a hold on the secret and intangible powers of witchcraft and that the two of them, the king and the head of the witch order, are thus in an excellent position to find any guilty individual.

From the chief's point of view it is naturally of great advantage to have an assistant who can check the activities of her fellow-witches and who can not only restrain the too obnoxious or too violent ones among them but who is forced, at the same time, to assume personal responsibility for the behaviour of the members of her order. Dr. Nadel insists, somewhat naïvely it seems to me, unless indeed he means to be ironical, that no *lelu*—such is the official name of the head of the witches—once appointed, neglects her duties, and that she finds means to fulfil her responsibility to the community as well as to discover the required victim. As head of the market, he insists, she always remains in sufficiently intimate contact with the sources of public opinion to respond properly to its suggestions.

Ostensibly then the alliance between the chief and the *lelu* has as its main objective the suppression of witchcraft in the interests of the whole community, and it does, of course, fulfil this function. But the important point to bear in mind is not whether witchcraft is detected but the degree to which it is allowed to flourish and the nature of the benefits that accrue to specific individuals and groups from the activities of those who practise it as well as the benefits that accrue to those charged with neutralizing and punishing it.

Among the Nupe, we have seen, witches are used to fight witch-craft. Yet of even more significance is the fact that, when the witches to any really marked extent get out of hand, so to speak, the campaign against them is entrusted not to a person like the *lelu* but to a special organization, an officially recognized secret society, that forms an integral part of the political structure of the Nupe kingdom. According to the official religious theory the members of this society received their supernatural knowledge and power from certain spirits and exercise their control over witches by means of this power. Their relationship to these spirits is of a specifically magical and coercive nature. They possess power over the spirits and not the reverse, and they can force these spirits to appear in certain magical ceremonies. The political and economic functions of this society are thus quite patent. The head of the society has complete control of membership, both his office and his title being confirmed by the king. All the social implications connected with this society are given in an origin myth—the nature of the paraphernalia of the cult, the fact that it is invoked against old women who mysteriously interfere with the proper order of things, and the culminating realization that it is a "magic of the king."

But on what occasions is the society asked to intermediate? There are two such occasions, one where a definite connexion with the actual needs of an afflicted community exists, the other where there is none. Let me paraphrase Nadel's description of the second method. It carries its own implications and needs no further comment.

The second method, he informs us, is employed on instructions "from above." It is then that the full power of the secret society as well as its relation to the political structure of the Nupe kingdom becomes apparent. It works in the following manner. At a given time of the year, usually around the harvest, the head of the society appears at the king's court with a report that the activities of the witches in the country have increased to a dangerous de-

gree, and he counsels the king to send the members of the society
to the various villages to rid them of this antisocial plague. If the
king agrees, and naturally he always does so, the head of the society mobilizes the various branches of the society scattered throughout the countryside. The members suddenly appear in the villages,
ostensibly to perform their dances and incidentally to "discover"
and punish witches.

Within a short time the terrified women, learning that the members of the society are in the neighbourhood, either flee and hide
in the bush or collect money to buy themselves free collectively.
This money is sent to the place where the society members are performing. The latter, after accepting this ransom, then perform
some of the "harmless" dance ceremonies connected with their
cult and omit the witch-hunting. However, the activity of the society has plunged the community into wild unrest. Households are
dissolved, women neglect their duties, and money becomes scarce.
As a result, a number of the village chiefs band together, collect a
large sum of money, and bring it to the king, beseeching him to
recall the members of the society. After three official but unavail-
ing attempts to force their recall the society members at last leave.
The head of the society himself appears at the king's court, this
time, however, to divide the spoils. The king receives one-third
while the head of the society keeps two-thirds. There are always
spoils to be divided because, as we have seen, the date of the ceremony is set for the harvest time, when money is plentiful everywhere in the country.

It might not be out of place to mention that the secret society
never operates in the capital of the kingdom. The official explanation is that here the king, helped by the *lelu*, can control witchcraft very well himself. It stands to reason that in the capital,
which is the king's own town, it would not be advisable to permit
the socially as well as economically disorganizing influence of the
secret society full scope. This is to remain a weapon in the hands
of the king and not one which may at any time be turned against
him and thus endanger his own interests.[5]

Our two examples from Africa must have made it clear that the existence of magic in societies that have long passed the simple food-gathering or fishing-hunting stage, and its persistence in civilizations where elaborate religious superstructures have been developed, are due, over and above psychological reasons, to its usefulness in economic exploitation. That it has other social functions as well goes without saying. But the primary reason for its consistent employment and for the high degree of systematization it has so frequently attained is economic.

There is, however, another aspect of our problem that merits attention. In a food-gathering society like that of the Yokuts described before, magic and witchcraft, we have seen, reign supreme. In so far as both are systematized, this may be regarded as a function of the struggle of the chief and the shamans to maintain their power and security against the layman and not as an expression of the systematizing mind of a religious formulator. Religion in any true sense cannot really be said to exist. Not only, for instance, are the supernatural beings drawn in the vaguest outlines but there exists no real fixity in the relations between them and their worshippers. The fears arising from economic insecurity, from disease and death, from the machinations of human beings, are not regarded as directly connected with the spirits. The latter are not responsible for them nor have they the power to allay them. Both these functions are in the hands of living individuals, of the practitioners of magic. Certain theoretical and theological consequences flow from this fact. Instead of the customary strife developing between different spirits either to gain the favour of human beings or to retain power over them, so frequent in the more complex civilizations, this strife takes place between the various practitioners of the magic art itself. That, too, has its interesting consequences, for so intense and embittered does this struggle frequently become that a good part of the energy of a shaman is absorbed in directing his evil powers against his colleagues and not against the general public. Here too the Yokuts data are very illuminating, as the following example will illustrate:

At the Tule reservation there was an old man named Tcehemsuk. He had supernatural power but was a poisoner as well. He had always been at odds with Sam Garfield who with his family lived at the reservation. Tcehemsuk asked one of Sam's boys, Pete, to come over to his house to drink some coffee. Pete did not want to go but at the same time was afraid to refuse. Tcehemsuk gave him some cold coffee to drink. The following day Pete developed a bad cold and complained that he felt "like he was burning up inside." They called a white doctor, but Pete's condition continued to get worse so they sent for Posoo (another shaman). When the latter arrived Pete's neck was swollen up on the outside. Posoo sang and danced for two nights. He cut and sucked the patient's neck but could extract nothing but blood. While he was doing his diagnostic singing none of his dream helpers spoke to him though he followed his formula perfectly. . . .

Now Posoo himself began vomiting blood. Pete kept getting worse and died in a few days. Finding his efforts useless Posoo returned [home]. . . . He kept vomiting blood. He got much worse and went to bed. He knew that Tcehemsuk was making him ill. He tried to kill Tcehemsuk with his supernatural power but his power was gone. He depended upon his own power and would get no other doctor to help him. He sang his songs while he lay in bed but nothing came to him. . . . Josie had him taken to the hospital where he died.

This Tcehemsuk was a big doctor, so was his brother. He had poisoned Pete, but it was with his supernatural power that he kept Posoo from curing Pete, and finally killed him too.[6]

Here a human being dies, victim of a quarrel between two shamans, in precisely the same fashion as, in the higher religions, he may die as a consequence of becoming unwittingly involved in a quarrel of spirits or deities. An instance of the latter is to be found among the Winnebago, where a faster is represented as bringing destruction upon himself and his whole village because, through divine trickery, he has been forced to decide in favour of one spirit as against another.

If then we will bear in mind that, in societies whose basic economy is food-gathering, the primary facts are the undifferentiated character of the religious manifestations, the all-inclusive use of magic and witchcraft, and the intense competition between the practitioners to maintain their power, then we can, to some purpose, turn to those cultures whose basic economy is fishing and hunting and see to what extent and in what form these particular religious manifestations are present and what new ones appear.

Tribes with true fishing-hunting economies, just as those with food-gathering economies, are extremely rare outside of North America. In North America, with the exception of the north-west coast of Canada, their cultures are all simple. Everywhere, except along this part of the Pacific Coast (but not southern California) and the Arctic, these are in close contact with agricultural tribes with fairly complex cultures. For this reason it is not always easy to be certain when significant influences have been transmitted from the complex to the simpler civilizations, particularly within the realm of religion. Yet, even allowing for them, there is a striking similarity to be found not only in the type of religion all these tribes have developed but in the kind of religious speculation they have failed to develop.

Like the food-gatherers, the fishing-hunting civilizations are all marginal. It is difficult, in fact, to imagine that the Eskimo, the Fuegians, the Andaman Islanders, or the Ainu arrived by choice at the inhospitable places where they now live or that they have stayed there otherwise than because it was impossible to migrate to other regions. Life is hard and, in spite of their technological advance over the simpler food-gatherers and their proximity to water, their food supply is insecure. Their fishing and hunting techniques do, however, considerably add to the economic security of such tribes. Inevitably the question arises, who, in a given tribe, profits most from this technological advance; who obtains the greatest security, acquires the most wealth, and secures some modicum of leisure? Only when we know this can we understand the particular developments magic and religion have made there.

Let us begin with the Eskimo. Their social organization is of the very loosest kind. No chief and no centralized authority exist there. Murder and blood feuds are the order of the day. Yet their adjustment to this most inhospitable of environments is almost perfect. It was made possible by an astounding series of inventions connected with the harpoon, the kayak, and the snow house. Where did these constructive forces come from? We naturally turn to the one group of individuals who are organized. We find that they are the *angakok* or shamans. They have managed to gather firmly into their hands whatever political power exists. This is evidenced in a number of ways, perhaps in none more dramatically than that, in a civilization where murder is extremely common, they are never murdered although they must be surrounded by people who hate them; and that in a country where women are often at a premium, the shamans' rights to cohabit with them at will are generally recognized. The mechanism they have devised to gain and retain this power is the organization of a religious "fraternity," carefully restricted in numbers, a complex religious theory, and a spectacular shamanistic technique. Their well-integrated system is designed to do two things: to keep the contact with the supernatural exclusively in the hands of the *angakok*, and to manipulate and exploit the sense of fear of the ordinary man. Here the environment plays directly into their hands. We can thus easily understand the reason for the answer an Eskimo gave to the great Danish explorer Rasmussen when he was asked: "What do you believe?" The reply was:

We do not believe. We only fear. And most of all we fear Nuliajuk, the mother of beasts. . . . All the game we hunt comes from her. . . . We fear those things which are about us and of which we have no sure knowledge, as the dead, and the malevolent ghosts, and the secret misdoings of the heedless ones among ourselves.

This is good *angakok* theory, an excellent and all-embracing integration of fear—fear for the food supply, fear of the general uncertainty, fear of the taboos that other people break, and fear, finally, of the dead and of the malevolent ghosts. What the *anga-*

kok have really done is to combine the fear of economic insecurity, first, with the magical formulae and taboos and, secondly, with the fear of deceased human beings. The dead are feared in all these simple cultures, we may surmise, not because they are dead but because they are human beings whose activities cannot then be controlled as well as when they were alive, inadequate as that control may perhaps have been. This we shall see later on also lies at the basis of ancestor worship.

The economic aspects of this *angakok* systematization are sharply and clearly outlined. Take, for example, the four main occasions where an *angakok* is asked to function among the Ammassalik and when he must summon his spirits. They are: the dearth of sea animals; the blocking of the hunting places by snow masses; a man's loss of his soul in illness; and a married woman's barrenness. It is also patent in the fact that around the food quest as such there has been built up a series of rites under the complete control of the *angakok*. That the emoluments are considerable is indicated by the fact that as much as 150 to 200 dollars will be offered for a familiar spirit, something, incidentally, that only an *angakok* can obtain.

The same sharpness of outline is exhibited in the delineation of the supernatural beings. There is no vagueness in the conception of Sedna, the deity of the sea, or of the moon and the air deities. However, this definiteness does not flow from any conscious interest in portraying them as distinct entities but from the fact that they are represented as having all once been human beings. The hardness and cruelty of their relation to human beings reflect this origin. And here too it is well to remember that it is the *angakok* who constrains the deities and that, although he may suffer cruelly during his initiation, once he has established the relationship with his helping spirit, life flows on for him in comparative ease. The deities are cruel specifically only to the people at large, not to the *angakok*.

It is thus the superior organization of the folkloristic background, and the more articulate expression of its relation to the food supply, that characterize the Eskimo and all other fishing-hunting economies, not the appearance of those new elements which play so great a part in the religions of the more complex of primitive cultures. There is no new evaluation of the subjective element—arctic hysteria can be discounted—and no appreciable change in the older conception that both the environment and the spirits must be coerced. In this respect it can be said the *angakok* as a thinker has adjusted himself completely to the attitude of his less sensitive fellow-tribesmen. Speculation he indulged in, but this was on the hardships of living and not essentially on any aspects of religion. Rasmussen has given numerous examples of this speculation, speculation which can be taken as representative of the thought of all primitive peoples living in economic insecurity, and this includes a large number.

In one of Rasmussen's interviews, an Eskimo turned one of his questions back upon him and asked:

Why must there be snow and storms and bad weather for hunting, for us who must hunt for our daily food, who seek meat for ourselves and those we love? Why must hunters, after they have slaved all day, return without a catch? Why must the children of my neighbour sit shivering huddled under a skin-rug, hungry? Why must my old sister suffer pain at the ending of her days? She has done no wrong that we can see but lived her many years and given birth to good strong children.

He answers his own rhetorical questions himself with a wisdom and a sense of reality rarely paralleled among ourselves [7] :

Even you cannot answer when we ask you why life is as it is. And so it must be. Our customs all come from life and are directed toward life; we cannot explain, we do not believe in this or that; but the answer lies in what I have just told you.

We fear!

We fear the elements with which we have to fight in their fury to wrest our food from land and sea.

We fear cold and famine in our snow huts.

We fear the sickness that is daily to be seen among us. Not death, but the suffering.

We fear the souls of the dead, of human and animal alike.

We fear the spirits of earth and air.

And therefore our fathers, taught by their fathers before them, guarded themselves about with all these old rules and customs, which are built upon the experience and knowledge of generations. We do not know how or why, but we obey them that we may be suffered to live in peace. And for all our *angakoks* and their knowledge of hidden things, we yet know so little that we fear everything else.

Among other fishing-hunting tribes, like the inhabitants of the Andaman Islands, the Ainu of northern Japan, the Fuegians, the Semang of the Malay Peninsula, and the fairly numerous tribes in North America, we find the same marked tendency for the medicine-men to organize and to develop the theory that they alone are in communication with the supernatural; we encounter the same tendency for the spirits or deities to acquire a clearer outline, because of their close relationship to the food supply, and we see the same attempt to stress fear as well as the same limitation of the creative-artistic energies to the elaboration of ethical-philosophical as opposed to purely religious speculations. In all these civilizations the pressing cares and problems of mankind are solved exclusively by magic and coercive rites, rites that are often quite elaborate and that are always completely controlled by the medicine-men and shamans. Where the latter have elaborated the concept of an original Supreme Power, a belief that actually exists among many of these tribes, it is only the shamans who share it and who enjoy any close relation to him. The Supreme Deity's function as a creator of all things, as well as his concern with ethics, can, under these conditions, be justifiably regarded as the attempt of an incipient intellectual aristocracy and a special class to buttress its own position and to develop a semi-sanctity for its representatives.

It is only where agriculture has become the principal method of food production, and where the technological advances are such that the threat of famine and starvation is not always imminent, that political and social units emerge which permit an analysis of the relation of the individual to the supernatural and a redefinition of the supernatural which can properly be called true religion. That this analysis and synthesis are the conscious work of the medicine-man, shaman, priest, or whatever you wish to call him, it is not difficult to show.

However, an agricultural economy does not necessarily imply a well-knit political and social organization. Among the Kiwai of British New Guinea, for instance, this does not exist in spite of the presence of both agriculture and clans. The land is extremely fertile there, and no difficulty is experienced in obtaining an adequate food supply. This holds for practically everyone. Accordingly there has been no opportunity for the medicine-men either to organize themselves or to seize power. As a consequence the folkloristic background reigns supreme. Magical practices and rites still remain the basic religious expression of the people, and the relation of the individual to the supernatural or the precise definition of the supernatural receives comparatively little attention. Such extreme cases are, however, rare.

Yet it is well to remember that only in exceptional instances is the religious formulator fundamentally interested in bringing precision into the delineation of the deities or emphasizing the subjective qualifications in the approach to the sacred and divine. Primarily he is occupied with gaining and maintaining power and security, and this is far more easily accomplished by various recombinations and reintegrations of the folkloristic-magical background than by refined analyses of spiritual concepts. Moreover, most agricultural economies permit a permanent seizure of power by organized groups of medicine-men more easily than do the simpler economies. This naturally introduces added difficulties. Where the profits are greater, the number of the contenders for power will, very naturally, also be larger. Alliances consequently will take place between the civil and the religious competitors for control. Classes and castes arise and stratified societies appear.

But the struggle for power between individuals or between groups and classes is only one aspect of the new conditions which this greater economic security and stability bring about. With agriculture there are almost universally associated—Polynesia and Malaysia excepted—totemic clans and a type of society in which the activities of the individual become subordinated to highly integrated social units with mystical associations. A communal ownership of the sources of the food supply develops which markedly restricts individual ownership. But the victory of the communistic implications of the totemic societies was never complete because of the presence within these societies of an organized group of individuals, the medicine-men, shamans, and priests, whose position depended upon individual and specific qualifications and who symbolized to the mass of the people the persistence of a past closely connected with a specific type of society and with a specific viewpoint toward the supernatural. The totemistic society was, at one and the same time, friendly and inimical to this religious viewpoint. In the resultant clash of forces, personal and collective, the medicine-man became far less independent than he had previously been. He found that he could not exist alone or without the protection of those who controlled the destinies of the group, generally the elders. Yet if he was less independent, his functions were more precisely defined and his position made more secure. In so far as he was a thinker, he now had more leisure in which to reinterpret the whole magico-religious complex and give it the impress of his creative imagination. At times he gained political power, and his new interpretations were generally accepted by the group. More frequently, however, they remained restricted to a small number of people or became enshrined in rituals representing a compromise between his point of view and that of the generality of his tribesmen and clansmen. . . .

Primitive religion has generally been treated with only the most partial and inconsistent recognition of this economic, as opposed to a vague societal, conditioning. Most students have discussed it as though aboriginal peoples spent their lives either revelling in a world of concepts or possessing no concepts at all. But if an analysis of religion is to mean anything, it must envisage the manner in which religion is embedded in life and not examine merely the beliefs, rituals, and speculations as such. Often it is expedient, in fact almost necessary, to study the religious expressions divorced from their economic conditioning and their social content. I shall do so myself, because frequently the religious phenomena that are fundamentally by-products of the social-economic order are precisely those most pertinent to the general history of religion and can be best envisaged when artificially removed from their functioning environment. But I must warn the reader to guard against forgetting the milieu in which they have originated and in which they have prospered. Paraphrasing our Eskimo philosopher, we must insist that religion comes from life and is directed towards life. In itself it is nothing.

4

The Magical Substratum

MAGIC is as old as man. It can in fact be said to have ante-
dated man, for the situation that it poses and seeks to resolve is identical with that by which apes and monkeys are confronted and which they are forced to resolve. It is briefly this:
how can a desirable object be coerced? The answer is to seize it as
effectively and expeditiously as possible and with as little danger
to oneself as possible. What differentiates man from the other animals is that, while he, largely, wishes to coerce this desirable object for purposes akin to that of the other animals, in part his objective is utterly different and not related to his purely vegetative
wants. Moreover, because he possesses articulate speech, he, himself, informs us of this difference. In man, then, not only can the
behaviour toward the desirable object be watched but the actor
tells us what he is doing, and his actions and his statements can, in
addition, be corroborated and explained by others.

Of these constituent elements the behaviour as such is rarely analysed. The individual acts themselves, the accompanying statements, and the explanations as to the nature of their relation to the
object acted upon, these, however, are all both analysed and elaborated. We are thus placed in an advantageous position for classifying and evaluating them both as regards their significance in the
history of thought in general and as regards their importance in
the history of religion in particular.

This, we know, was the favourite preoccupation of the ethnological theorists of the nineteenth and early twentieth centuries: Tylor, Robertson Smith, Frazer, and Marett in England; Durkheim, Hubert, and Mauss in France; Preuss in Germany. They
all seem to have agreed upon one fact, namely, that in the extended

learning process called civilization, magic constitutes the first application of the principle of causation, the first explanation of the interaction of the ego and the object. All, of course, except Lévy-Bruhl, who, as is well known, refuses to credit primitive people with any understanding of the elementary logical processes. He does not feel that they actually do polarize the subject and the object in such a fashion as to make the principle of causation, as we conceive it, meaningful. Into that interminable discussion we cannot enter here except to say that no ethnologist with any long experience among aboriginal cultures agrees with him. This disagreement in itself may not represent a valid refutation of his views. It does, however, constitute a pertinent fact in the discussion of primitive mentality and one that merits some consideration, a consideration which he has signally failed to acknowledge.

Thus, in the beginning, there was magic and magic was with God and God was magic. But who here, in this historic formula, is God? Translated into more concrete form for the purposes of discussion, this equation signifies that the ego is with the object and the ego is the object. And indeed it is the fundamental concern of every magical act and rite to establish a relation of such a kind to the object that it can literally be at one with the ego, be unreservedly absorbed into it. The apparent primacy of such an equation in the history of mankind has, quite legitimately and quite naturally, appealed to the psychoanalysts. For them it is a manifestation of those neurotic compulsions that are today so prominent in the actions of children and of psychopathic individuals and which they interpret as regressions to a generalized infantile mentality. In so far as all human thinking is a neurotic compulsion, they are right. And there can be little question but that considerable significance should be attached to this resemblance. However, the interpretations and the conclusions of the psychoanalysts in the realm of cultural history are, even if we wish to be very generous, only vaguely anticipatory of the true ones rather than the true ones themselves, and their method of demonstration is false and highly repugnant to all our critical and logical instincts. They should, one would surmise, feel perfectly at home with Lévy-Bruhl's "prelogical mentality." [1] Most of them do, particularly Jung and his followers.

The essence of magic then is admittedly coercion, coercion in the interests of our imperative organic needs—the satisfaction of hunger and the gratification of the sex instinct. Around the food supply and around woman we consequently find clustered the oldest and most insistent magical formulae and practices. Yet the dangers inherent in coercing an object, they, too, are the concern of magic and become crystallized early in the history of mankind, in rites and observances designed to ward off whatever harm is likely to befall the performer consequent upon his attempting any coercion. Both types of magic, the positive as well as the negative, persist long after magic as such has ceased to be the only method predicated by man for establishing a relationship between himself and the outside world.

Religion is, accordingly, replete with it. Retroactively, in its turn, religion influences and reshapes the magical materials and, since it is a higher type of thought and analysis, this reshaping always takes the form of a systematization and a symbolical reinterpretation. Magical incantations, spells, formulae, and rites, as they are encountered today in all but the very simplest cultures, have consequently already been subjected to the definite influence of the religious formulator. This influence has its economic as well as its ideological side. It is both to his personal interest as well as to the interests of the group or groups with which he, as a medicine-man or shaman, is allied, that he emphasize the difficulties and the dangers attendant upon this coercion of the world of necessary and desirable objects. These difficulties are expressed in a number of different ways—in the insistence upon meticulous accuracy, in an excessive care lavished upon formal details, and what not, all of them designed to extend the period of time between the initiation of the rite and the successful achievement of its objective.

Psychoanalysts will obviously object to such an interpretation, for to them the similarity between the magical rites of primitive peoples and the neurotic compulsions of individuals in our own civilization is so great that it seems far-fetched and falsely rational to imply that economic factors have been operative here. To them magic is the normal functioning of the psyche at an early stage, at a period in its evolution where man was still fairly exclusively dominated by the unconscious and consequently an easy prey to the tyranny of thought. There is, however, no validity to their contention, for, as we have shown, sufficient economic insecurity prevailed in early primitive society for this to have produced the psychic insecurity which lies at the base of those neurotic disturbances to which they have reference. The similarities between the magical rites of primitive peoples and the behaviour of neurotic individuals in our own society cannot then be attributed to the fact that the former represent an archaic form of thought to which modern neurotic individuals revert. At best this similarity may be interpreted as evidence that both have reverted to an infantile mentality. But even if the psychoanalysts were remotely correct, that would not interfere with the economic utilization of magical rites for the purposes and along the lines indicated above. The craving for power and the longing for security have always made strange bedfellows, and they must have done so then as they still do today.

How all the multifarious components of magic, as well as the extent to which the magical situation—the behaviour of the performer, the formulae, the articulation of the purpose—can become a work of art, and how conscious political and economic implications can, nevertheless, interpenetrate them, this has all been beautifully illustrated by Malinowski for the Trobriand Islanders. According to him, magic represents, to the natives, a specific power which, in its action, is essentially human, autonomous, and independent. The magical power itself resides in certain words, accompanied by specific acts, which can be performed only by an individual entitled to do so through his social position. The words and the accompanying acts possess this power of their own right. Their action is direct and is not mediated by any other agency nor is their power derived from any supernatural beings, any more than can, theoretically, any component of this magical unit be tampered with.

As a specific example of such a magical unit I shall take an incantation connected with the *kula*, the system of social-economic relations which forms the novel feature of Trobriand society. The spell itself is connected with the rite performed over a sprig of aromatic mint a few days before a new canoe is ready to sail. The spell has three parts, each with technical names: an initial part, the foundation; an intermediate part, the body; and a third part, the top. The names have reference to a tree or post. The actual words are as follows:

Foundation or initial part: "Who cuts the mint plant of Labai? I, Kwoyregu, together with my father, we cut the mint plant of Labai. The roaring *sulumwoya*, it roars; the quaking *sulumwoya*, it quakes; the coughing *sulumwoya*, it boils."

The body or intermediate part: "It boils, it boils, it boils, my mint plant, it boils. My herb ornaments, they boil; my lime spatula, it boils; my lime pot, it boils; my comb, it boils; my mat, it boils; my presentation goods, they boil; my big basket, it boils; my personal basket, it boils; my magical bundle, it boils; my head, it boils; my nose, it boils; my occiput, it boils; my tongue, it boils; my larynx, it boils; my speaking organ, it boils; my mouth, it boils; my *kula* courting, it boils."

The top or conclusion: "New spirit, my maternal uncle, Mwoyalova, thou breathe [the spell over] the head [of] Monikiniki; thou breathe [the spell over] the head [of] my light wood. I kick the mountain, it tilts over, the mountain; it subsides, the mountain; it opens up, the mountain; it jubilates, the mountain; it topples down, the mountain. I breathe [a spell over] the head [of] Koyarau; I charm the inside [of] Siyaygana [canoe]; I drown the *waga*, I submerge the lamina. Not my renown, my renown thunder; not my treading, my treading noise made by flying witches, tududu." [2]

The incantation is recited in a highly formalized manner. The voice of the magician rises and falls at specified places. Some of the words are recited slowly, some rapidly, and some are definitely chanted. Certain words are repeated, others not. Beyond such rhetorical details, however, no demands are made upon the performer. His emotional condition never becomes the object of any interest to the group.

Superficially nothing further removed from religion can well be imagined than this incantation, and yet no great changes are required to change it into an invocation and a prayer. Indeed the likelihood of its being incorporated into a larger whole, with specifically religious implications, is overwhelming. Its transformation into a true prayer, the addition of offerings and sacrifices, and, finally, the presence of supernatural beings who are either to be invoked or warned away, these are all inevitable developments in a civilization as complex economically as is that of the Trobriand Islanders. Practically all the various stages through which a spell can pass in order to be transformed into a prayer are, in fact, found here. Malinowski, himself, lists numerous spells in which spirits are invoked and offerings made to them. That such spirits are not regarded as the agents of the magician in carrying out the bidding of his magic does not invalidate our right to interpret an invocation or incantation as a true prayer. What more complete remodelling, for instance, can exist than this: "Partake, O spirits, of your payment [food] and make my magic thrive"; or the belief that when something has gone wrong with the magic, the spirits will become angry?

At times the spirits are even supposed to appear to a magician in dreams, to advise him what to do. In such cases the magical formula becomes definitely secondary to religion as, for example, in the following account:

The owners of fish magic will often dream that there is plentiful fish. The cause of it is the magician's ancestor spirit. Such a magician would then say: "The ancestral spirit has instructed me in the night, that we should go to catch fish!" And indeed, when we get there we find plenty of fish, and we cast our nets.

It is only then that the magic is practised.

But more significant than even the influence of the religious re-interpreter is the fact that the magic connected with the main economic pursuits is the one particularly affected—the garden, the fishing, and the weather magic. In fact it is in connexion with their most important socio-economic undertaking, the *kula*, that the religious formulator is at his best.

One thing surely must have become clear in this description of Trobriand magic, namely that, wherever the religious viewpoint is present, an inevitable tendency develops to mitigate the coercive aspect of a rite or the obsessive intensity of an attitude. In other words an individual's obsessive subjectivism becomes disturbed and we begin that long and tortuous journey which is to lead us in the domain of religion to exactly the opposite pole, the conception of a Supreme Deity in whose hands man is as wax, a helpless reed.

Thus far we have been discussing only that phase of magic which deals with the food supply and the assurance of economic wellbeing. The magic connected with the physiological functions and needs of man is, we know, just as fundamental and has had possibly even a longer history. Its persistence through all the stages of man's evolution, even into our own highly sophisticated modern cultures, is well known. Unfortunately we cannot dwell upon it here, for in the present book we are interested in magic only in so far as it bears on religion. We shall confine ourselves accordingly to indicating the manner and degree to which the magical formulae and rites have been remodelled and transformed by the religious thinker, and the extent to which they have become incorporated into a strictly religious system.

Only in the vague sense implied in the general theory that a spirit or deity has created the whole social environment can it be said that such basic physiological facts as birth, the changes at puberty, pregnancy, and cohabitation have ever been specifically attributed to the agency of supernatural beings, even in those cultures that possess well-integrated religious systems. Gods presiding over childbirth, pregnancy, and cohabitation do exist among some of the higher religions like the ancient Greek and Roman. They are not, however, to be found among any primitive peoples. Yet, if deities are not found presiding over such functions among primitive peoples, this does not mean that they bear no relation to them. Obviously they must. But the relation to these physiological facts belongs to what we may justifiably regard as the earliest stratum in human history. It is apparently of the most tenuous description, different altogether from that which prevails toward the assuring of the food supply.

The first thing to be remembered is that the magical formulae and rites connected with them were elaborated in the interests of the community and that they were made definitely subservient to that aspect of societal evolution concerned with the factor of age and the establishment of status. Birth became correlated with the introduction of an individual into the world, puberty with that into the tribe, and cohabitation, as expressed formally in marriage, was given the secondary meaning of an introduction into the status of a fully functioning social being. There thus arose that series of rites and rituals clustering around the primary physiological periods of life to which Van Gennep has so aptly applied the term "transition rites" (*les rites de passage*). To those of birth, puberty, and marriage we may justifiably add death, for that, too, is connected with the passage from one specific physiological and social status to another.

The rites to which the religious thinker seems to have paid most attention were those clustering around puberty. It is perhaps not speculating unduly to say that this interest on his part must have begun at a time when the specifically religious concepts were still in a fairly inchoate condition and when magic was still universally dominant, for initiation rites are already found in somewhat luxuriant elaboration among tribes possessing the simplest economic organization, among the food-gathering and fishing-hunting cultures, for instance. I need only mention the Australians, the Andaman Islanders, the Fuegians, the Ainu, and the Central Californians. No greater demonstration of the primacy of socio-economic, as opposed to all other factors, can very well be given. Subsequently we do, it is true, find supernatural spirits associated with these rites, but this never seriously affected their older meaning or function. One consequence of fundamental importance has flowed from this fact, namely, that the magical formulae and practices were left essentially untouched and that they were not subjected to any marked religious reinterpretation and revaluation. But even if such an explanation is rejected as inadequate, its rejection would not seriously militate against our conclusion, for other factors were at work which would have effectively excluded these magical practices from special consideration. Physiological facts cannot of course be coerced. They appear of themselves and are subject to their own autonomy. It is not strange, then, that only in myths, and then only in the most archaic sections, is either their first appearance or their continued functioning attributed to any outside agency or agencies.

The situation is quite different with physiological conditions such as disease and death. These can be coerced; they can be brought about. Yet manifestly no one wishes to inflict calamity and destruction upon himself. The ego is consequently thought of as being himself coerced. All his energies are, accordingly, devoted to protecting himself and to so constraining an object that its malign influence may be directed toward someone else. Around disease and death, from the very infancy of mankind, magic in its negative form has thus predominantly clustered. In the history of religion this negative form of the coercion formula, where the ego is coerced instead of himself coercing something, has always been of the utmost importance. As can readily be understood, it is the one aspect of thought which, even in the very earliest periods of society, could not easily or permanently become an integral part of the subjectivist obsession. That both death and disease can be regarded as self-caused, that destruction can be conceived of as self-conditioned and as emanating directly from the ego, this we know. But such an interpretation would manifestly disrupt the subjectivist obsession. Such a view did, as a matter of fact, develop but at a comparatively late period in the history of primitive religion.

How difficult it was, in the childhood of thought, when thinking was fairly exclusively a form of not-understood coercion, not to postulate an intermediate something between the subject and the object or to conceive of any relation between the two except in a mediated form, is best proved by the various theories of disease and death then current. Although disease was almost universally regarded as due either to a disease-object within a person or to the temporary absence of the soul, and although death was often interpreted as due to the lodging of a foreign object within the body, in both instances it was believed that this could not have taken place except through the direct action of another agency. Disease and death were never thought of at any time in the history of mankind as simply lodging themselves in a man, nor were they personified as spirits until a comparatively late time. Such a conception is the direct antithesis of the basic postulate of magic, where the individual must of necessity be the coercer. It is because of this characteristic of magic in its relation to disease and death that religion may be said to have started with the attempts to understand and explain, specifically, the disease and death situation.

The agency to whose activities they were attributed was, in the simpler societies, almost always regarded as human. Even where the spirits or deities were regarded as having directly or indirectly instituted disease and death, it is man himself who is thought to be responsible for their lodging in a particular individual, i.e., it is he who stands behind the disease-bringing or death-dealing object. At all times society has, accordingly, had witches, men and women. Their specific role in the evolution of primitive religion we shall discuss later. Here we shall limit ourselves to some general remarks on the nature of the magical practices connected with disease and death in so far as they have either influenced or have been incorporated into religion proper.

Of the two most general theories of disease causation—the intrusion of a foreign object into the body or the temporary loss of the soul—the first has probably persisted with few changes and transformations from palæolithic times to the present.[3] The second, on the contrary, seems to have been subjected to consistent and insistent elaboration. The magical practices and formulae clustering around it were all naturally concerned with methods for inducing the soul to return. These the religious formulator took over bodily, we may surmise, and without much change. It was easy enough to attribute the loss of the soul at death, or its temporary loss during illness, to the action of some deity. For the present discussion, what interests us, however, and what indicates the magical mentality still at work, is the fact that the supernatural spirit regarded as responsible is frequently pictured as appearing not of his own volition but through constraint, that he is often, in fact, captured and coerced into returning the soul. The following example, which I shall give at considerable length, will illustrate the extent to which the whole magical apparatus can exist significantly, even where religious beliefs and concepts are already fully operative:

Once there was a young girl who was sick, and the parents did not know what was the matter with her. They used to give offerings to a medicine-man and beg him to cure her, but he always found that his method of curing was not strong enough for the purpose. Then they called in a conjuror to find out if anyone was making this girl sick. But the first one they called could not find out. Many of these conjurors attempted and failed.

Finally they heard of a man who was a wonderful conjuror. There never was anything he failed to know when he was asked. So they sent for him. They offered him a horse, broadcloth and tobacco if he could find out what ailed the young woman. He said he would try, but he told them what he wanted them to do. First to get twelve very strong poles and stick them in the ground about four feet, for if they did not have them deep, the poles would not stand the strain. Then they were to tie a strong grapevine around the poles. They were told to put up three of these little structures, having four poles in each. When they had those structures up, they told the conjuror that they were ready for him to come.

That night there were many people who watched him try to find out why the girl was sick. He sang a song at the first little structure, then threw his shirt inside, for the structure was open above.

Suddenly a gust of wind blew and the little structure started to shake. Soon they heard a noise. This was when the animals and insects were arriving who had come to tell why the girl was sick. Then the man went to the next house and sang a song. Then he threw some of his clothing inside again. Soon the wind became stronger and the house started to shake again. They heard more noises, for more of the animals were arriving. Then he went to the last one and sang a song. Finally he went in. The wind blew still harder and the three lodges shook very much, the poles almost being pulled out and the vine by which they were tied broken. Soon they heard a voice inside that asked why they were called, and the man told them that a girl was sick and that he wanted to know why she was sick, that no one seemed able to say. They heard someone say that the right one was not there yet, but that he was on his way. When this one arrived they asked him if he knew why the girl was sick, but he too did not know. Again they heard someone say that the right one had not come but that he would soon be there. Soon they heard another arrive, and the turtle asked him if he knew why the girl was sick, and the answer was, "Yes. I know. It is the moon who is making the girl sick."

The conjuror then asked the parents what they wanted him to do, either to ask the moon why he was making the girl sick or to let her go. So they said, "Ask the moon." Soon some of those strong animals left to go after the moon. The turtle was among those that went. The people said when these got to the moon it was dark and they could not see the moon. When they arrived at the moon, the moon asked them what they wanted. They told him they were coming after him.

The moon was willing to come, but when they were halfway, refused to go any further, so they had to pull him along. The people heard the turtle tell the others, "Be strong; pull hard." Soon they got the moon in the little structure where the conjuror was staying. The man asked the moon, "Why do you make this girl suffer?" The moon said, "Why, when this girl was fasting, I blessed her, so she will have to suffer as long as she lives, for I am all the time suffering and she will be the same way." The man could do nothing with the moon so they let him go. So the girl suffered till she died. . . .[4]

In this example the moon-spirit is captured exactly as is an evil sorcerer. Now in the evolution of religion the task of the religious reinterpreter is, ideally speaking, to consist of three things: the elimination of such analogies, the transformation of the coercion into a willing acquiescence, and the substitution for the older interpretation of disease of a new one, according to which it is to be ascribed to the mistakes or sinfulness of the man afflicted. Such a thorough reinterpretation, however, develops late and is never complete. The attribution of disease to mistakes committed by an individual is, by itself, rare. It is clearly connected with the whole concept of taboo and is extensively held wherever taboos are strong as, for instance, among the Eskimo, and in most totemistic societies. But in all these societies, the belief in its connexion with spirits is palpably a priest's or medicine-man's reinterpretation and is predominantly confined to them. For the ordinary man disease and death are regarded as specifically caused by man. This is to be explained as due to the fact that not only is it manifestly one of the oldest beliefs in the world, but it has, at all times, been strongly reinforced by the belief in the evil machinations of the souls of the dead and by ancestor worship.

Yet the belief that death is caused by a spirit, even in societies completely dominated by magic, is far commoner than is customarily supposed. Nor should this occasion any great surprise. Death, it must be remembered, is never looked upon as the reduction of the individual to nothingness. It is simply a change in the manner of communication between one individual and another. Essentially it is a separation—just as is disease. But if disease is a temporary separation of man from the group of the normal human beings, death is a permanent one. The problem of the living is to make this separation permanent and complete and to attempt to remove the dead from the world absolutely and irrevocably. This, however, is difficult and dangerous, for the bonds that attach the dead to the living are numerous, intimate, and palpable, and they cry out for recognition. The dead have had possessions; have had parents and children, husbands and wives. More than this: each one has had a definite status in the community; to each one life on earth had become endeared by the memory of a thousand and one activities shared with others, by gifts and acts of kindness, and embittered by unkindness, hatred, and envy. Such things are not easily forgotten by the dead or by the living. It is easy to understand then why the dead should not wish to forget and why, if persuasion and conciliation fail, the living should, as Frazer has justly remarked in his recent work, *The Fear of the Dead*, employ force and fraud. Forget they must, and if they will not do so willingly, then they must be compelled to do so.

Into the enumeration and discussion of the magical formulae and rites man has devised to speed the departing ghosts, we cannot here enter. Frazer has enumerated them in detail in the work just referred to. Nor is it really necessary for our immediate purpose. That purpose is to determine the reason why the spirits, at an early period in the history of mankind, are connected with the observances and rites centring about death. The answer to that question must now be clear. They are connected with them because the dead and the ghosts of the dead were the materials out of which the notion of spirits actually developed. This is, of course, a very old theory, associated with the name of Herbert Spencer. Because of the popularity of essentially psychological interpretations since the appearance of Tylor's *Primitive Culture* in 1871, it has been somewhat unjustly relegated to the background. Yet its fundamental soundness and correctness seem to me to be beyond doubt. In the relationship of human beings toward one another, living and dead, there are present all the constituents necessary for religion.

Let me again enumerate what these are. There are fundamentally only two: specific emotional reactions, and the offering of gifts which entail the assumption of obligations by both parties, the giver and the receiver. Why should we believe that these will change immediately a man dies? Are not investigators and theorists simply reading the implications of our own Western European civilization into the facts when they make the assumption that a change of attitude is an ultimate human response to this particular situation? Not all of them do of course. Lévy-Bruhl is a shining exception.

The psychoanalysts, following Freud's interpretation as given in *Totem and Taboo*, have, in the interests of their general viewpoint and their specific theory of symbolism, polarized the whole situation to such a degree that it completely distorts the facts. There is no justification for the sharp contrasts they postulate. The only change in attitude, so we may surmise, that must have taken place immediately upon the occasion of a death was the recognition on the part of the living that the customary type of communication between the dead man and the living had changed. But nothing else. Human beings being what they are, that was, of course, fundamental enough. The living must have realized that, whatsoever was the nature of the dead man's presence as a resident in the universe at large, he was absent in the ordinary and somewhat important practical sense of the term. And since it was but natural for certain people to take advantage of a living individual when he was temporarily absent, so it was only natural to do so when he was dead. In the latter case there seemed indeed to be more ample justification for doing so. The dead man was no longer making use of his possessions, tangible and intangible, and it could, for that reason, be claimed that he had thereby lost his rights in them. Primitive people credited the dead man with sufficient sense of the realities to understand this.

The most baffling contradiction of emotions resulted from the interplay of these factors. The ambivalence of feelings and emotions this generated is illuminatingly brought out in the strange medley of magical rites and observances connected with death, in the early reinterpretations of these rites, and in their equally early incorporation into the religious unit *per se*.

The reason for the presence of positive and negative magic in death ceremonies thus lies, we have just seen, in the fact that the dead had to be both propitiated and warded off. Both these attitudes also became essential constituents of religion proper. Their omnipresence there can hardly strike us as strange, for they are, after all, essential constituents in the intercourse between living human beings. Religion itself, in contrast to magic, can very well be regarded as having been originally differentiated from magic, and subsequently fostered, by this extension to the dead of all the attitudes and types of intercourse and behaviour that had been characteristic of the living. Everything is present here—a strong initial emotional intensity, offerings and propitiation, obligations, ambivalence of feeling. The dead thus became easily transformed into supernatural beings and served as the prototypes for that personification and deification of the external world that play so fundamental a role in primitive religion. It is not at all necessary to assume that ancestor worship followed immediately in the wake of the worship of the ghosts of the dead. Ancestor worship is, in fact, a comparatively late development. No well-authenticated instance of its existence can, for example, be found among either food-gathering or simple fishing-hunting peoples.

The religious formulator has taken these contradictory and complementary types of magic and attempted, in the course of time, to restate them completely in terms of his favourite preoccupation: the reduction of the element of coercion inhering in them to its lowest denominator. When we realize the number of obstacles against him, it is clear that he could naturally succeed only to a moderate extent. The explanation for the cause of death, as well as the innumerable customs clustering around it, always remained, accordingly, dominated by the magical mentality.

On one aspect of death, however—the fate and the adventures of the ghost after it had left its earthly envelope—he was at all times permitted, even possibly encouraged, to speculate. To this, and not to the operation of any folk imagination as such, must we attribute the exuberant development of native theories of the soul, of immortality, and of the abode of the dead.

Our purpose in this book, however, is, as we have already indicated, to discuss magic only in its relationship to religion. To say that religion grew specifically out of magic is manifestly wrong. But that magic very definitely preceded religion is beyond the shadow of a doubt. The precise relation the two bear to each other genetically has now been the subject of heated discussion for almost two generations, and a few remarks about the history of the various interpretations of this interrelationship will not be out of place. Space forbids me to do more than touch upon this subject.

Modern anthropology can be said to have begun significantly with the publication in 1871 of E. B. Tylor's *Primitive Culture*. Barely a generation afterwards, Tylor's main contribution, the theory of animism, was subjected to the most far-reaching criticism by a number of scholars. It was pointed out that Tylor had neglected what seemed to them the most characteristic aspect of primitive culture, namely, the role of magic. To the elucidation of this role and of its relation to religion they accordingly devoted themselves. All these new interpretations, it is well to remember, had as their starting point two ethnological areas: native Australia as revealed in the famous monographs of Spencer and Gillen and of Howitt, and native Melanesia as revealed in the equally famous work of Codrington. That the problem was ripe for discussion, however, is indicated by the publication within a year of Codrington, that is, in 1892, of J. H. King's *The Supernatural, Its Origin, Nature and Evolution*.

On the basis of the data for these areas the major theoretical preoccupation of ethnologists of the last forty years has developed. For religion it began with the theory of preanimism, which was first significantly stated in R. R. Marett's article on "Preanimistic Religion" in 1899, and with the specifically magical interpretations of religion first formulated in J. G. Frazer's great work, *The Golden Bough*, published originally in 1890 and completely revised in 1900. Since the appearance of these two works the conception that a preanimistic state preceded the animistic in religion and that the belief in magic was a form of thought preceding so-called rational thought has been generally accepted. Only in England and France, however, have they been thoroughly analysed. The one German ethnologist who occupied himself with the subject, K. T. Preuss, did so in such a sketchy and arbitrary manner that he can be left out of account.

Intelligibly enough the only systematic and serious criticism of these preanimistic and magical theories has been made by the well-known Austrian priest and theorist, W. Schmidt. Many of his strictures are quite pertinent. But he is so obviously a Catholic apologist that their force is thereby greatly diminished. In spite of his admittedly great critical powers one is, quite naturally, deeply suspicious of his treatment of the facts wherever they would seem to militate against the dogmas of the church, and that, in the realm of the history of religion, unfortunately is practically everywhere. Apart from this he has become intimately identified with a highly problematic and dogmatic theory of the evolution of primitive cultures.

In France the number of scholars who have contributed to the elucidation and clarification of these theories is quite large. They include among others such distinguished thinkers as S. Reinach, E. Durkheim, M. Mauss, H. Hubert, and L. Lévy-Bruhl. With the exception of Reinach they are all connected with the well-known viewpoint of Durkheim, so completely and admirably expounded in his famous work, *Les Formes élémentaires de la vie religieuse,* and in the various volumes of the great *Année Sociologique.* Special mention must be made of what is, in many ways, the most stimulating and best presentation of the Durkheim school, Hubert and Mauss's monograph published in *L'Année Sociologique* in 1904 entitled *Esquisse d'une théorie générale de la magie*. Lévy-Bruhl's work we have already mentioned.

The fundamental objections to the point of view of the members of the Durkheim school are the well-known ones. It is aprioristic; it is arbitrary in its choice of information; it is not always critical of what it does select; and it eliminates the individual. These are formidable criticisms to advance against a synthesis that is avowedly concerned with the history of mankind and of religion. All this does not signify that the viewpoint of these writers has no merit. It does, however, mean that most of what they say is strangely unreal and largely beside the point, in any examination of the evolution of human society which is not of so general a type that it loses all concrete intelligibility. One has the feeling that their generalizations, instead of being pauses and vantage points from which to contemplate the known facts that have been subsumed and the unknown that the future still has in store for us, have become end-points which have crystallized in the very process of their formulation. Not only is this an unhealthy condition but it reacts unfavourably upon the very nature of the facts that are actually to be studied and brings about confusion and an unconscious falsification of the record.

5

The Crises of Life and Transition Rites

SOME awareness of the significance of the changes that take place in the life organism, beyond that of their being specific physiological conditions, can be credited to most vertebrates, certainly to most mammals. Among the higher mammals, in fact, the successive activities covering the whole period between sexual maturation and the development of the young into independent beings no longer in need of parental care, have certain characteristics that might very well be interpreted as in the nature of compulsive rites. For few other facts in life is it indeed possible to show so direct a relationship between man and his animal forebears as for those of the sex cycle. It is not strange then that they should have been the first to become socially crystallized, reorganized, and reinterpreted. Nor is it strange that this reorganization and reinterpretation never attempted to disguise the biological facts and acts involved. This is particularly true of the physiological indications of puberty and of sexual intercourse.[1] Even in the most sophisticated religions the symbolism in which this reformulation is expressed has always remained threadbare. Equally significant is the manner in which this sex symbolism was extended to the universe in general. Not only was there a polarization of nature into male and female—the male sky and the female earth, the male sun and the female moon—but sex and its secondary ramifications were brought into immediate and fundamental connexion with the whole life of the group, particularly with regard to the assurance and the perpetuation of the food supply. Pantomime dances and coercive rites were its social expression.

There was, however, another side to this socialization of the

sex cycle which has had a direct bearing on the history of civilization. One of its constituent elements, puberty, became not simply
the recognition that an individual had reached the age of sexual
maturity; it became dramatized as the period of transition *par
excellence*, the passing of an individual from the position of being
an economic liability to that of an economic and social asset.
Two distinct sets of circumstances, one physiological, the other
economic-social, thus conspired to make of puberty an outstanding focus which was to serve as the prototype for all other periods
interpreted as transitional. It was certified and authenticated by
magic and subsequently sanctified and sacramentalized by religion. Its social and economic significance and evaluation are at-
tested by the fact that the simplest tribes, the food-gatherers and
fishing-hunting peoples, have already developed intricate and
complex initiation rites around it. They are the fundamental and
basic rites of mankind. They have been reorganized, remodelled,
and reinterpreted myriads of times, and on their analogy have
been created not only new types of societal units, such as secret societies, but new ideological systems as well.

So fructifying a source of social and religious inspiration must
manifestly have gained its hold upon man's workaday life and
imagination for more than one reason. We have mentioned the
primary one, the fact of its being encased in a physiological, social-
economic, and magical envelope. But certain secondary physiological elements were also involved. The period included between a woman's first menstruation and her pregnancy and
childbirth—they must have followed in rapid succession in the
first phases of civilization—necessitated her complete separation
from the group activities for a varying length of time, a separation that became duly ritualized and dramatized very early. Similarly puberty separated the young boy from the care of his mother
and the older women who were bringing him up. This too became
ritualized and dramatized in diverse ways. In both cases the separation constituted the prelude to a new reintroduction to the life
of the group. It was at the same time a personal and social rein-

tegration. As such it was seized upon by the medicine-man and thinker for the starting point of a series of symbolical interpretations. Of these the principal one was the idea that the individual had died and had been reborn again. This became the favourite theme of primitive man's philosophical and ethical speculations.

I well realize that most students of the history of religion have sought to connect the almost universal presence of this theme in early society with man's almost innate recognition of the processes of nature. They would seem to contend that the very first thing man must have noticed was the annual death and rebirth of the organic world around him, of the daily setting and rising of the sun, of the waning and waxing of the moon. Yet it cannot be too firmly emphasized that this is really reversing the actual order of recognition. Man first analysed himself, and this analysis was stated in terms of his relation to the social-economic world as vitally determined and circumscribed by his physical environment. The results of this analysis or awareness he subsequently extended by analogy to the physical world around him. Only then can it be said that he became significantly conscious of nature dying and being reborn again every year. This was not at all necessarily apparent to non-agricultural peoples, quite apart from the fact that in the first epochs of the palæolithic age man was probably not living in a portion of the world where the changes in season were particularly marked or where nature did, in any very overt manner, die and then become reborn again. The fertility rites that express this recognition most clearly and that play a predominant role in so many primitive tribes and civilized nations are all closely interlinked with agriculture, which is, of course, a comparatively late phase of cultural evolution.

Of the two other major physiological events of life, birth and death, only death became a centre for social and ritualistic associations. Birth was, after all, but a special event in the central sex cycle whose focus was puberty. Yet that, in many cases, it never attained any real independence was not entirely due to its intrinsic connexion with puberty but to the circumstance that it was merely a biological fact and, in a society where economic security was at its lowest, not always the most welcome one, as the great prevalence of infanticide attests. Whatever potential future advantage it held for the group, an individual at birth constituted no immediate asset. The observances and rites that clustered around birth were concerned accordingly more with the parents than with the child. It could develop into a true transition rite and become socially significant only when it did truly represent a transition, that is, after the theory of rebirth had become widespread and an individual was welcomed back into a world from which he had merely been away on a protracted leave. This is not to say that birth passed unnoticed ritually. But it was noticed over a prolonged period of time extending from the day of the child's advent into the world to the age of puberty. Birth was never regarded as a single dramatic fact to which an immediate and clearcut recognition was to be given.

The rites centring around puberty had as their objective the preparation of an individual for a full life as an integral part of the community and his initiation into a new status. The same held true, in a sense, for the death and funeral rites. But the new activities for which the dead man was being prepared, and the new status into which he was being initiated, had a twofold reference. In part they still pertained to this world, in part to a world of the imagination. The cardinal difference between the two lay in the fact that, whereas the puberty rites were positive and symbolized the separation of a youth from a life of social inactivity in order that he might be conducted into one of activity, the death rites were negative and symbolized the separation of a man from a life of activity so that he might begin one of inactivity. At least that was the goal sought by the living. Of course we do know that in these death separation-rites the wish was father to the thought. It was soon realized that the complete elimination of the dead was not an easy task. Instead of his complete separation and relegation to inactivity a compromise was arrived at which corresponded more accurately to the strong ambivalence of feeling with which the living regarded the dead. The separation between the dead man and the living world was accordingly made partial and gradual and the inactivity transformed into a latent hostility.

Yet the rites for the dead, in spite of all other constituents, remained basically a ritual of separation to which there was soon added the ritual of the soul's entry into a new non-human and altogether desirable world. Here was a field as if made to order for the creative imagination of the medicine-man and poet-thinker, and the voluminous treatment received by the ritual drama of the soul's separation from the land of the living, and of its journey to the land of the dead and the blessed, indicates only too clearly the extent to which he took full advantage of it. Manifestly it was in the interests of people who craved that the dead be separated effectively and irrevocably from the living, to paint the haven to which the deceased were to be directed as free from the hardships and the insecurities of this world. Perhaps then they would stay there. Innumerable variations were rung on this theme. They were all largely concerned with rebirth. Was death to be taken as a reintegration of the ego for renewed activity in a new supernatural world or, ultimately, for renewed activity in this? Was the realm of the dead to become autonomous and co-equal with our own? Were the dead to become reincarnated? Was the distinction between life and death to become blurred or was it to be blotted out? Such were some of the problems for speculation.

In the simpler cultures, before the rise of full agriculture, the first view seems to have prevailed, and this belief in transmigration and reincarnation found its expression in such a conception, for instance, as that of the Winnebago, where death was interpreted as a momentary stumbling involving no loss of consciousness although signifying a break in the means of communication between the dead and the living but which the dead, or at least the favoured dead, will, after considerable hardships and suffering, eventually restore.

Birth, puberty, and death were thus, very early, recognized as an unending cycle, in which an individual passed from one level of existence to another. Of these the highest level was the period between puberty and the first signs of physical and social senility, that wherein a sexually mature individual began his full social realization. Death was its negation and birth its new affirmation. It is in this emphasis upon man as functioning in our workaday world that we find the clue to the ambivalent attitude toward death. As a biological extinction death had no terrors. The evidence for the correctness of this statement is overwhelming. Death conceived of as annihilation was, however, a denial of the highest and most meaningful functioning which an individual knew. It was consequently to be interpreted as simply a temporary cessation of activity just as the period between birth and puberty was to be regarded as an abeyance.

The puberty situation was thus the central and vivifying focal point from which rites and observances radiated in all directions. It was soon broken up into its constituent elements, most of which received special treatment. In the case of women the physiological facts—the first menstruation, pregnancy, and childbirth—at first dwarfed the social-economic factors; in the case of men the social-economic factors from the very beginning dwarfed the physiological. This was natural enough at a period in man's existence where woman's position was at best undifferentiated, politically and economically. The social-economic implications of this situation thus being so much more important for the man, it is not surprising that the puberty rites for him have always remained far more complex and differentiated than those for the woman. The latter became progressively more complex as her economic functions became more important, after the introduction of agriculture, for instance. Occasionally, as in some West African tribes, puberty rites exist for her only.

To these puberty rites we shall now turn, taking as our examples the Arunta of Australia, the Selknam of Tierra del Fuego, the New Caledonians, the Ashanti of West Africa, and the Thonga of South Africa.[2] Space will permit us to describe in detail only the Australian and Thongan rites. The justification for dwelling at such length upon rites that are primarily magical is to give the reader some conception of the materials from which were subsequently developed those specifically religious ceremonies and dramas that form so vital and integral a part of the life of most of the agricultural civilizations found among primitive people. To reject by stressing too insistently the magical and folkloristic nature of much of what is contained in these ritual dramas would be equivalent, on a different level of course, to chiding the great classical drama of Greece for its retention of uncouth superstitions and for its often archaic delineation of the Greek deities, or to dismissing as utterly magical the whole ritual of the Christian Passion because it obviously contains elements that hark back to a primitive and unintegrated past.

Before proceeding to a description of the initiation rites, it might, however, be well to review briefly the point of view of M. Van Gennep, to whom we owe the first complete and certainly the most stimulating survey of the various transition rites.[3]

According to him all transition rites can be divided into three groups: separation, marginal or intermediate, and reunion. The validity of this division all will concede. But Van Gennep—and a large number of scholars are in agreement with him—assumes that in primitive religion there is a sharp distinction between the workaday world and the supernatural world. I cannot follow him at all in his definition of the sacred and the profane nor can I accept the concept of marginal or intermediate as being either valid or fruitful. Yet the view that the life of an individual in primitive society fluctuates between the profane and the sacred and that it is largely concerned with the attempt to attain to a holy state, even if only temporarily, is widely accepted by all students of primitive culture. With that interpretation we are in complete disagreement, the reasons for which must have already become apparent to the reader.

We shall begin with the Arunta of Central Australia.

The Australian economy is based on food-gathering, fishing, and hunting. Because of the apparent simplicity of the whole mode of life, the Australian civilization became, very early in the history of ethnology, the classical example of an archaic primitive culture. As such it has been utilized repeatedly by all theorists, particularly by J. G. Frazer and E. Durkheim. During the last few years, however, it has become increasingly more obvious that a fairly complicated evolution lies behind the present-day native culture. But whether this is so or not, the extreme antiquity of the initiation rites is not to be questioned.

Every Australian boy when he reaches the age of puberty must submit to circumcision and subincision and participate in the series of ceremonies centring around them. In spite of the painfulness of the operations involved, particularly as they are carried out under the very primitive conditions prevailing, the young boys submit to them cheerfully, for in no other way can they acquire full social status. The German missionary Strehlow has described these rites with admirable understanding and, since he brings out their salient traits and purposes more clearly than his famous predecessors, Spencer and Gillen, and gives a better insight into the native viewpoint, his account will be followed. The series of ceremonies constitutes distinct acts in a long ritual drama and as such I shall present it:

Act I. This act is given the generic name of *Thrown-toward-Heaven* because the essential part of the ceremony is the throwing of the novice into the air. As he falls to the ground he is then subjected to a severe beating. The throwing in the air is supposed symbolically to assure him growth of stature and the beating to inspire him with fear for his elders.

The boy is then immediately separated from the camp of the married women and older unmarried girls and compelled to stay in that of the unmarried men. This separation is the first of many acts designed to wean him from the conception of women as mothers and as non-sexed and to substitute for it that of women as wives and as sexed. After being properly painted and smeared he is led before the elder men who throw him in the air, beat him, and then order him to retire into seclusion, to a place near their camp. There he must light a blazing fire. He is allowed to eat only plants. To symbolize this initial stage in his passage from the status of a boy, he is given various names, first, The-Fat-Besmeared-One, and second, The-Morally-Good-One.

Act II. This often consists of two parts: the Ltata dance and the issuance of invitations to the neighbouring camp to attend the initiation rites. The Ltata dance has as its purpose the mitigation of the boy's fear of the operation to be performed on him and to induce him to believe that he is really to be shown some new and interesting ceremonies. Its secondary purpose is that of acting as sex magic to interest the women in the men participating.

Act III. The Circumcision. Before the elders proceed to the circumcision ceremonies proper, the boy is initiated into the knowledge of those secret rites that are in some manner connected with the mythical history of circumcision. After an all-night dance of the women, the young boy is first taken away from the camp and then brought back and ceremonially led to different parts of the initiation place. Before evening he is shown for the first time in his life the sacred *wonninga.* The next day he is newly decorated, given another name, and initiated into the knowledge of a few more secret rites. The one who is to perform the circumcision is then selected. Everything now is in readiness for the circumcision rites proper.

At a signal agreed upon, the novice, who has been sitting quietly with his head bent over his folded arms, suddenly jumps up and seats himself on a shield which his father's brother is holding. Two old women relatives then approach and efface the decoration which had been painted on his forehead just before he had been given his last name and which was to symbolize that his separation from the women and from his former life was now complete. They then warn him to avoid thereafter the footpaths used by women or any other place where he might encounter them. The novices are now driven away in fright by two men whirling bullroarers. Six men are thereupon designated to build up a human "platform" upon which the novice is to lie when he is circumcised. This "platform" is formed by having one man stand on the ground on all fours while five other men lie across him, at right angles. Finally the operator appears, his eyes rolling and his whole behaviour indicative of a madman. As he seizes the prepuce of the young boy, the audience of older men shout in chorus:

"Behold the maddened one! Let him circumcise the heaven-raised one!"

He then performs the circumcision. The blood flowing from the wound is caught in a shield and buried in a hole. The prepuce is then pressed against the abdomen of the boy's father and older brother in order to mitigate the pain that the sight of the novice's suffering may have caused them. It is then buried in some secret place.

The boy has now become a man, and to symbolize this fact he is initiated into the true nature of the bullroarer in the following manner:

We have always told you there was a spirit called Tuanjiraka and that he it was who had caused you pain. But you must now give up this belief and instead realize that the Tuanjiraka and the bullroarer are one and the same. When you were a child we spoke to you and to the women about you as though the two were distinct. Now the time has arrived for you to know that they are identical. Yet what we told you when you were a boy, that you must now in turn pass on to your children, so that the knowledge that Tuanjiraka does not really exist is not divulged to them. If this information were to become generally known then we would all disappear from the face of the earth and those below the skies would know that we had been wiped out. So, young man, you, like us, must never spread this information and must never allow children to hear about it. Keep the knowledge of the bullroarer secret and spread the myth of Tuanjiraka. Like our ancestors, so you, too, have now become a man. Remember again that if the children were ever to hear the truth about it you would become deathly ill. So you must, like us, continue to lie and say: "Why, of course, Tuanjiraka exists." [4]

The main male participants now leave the scene of operations, and the novice is taken to a place outside the camp where he is carefully watched by specially appointed relatives. He receives two new names from the men, He-with-the-Wound and He-Who-Hides-Himself, and two new ones from the women and children, respectively The-Child and The-Hidden-Little-Man. The youth himself applies special names to all the individuals involved in the ceremonial. He calls himself the Dog; the operator, the Pain-Instigator; he who holds the prepuce during the operation, He-in-Whose-Presence-We-Must-Observe-Silence; and those who caught the blood in their shield are designated as Bound-to-Each-Other-by-the-Shield or Bound-to-Me-as-a-Father. He must remain silent in the presence of a number of these people until his wound has healed and he has presented them with a gift of meat. Then a short harangue on morals is delivered and a long series of food taboos imposed on him. As a matter of fact he is allowed to eat only roots and the meat of a few animals, and threatened with being thrown into the fire if he disobeys. Finally he is taught an entirely new vocabulary, which he must use throughout his forced exile. Then he is removed to a place at a considerable distance from the camp and Act III is over.

Act IV. The Subincision. This begins about six weeks after the circumcision. The young man is sent away on a hunt while his father is informed of the healing of the wound. Then the boy returns and is asked to sit in the midst of a circle formed by old men. He holds his head in his hands, and as he does so all the old men in succession bite his head till he is all covered with blood. The reason given by the natives for this very painful operation is that it insures the growth of head-hair. On the following day a long pole made of a eucalyptus limb is carefully wrapped with string fashioned from hair, decorated with black charcoal rings, and covered with birds' down. After it has been set up and duly admired, it is hidden just before evening, to be brought back again after midnight.

In the evening a group of men conduct the novice to a secret place. There the young men paint and decorate themselves to the accompaniment of songs sung by the old people. Ten young men then hide in the neighbourhood only to rush back within a short time to perform an intricate pantomime dance. A long spear is now placed over the neck of the ten dancers and all go to join the old men. Shortly after midnight the old men, who have been resting until then, rise and start for a specially designated place near the camp, where, after a blazing fire has been started, they plant the decorated eucalyptus pole. This pole is supposed to symbolize the spear of one of their ancestors. At the first sign of dawn the novice is brought in from the camp. His father now presses the eucalyptus pole against the boy's abdomen, supposedly in order to drive away the fear of the impending pains and to give him courage. "Do not fear; remain quiet, for today you will become a man!" the boy is assured. Then he is placed on a human platform as in the case of the circumcision rite and the operation is performed.

The next two acts of the drama, the smudging rite and the rite to induce the growth of a long beard, are not of great importance.

Act VII. The final act is called *Inkura.* This is a series of rites and dances which may take place as much as two years after the subincision. It often lasts more than two months. Women take part but only at the beginning and at the end.

A special piece of ground is prepared near the camp where the main festivities take place and in which are hidden bullroarers borrowed from neighbouring camps. After this has been done, the chief returns to the main camp and distributes spears and spear-throwers to the various novices, who, carrying them on their shoulders, march to the specially designated place for the final act. They are almost immediately sent out on a hunt, and after they have returned with their booty, a meal is prepared and they are initiated into the knowledge of a few more secret rites. In the ceremony that follows the women and children may take part but they must keep at some distance from the novice. At an arranged time the chief calls the novices, and they appear running and throw themselves upon the ground in front of him. There they are placed on smoking branches of eucalyptus until they are covered with perspiration. When this is finished they rise and run away, pursued by their official guard. When they return they find that a long decorated pole has been erected to which small bullroarers have been attached. Near it is a large pit in which sit the ceremonial chief and his helpers. The novices rush toward it, one jumping into the pit and, at the same time, pressing the head of the chief down to signify that the ceremony is now over. Other novices sit at the end of the pit with their feet inside. A number of rites take place at the pole and finally, toward evening, a messenger is sent to the women to inform them that they are now to come and view their future husbands. When they arrive, the old men paint and decorate the novices and the latter climb up the poles and slide down again. Shouting and shrieking, holding their hands on the back of their necks, they march in a goose-trot around the women. Then the women retire.

The old men now distribute bullroarers to the novices, and the latter scatter in all directions, swinging their bullroarers continuously in order to inspire the women with fear. It is also believed that this will awaken their passions. The boys have returned by this time and now lie down to sleep. While they are asleep the old men bury the pole. During the night the chief starts a fire at each of the cardinal points. At dawn he awakens the women and orders them to dig a small pit, light a fire, and throw branches into it. The novices now come forth, two at a time, and are placed on top of the smoking branches. After this smudging ceremony the women press their hands on the chests and the backs of the boys and take off their various finery. The fire is extinguished and the lengthy drama is over. . . .

Before we turn to our next example a few general comments

might perhaps not be out of place. The native interpretation of these ceremonies is a model of realism. Their purpose is to insure the authority and wealth of the older men. Of the main native reasons enumerated by Strehlow [5] only one, for instance, is entirely magical, the reason for subincision. This rite is supposed to make the youth lithe and nimble so that he can ward off the spears of the enemy. Circumcision itself is interpreted in a number of ways: to prevent the prepuce from growing together, to reduce sexual excesses, and to inculcate respect for the elders. But over and above all other reasons is the somewhat cynically expressed purpose of the old men of having the novices supply them, for many years, with regular presents in the form of animal food, of reserving the choice dishes for themselves by the utilization of the numerous food taboos imposed on the younger people, and, finally, of keeping the young women for themselves.

The psychoanalysts, naturally enough, will have none of this. To stress economic-social factors is for them quite irrelevant and ludicrously beside the point. Their romantic proclivities are thereby only outraged. These Australian initiation ceremonies are accordingly welcome grist for their mill. The bullroarer, regarded by the natives themselves either as the ancestral ghost or its materialization or as being what it actually is, this a Freudian like Róheim has no hesitation in identifying with the penis. A penis-shaped object found marking the graves is interpreted as

the representative of a second body or soul which springs up when one of the *Alcheringa* ancestors dies and is derived from a mitigated ceremonial castration [subincision]. . . . It indicates the passage from and to the land beyond the grave. . . . Our sources call the something that is separated from the body at the moment of death a soul. But various features of world-wide belief, such as the serpent-shaped soul and the other phallic symbols for the soul, the analogy felt in many places between cohabitation, i.e., the egress of semen and extasis, i.e., the egress of the soul, together with the procreative faculty attributed to the latter—all these show that the eternal idea of the soul is but the sublimation of a male member pure and simple. . . . After all this is not a very surprising conclusion . . . [for] supernatural ideas are but the symbolic representation of biological facts.[6]

No one of course will deny the strong preoccupation with sex to be found in all puberty rites. That is, after all, only natural. But what we are dealing with there is simply the sex imagery and the sex symbolism of the moment. There is nothing ancient or archaic about it. To assume that we are concerned here with "the survival of the archaic multiplication by fission, the phase of development in which the propagation of the species was also the death of the individual," as Róheim following Ferenczi does, such a conception can only be characterized as sublime romanticism.

That rites of so vital a nature would early become associated with religious beliefs goes without saying. But here in Australia this association is manifestly secondary. Everything is definitely subordinated to a general social theme ceremonially conceived of as a progressive separation from one type of life and an entry into another, a progression which includes a number of steps recurring in all puberty rites whenever they have attained any complex expression.

Among the Selknam of Tierra del Fuego we find this theme even more dramatically stressed. The separation of the boys from their mothers is attended with all the signs of intense grief. The boys are there initiated by masked men impersonating spirits with whom they have to wrestle. They are overcome, the struggle symbolizing their death and rebirth. In spite of its marked penetration with definite religious beliefs the social-economic purpose is brought out with the same incisiveness as was the case for the Australians. The fundamental and immediate objective was to maintain power in the hands of the older people and to keep the women in proper subjection. But through it all the larger social-biological formula is still clearly visible—the death in one status and the rebirth in another, on a higher level. The completion of this formula, the conception that actual death is really a protracted sep-

aration to serve as a transition to birth and for a repetition of the
whole life cycle, that is unknown here.

But let us now turn to an entirely different culture, that of New
Caledonia, which is based on agriculture and which possesses a
specialized economic system. In general it can be said that wherever full agriculture has developed the puberty ritual becomes
considerably simplified because there are then other and newer
rituals more specifically bound up with this mode of life to take
the place of the older and to serve as the ceremonial focal point.

As in other parts of the world the separation of the young boys
from the women is strictly enjoined. Léenhardt says:

The ceremony always takes place near some isolated body of water
lying concealed under trees and where no strange eye can through
chance penetrate. No woman is allowed to approach this retreat. The
euphemistic expression employed in conversation with women to describe circumcision clearly indicates the secret character it was supposed
to possess. . . . The pilou are thus located in a place entirely cut off
from the rest of the world. They lie within an area circumscribed by the
body of water wherein the initiated bathe and where the skulls of ancestors are piled up. Here it is that the hut prepared for the newly circumcised boy is to be found and where they rest during their convales-
cence.[7]

Chastity is regarded as essential not because of moral scruples
but because it is believed that sexual indulgence before initiation
might prevent a successful circumcision. Great care is taken after
the operation to prevent any inflammation. As soon as the novices
begin to convalesce, old women bring them food every five days.
But they must eat by themselves and observe two main rules: not
to allow themselves to be seen by the public and not to eat certain
proscribed foods. As soon as possible they obtain their own food
in order to demonstrate their skill to the community.

At night they go along the roads frequented by the people during
the daytime and dig ditches in the earth in the shape of the birds, bats,

and fish which they have succeeded in catching and eating. . . . As a proof of their exploits they place at the bottom of the holes the fish-bones and the remains of their game. The people are all excited when they come upon these things as they pass along the paths the next morning. . . . Finally, as a still more marked indication of their vitality, the young novices plant a large pole on top of a hill. This high pole is in the nature of an announcement that the young men regard themselves as almost cured and that they are about to re-enter the world of everyday life. It marks the "finale." The pole itself is called *ti* and is a replica of the *karoti* tree that is planted as a memorial of the dead and which effectively closes the road to him. The tree that is thus cut and planted, the *ti*, is supposed to recall the dead to one's mind. The *ti* itself decays and falls down. The circumcised *membrum virile*, which is its analogue, that too is a memento for the dead, but it endures for ever. . . .

Through this communion with the ancestors that is called to mind by the mutilation, the newly circumcised youths attain to their social maturity. They leave the tutelage of the women and are admitted to the society of men. But they still are not authorized to touch a woman except at their own risk and peril. For this they must await the decision of their elders. This is of course accorded them. . . . The woman that they then marry must be given a purification drink in order to remove the dangers attendant upon their union.[8]

The above account indicates clearly that both the separation and the circumcision are conceived of as a temporary death which is to be succeeded by a new and more mature life.

Among the Ashanti [9] of West Africa, in a civilization of the most complicated type both economically and politically, the basic formula is still definitely visible. Here only girls go through a puberty ceremony. The theme of birth and death is repeated at every turn. An old woman told Captain Rattray, for instance, that the reason why women are carried at certain parts of the ritual is that they are newly born and cannot walk. Similarly the old women in the tribe regard the ceremony with a note of sadness, taking it as a portent of their own death. "A birth in this world is a death in the world of ghosts; when a human mother conceives, a ghost-mother's infant is sickening to die." So runs an Ashanti proverb. There is no separation from the community here as in the other instances given because, among the Ashanti, this theme has been transferred to the rites connected with birth. In a way the Ashanti puberty ceremony can be regarded as the positive phase of a lengthy initiation rite beginning with birth and of which birth is the negative or perhaps neutral side.

For our purposes the most important aspect of these Ashanti rites is the marked persistence of the magico-folkloristic background, on the one hand, and the intimate connexion with religion, on the other, a connexion not always apparent in the simpler cultures of primitive people. But even here the gods enjoy no specific role. They are not even protectors. They are simply listeners to be informed, in ceremonial fashion, that something fundamental to the lives of human beings has taken place. The magico-folkloristic background still retains its autonomy. Only against death, death at the hands of the Mother-Who-Dwells-in-the-Land-of-Ghosts, do they ask protection. Thus as soon as the girl has told her mother that she has begun to menstruate, the latter takes some wine and, spilling it upon the ground, makes the following statement to the gods—it can hardly be said to be a prayer:

Supreme Sky God, who is alone great, upon whom men lean and do not fall, receive this wine and drink.

Earth Goddess, whose day of worship is a Thursday, receive this wine and drink.

Spirit of our ancestors, receive this wine and drink.

This girl child whom God has given to me, today the *bara* state has come upon her.

O mother who dwells in the land of ghosts, do not come and take her away and do not have permitted her to menstruate only to die.[10]

Turning now to another region I shall select as a final example of the formula the well-known puberty rites of the Thonga of south-east Africa so admirably described by Junod.[11] Here we find every element of the formula fully preserved. As in so many African and Oceanic tribes, all the rites centre around circumcision, and the complete ceremonial is, as a matter of fact, regarded as belonging to "the circumcision school." The economic aspects of the "school" are brought out very neatly at the very start. The ceremonial is controlled by the chief and the arrangements are made by the council of headmen over which he presides. It is the chief who supervises it and who receives the fees paid by those who are to be initiated. The highly profitable nature of the ceremonial is also brought out by the fact that all those young men who were initiated on the previous occasion—the intervals are generally four years—have to attend the school as shepherds and act as servants of the leaders.

What we have here then is a true ritual drama of impressive significance. As such I shall describe it.

Act I. The Circumcision. The time of the year for the opening of the school is the month in which the morning star, Venus, appears in winter. A lodge is built at a considerable distance from the village and then, as the morning star rises, the young men leave the inhabited world for what is the equivalent of the wilderness, to enter the lodge or, as it is called, "the yard of mysteries." That is the first rite. Then as they pass along the road they come upon a fire made of scented wood. Across this they must jump. Shortly after, they hear a tremendous noise made by the beating of drums and the blowing of antelope horns accompanying a song. This song the boys must pretend not to understand. Here they are stopped, and eight of them are pushed forward between two rows of singers who give them a good whipping at one end and deprive of their clothes at the other. Then their hair is cut off and they are made to sit on eight stones placed near the entrance of the yard, at a spot called "the place of the crocodile." On eight stones directly opposite them are eight men called lion-men, their heads covered with lion manes and presenting a terrifying appearance. As a boy is seated he receives a severe blow on the head from behind, and as he turns to see who has struck him he beholds a shepherd laughing at him. This is the opportunity the circumciser has been waiting for. As the boy's attention is diverted, the operator seizes the foreskin and with two swift movements cuts it off. Often the boy falls down unconscious and is restored by having cold water thrown on him. In the expressive phrase of the Thonga the boy has now *crossed*. He is brought into the lodge.

Act II. The Trials. (*a*) *The yard of mysteries*. The yard of mysteries or *sungi*, where the second part of the drama takes place, is replete with symbolism. It is surrounded by a high fence made of thorny branches, to indicate that all that takes place within must be kept secret. This fence is prolonged at the entrance so as to make a long avenue through which one passes in order to penetrate into the yard. Then the way is continued by twelve poles, six on each side. The road between these poles is intended only for the inmates of the yard. Visitors, men of course, turn around them and cross the road five times in order to reach the men's entrance at the end. They do not use the candidates' entrance, which is on the other side. In the central court there is a long fireplace of stones called the Elephant, around which the boys sit to warm themselves. In the middle of the yard is often found a tree, which the instructor climbs when he is imparting his teaching.

(*b*) *Sexual and linguistic taboos*. Sexual intercourse is, of course, prohibited to all the inmates of the enclosure. It is permitted for married people in the village, but there should be no noise and, particularly, no quarrels between jealous co-wives. It is interesting to note that the consequences of any disturbance of the peace are purely economic, namely, it would give the shepherds an excuse to come to the village in the evening and plunder it. The most interesting aspect of the sexual taboos, however, is connected with the use of obscene language. Even mothers have the right to sing obscene songs when they are pounding the meal for the occupants of the yard. As in the case of the Arunta, many words and expressions are used that have nothing in common with the everyday language.

The whole purpose of the arrangements in the enclosure and of the observances just enumerated is manifestly that of emphasizing the completeness of the separation that has occurred from the workaday world. The existence of taboos for old words and the freedom to use obscene language, customs frequently encountered in rites for the dead, heighten this feeling of the gulf between the old life and the present, both for the boys and for the other participants and the relatives.

(c) *The six trials.* As the Thonga proverb goes, "Ngoma [the circumcision school] is the shield of buffalo's hide! It is the crocodile which bites," i.e., candidates must be prepared for the hardships of initiation because they are only a rehearsal for the hardships of life. The trials to which they must submit are six in number—blows at the slightest pretext, cold, thirst, unsavoury food, punishment, and death. Space forbids our describing more than a few of these tests.

Every day the novices sit around the Elephant and pretend to lunge at some object with a stick while the men and shepherds dance around them singing the following song with a symbolical implication: "The black cow kicks! It kicks against the jug of the baboon!" The shepherds themselves are supposed to represent the cow which the boys are to milk and who is to kick them.

Nothing is done to protect the novices against the cold. They must lie naked in their shed, light a fire but only near their heads, and lie flat on their backs. No blanket is permitted. In the morning they are led to the water and often must stay in it until the sun rises. Not a drop of water is permitted them throughout the initiation. The main food is a kind of unsavoury porridge without seasoning. This they must devour almost in the manner of animals. Punishments are meted out at the slightest provocation. Death not infrequently results from infection following the circumcision. In such a case no mourning is permitted.

(*d*) *Teaching the formula*. When the trials are over, the words of the secret formulae are taught. The words are generally unintelligible and are subjected to symbolical reinterpretation. Thus, for example, in one such formula we find the following wellnigh meaningless phrases: "The little bird has sung; it has stirred the handles of the lances which are like lions; they pierce each other; the running of the wild pig; of the frog which cries . . ."

According to Junod these phrases are to be explained in the following manner:

The lances which are like lions ready to tear each other represent the school, which is starting, *awakened by the bird of winter. The running of the wild pig* is the description of the life of the boy who was idling his time away and waiting until the initiation would make a man of him. *The croaking of the frog (shinana)* is his childish stupidity. The *shinana* is a strange animal indeed, a small batrachian which when attacked swells to considerable proportions; then it becomes so hard that its enemies, even a cock with a sharp beak, so they say, cannot pierce it. The now circumcised boy, before initiation, was a *shinana* before it swelled up.[12]

Act III. Return to the World. There are four parts to this act: the raising of the so-called *mulagaru* pole, a masked dance called *mayiwayiwane*, the waking test, and the chameleon procession. They represent a graded series of reintroductions to a new world and to a new status.

(*a*) The *mulagaru* pole is erected in that part of the yard where the formulae have been taught. At its extremity a man is placed half hidden by white hair. Then the boys are awakened and brought to the pole, told to lie on their backs, and instructed to address the pole as follows: "Good morning, grandfather." The man at the top answers: "I greet you, my grandchildren." This conversation with the "grandfather" is repeated for a number of days. As an indication that the separation is soon to give place to a reunion with the world is the fact that the boys are now allowed to complain of their sufferings and to ask permission to return home. The man at the top of the pole, so runs the official interpretation, is the ancestor of the clan, and by talking to him they begin their admission to the adult life of the community. Then come a purification drink and permission to drink water.

(*b*) In the *mayiwayiwane* dance the boys are masked and execute high jumps before the women, who are summoned for this special occasion. The women must not be allowed to recognize the masked dancers, who are supposed to be supernatural beings. If, through chance, any of the dancers falls down, he is immediately covered with a heap of grass and pronounced dead. The official theory is that a circumcised novice cannot fall and still remain alive.

(*c*) Following the *mayiwayiwane* dance comes what is considered the greatest of all the trials through which the youth must pass, that of not being allowed to close his eyes for a whole night. The following morning the bits of skin still remaining from the circumcision are picked up, burned, and made into a powder with which the *mulagaru* pole is smeared. Then the masks and mats are thrown on the roof of the shed and at dawn all the boys are driven, at a trot, to a pool. They are not allowed to look back. The whole temporary establishment is then burned up and the boys wash away the white clay, cut their hair, anoint themselves with ochre and put on new clothing. The women now bring seasoned porridge and, as a final indication of the break with the licence that prevailed when the "yard of mysteries" still existed, the shepherds who receive the pots from the women are not allowed to use insulting words to them.

(*d*) Then comes the last rite, the final affirmation of the new life that has been attained. This is the chameleon procession undertaken by the initiated to the capital of the chief. Covered with ochre, marching on mats spread out on the ground, the boys advance slowly at first, bending their bodies forward. Suddenly they change into a brisk motion and, stretching out first one leg and then the other, they press forward, imitating the stately gait of the chameleon. Finally they enter the capital. There, with heads bowed, they sit in the central place. Now it is that their mothers and sisters are expected to recognize them. Each mother, carrying a bracelet or whatever present she may have brought, searches for her son and, when she has found him, kisses him on the cheek and gives him a gift. The boy then rises, strikes his mother a good blow on the shoulder, and utters the new name he has chosen, and the mother, in answer, begins to dance and sing the praises of her son. The ritual drama is over.

As I have already pointed out, the puberty ceremonial is the transition rite *par excellence*. Innumerable beliefs and observances cluster around birth, marriage, and other events of life but they rarely receive the same elaborate ritualistic treatment accorded puberty. Where they do receive such elaboration, as in complex agricultural societies with marked social stratification, the formula so prominently discerned in the puberty rites is, however, still found in full evidence, although naturally distorted and reinterpreted by the new economic environment to which it must adjust itself. Again we find the passage from one condition to another, from a lower status to a higher one, and again we find this symbolically designated as death and rebirth. The frequent occurrence of rites connected with death in the simpler societies is not really an exception to our generalization, for death, like puberty, has, from the very beginning of human society, apparently been regarded as a transition rite. Nevertheless, a really elaborate ritual drama portraying death and rebirth is found only among the more advanced cultures. For a discussion of it I must, however, refer the reader to the voluminous information on the ritual drama found in such works as Frazer's *Golden Bough*.

No one can possibly read the descriptions of the puberty-drama given above without being impressed with the manner in which heterogeneous elements of all kinds, most of them evidently derived from the most archaic stratum of the magico-folkloristic background, have been integrated into a consistent whole and how obviously this integration has been made to serve direct social-economic purposes. It is equally apparent that these economic purposes do not always or even generally have only the good of the community as their primary objective and that, not infrequently, they directly serve the interests of certain groups or classes. In the simpler cultures they are the elders; in the more complex ones, definite coteries or groups, whether we call them economic classes or not.

Manifestly this is not the work of the group as such nor the folk-soul expressing itself unconsciously in obedience to some mystical urge. Rather it is the accomplishment of specific individuals banded together formally or informally, of individuals who possess a marked capacity for articulating their ideas and for organizing them into coherent systems, systems naturally which would be of profit to them and to those with whom they are allied. Here again we have the religious formulator at work. If, in the drama connected with the transition rites, his religious activities seem to be in abeyance, that is due to the patent fact that he has there to contend with the viewpoint of the non-religious man and because the social-economic purposes of the rites outweighed all other considerations.

Yet obviously something reminiscent of a religious feeling permeates the attitude of many of the participants in and beholders of these rites. But what is it that so permeates them and how shall we describe it?

Since the belief in spirits or gods forms no integral part of these rituals, we must seek for the religious implications elsewhere. To the author they inhere in the attitude of individuals toward their life-values. Religious implications are of course very easy to find if we think of the religion of primitive peoples in the somewhat elastic fashion so customary among recent theorists and ethnologists. Take for instance Van Gennep's definition as it is restated by Rattray. It may be regarded as representative. Rattray, in speaking of transition rites, says:

Hence, regarded from the side of what we should call religion, namely the side of taboo, the typical rite not only expresses the central purpose of attaining to a holy state but likewise dramatizes the entrance and the exit, whereby the worshipper abandons and in due course resumes the tenor of his workaday.[13]

Rattray, as we might expect from so consistent a realist, has his doubts about the correctness of such a definition. It is, however, the currently accepted one.

According to this conception, apparently any stoppage in the even tenor of the workaday world is to be construed as incomprehensible and non-natural in origin and therefore as partaking of magic and religion. Stoppage, separation, taboo, they are all to be equated and regarded as essentially akin, if not identical, in the view of these theorists. They would have us believe that this interpretation is confirmed by the existence of such marked contrasting categories as the concept of the profane and the sacred. But I cannot help feeling that they have unconsciously been led astray by the prominence of these categories in the great historic religions. Rattray, as we have just mentioned, and there are many ethnologists proper who share his doubts, is extremely sceptical of the degree to which primitive man is aware of the taboo condition and of the extent to which he regards it as indicative of a spiritual retreat which is to be followed by a readjustment to life through what he calls a disciplining of the soul. Had Rattray himself, however, looked at religious phenomena as the expression of a certain type of temperament and not simply as an expression of individuals indiscriminately, he would undoubtedly have phrased his doubts somewhat differently and have realized that, while the concept of a spiritual retreat and of the sacred and the profane does undoubtedly exist, it is a construct of the religious formulator and is only inconsistently shared by the people at large; that not even the former can be, or, for that matter, regards it as desirable to be, himself wholly consistent.

Yet his creation is of sufficient consistency to act as a point of crystallization for all those vague fears and emotions that arise from the conflict of man with the workaday world and from his recognition of the outstanding physiological events of life—birth, puberty, sexual intercourse as stabilized in marriage, and death. The intervals between them came to be interpreted as "profane" and the events themselves as "sacred." On the basis of this distinction there were eventually to develop true sacraments. In other words, life was to become completely sacramentalized. Yet this sacramentalization must not be looked upon wholly through ideological spectacles. It is in fact prevailingly practical and realistic. How could it very well be different? For, to whom do we owe it, whose temperament does it express and whose interests does it specifically serve? The answer is simple enough. We owe it to the same group of individuals to whom we must credit all the significant articulations of religion—the shaman, the medicine-man, and the priest. Let us accordingly turn to a consideration of the role of these men and women and study the manner in which they worked.

6

From Magicians to Priests:
Their Nature and Initiation

FROM the very beginning of our contact with primitive peoples Western Europeans have differed in their attitude toward the medicine-man and shaman. Some have felt that they were, in the main, conscious impostors; others that they were sincere but the dupes of their own beliefs and imaginings. What Europeans think on such a matter is perhaps of minor importance. It is of some consequence, however, to know that a similar division of opinion has apparently always existed among aboriginal peoples themselves. How is this to be interpreted? Are we to seek for an explanation along social-psychological lines, such as the average man's resentment against the shaman's occasional lack of success or against the power and prestige he possessed? Or shall we seek it in an even more specific context, his jealousy of the shaman's economic security, his resentment at the fees he is forced to pay or at the fact that these fees save the shaman from part, at least, of the hardships connected with the securing of food? All these reasons clearly enter. But it is not only the average man who voices his doubts concerning the shaman's sincerity. Shamans themselves do. This too we must expect where rivalry and competition between them are as great and as intense as is the case among practically all primitive tribes. After discounting for all these possibilities, however, something still remains unexplained, and for that we must fall back upon the temperamental characteristics of the medicine-men themselves.

The two temperaments, that of the thinker-artist and that of the layman, whose influence is so marked in the actions and thoughts of our own civilizations, are encountered among aboriginal cultures as well. Let us call them introvert and extravert although, naturally, no characterization in this simple fashion is correct or adequate. Far from being less marked the contrast between these temperaments is, in primitive cultures, often sharper and more clearcut than in our own. Nor do we have to rely upon white ethnologists to point it out. It has been noted by the natives themselves. I cannot, for instance, think of a better description of this opposition than the one Rasmussen obtained from a Caribou-Eskimo shaman:

"We shamans of the interior," said the old man, "have no special spirit language and believe that the real shamans do not need it. On my travels I have sometimes been present at a séance among the saltwater dwellers. These shamans never seem trustworthy to me. It always appeared to me that they attached more weight to tricks that would astonish the audience, when they jumped about the floor and lisped all sorts of absurdities and lies in their so-called spirit language; to me all this seemed only amusing and as something that would impress the ignorant. A real shaman does not jump about the floor and do tricks, nor does he seek help by the aid of darkness, by putting out the lamps, *to make the minds of his neighbours uneasy*. For myself, I do not think that wisdom or knowledge about things that are hidden can be sought in that manner. *True wisdom is only to be found far away from the people, out in the great solitude, and it is not found in play but only through suffering. Solitude and suffering open the human mind, and therefore a shaman must seek his wisdom there.*" [1]

Wisdom is attained only in solitude and through suffering! What manner of man is it who speaks thus? When we have learned something about him, we shall understand much of what is, at first, bewildering in primitive religion.

Throughout the world of primitive man some form of emotional instability and well-marked sensitivity has always been predicated as the essential trait of the medicine-man and shaman. This is particularly true of the simpler cultures where magic plays the dominant role. Such instability may take a large variety of forms. Throughout Siberia we know that it assumes pathological proportions and that a shaman there is preferably selected from among those suffering from *menerik*. This is a nervous affliction in which the patient falls into trances and where he is subject to fits of unconsciousness. Although manifestly *menerik* itself is a disease, the insistence that shamans be selected from individuals subject to it has a definite bearing on the fundamental trait of all shamans and medicine-men everywhere. *They must be disoriented and they must suffer.*

It is not difficult to surmise why, in early civilizations, the more or less normal man should have insisted that the medicine-men possess such a temperament. Thought was then obsessively subjectivistic and coercion the only type of relation that seemed to exist between the ego and the objective world. The shaman, the medicine-man, and the magician incorporate this attitude in its purest and most undiluted form. But of far more importance is the fact that he alone was sufficiently articulate to describe how he felt, what he saw, and what he was doing. Now the world he described was that of a man neurotically susceptible to all inward stirrings, physical and mental. Whereas his more insensitive fellowmen were exposed to only a selected number of the impacts and shocks of his external and internal world, he was exposed to all of them and had to make an adjustment to all of them. The very intensity of his inward life spurred him on and aided him in the attainment of his goal. It is only natural then that he should regard his success in thus successfully coping with the outside world as a validation of both his inward life and his specific type of temperament and that the same inference should have been drawn by the ordinary man in observing him and passing judgment upon him.

The medicine-man was thus constrained by his own temperament and by the attitude of his fellowmen to make an analysis of his inward life that would properly mirror his own special personality and that would, at the same time, be intelligible to the layman. Such an analysis would naturally have to stress the salient characteristics of the shaman's mental state when he was engaged in the practice of his profession—his trances, his neurotic susceptibilities, and the conditions necessary to the attainment of this state. That meant the stressing of his fantasy life, of his illusions, and of his hallucinations. These differed only in degree, assuredly, from those of his normal fellowmen. However, consciously to focus attention upon the epileptoid side of his make-up entailed pain and suffering, meant a break with the normal activities of the workaday world, and this led to the avoidance and the temporary abeyance of the latter. If, consequently, we find a strong insistence on initiation through suffering, on the need for solitude in order to concentrate, and on what might be called a sanctification of avoidance taking the form of taboos, we know where they came from. To all this must be added certain unpredictable fantasies and hallucinations peculiar to the shaman and which indicated the immediacy of his relationship to the supernatural world and his identification with specific objects in it, such as with animals, as well as his power to transform himself into them.

The shaman was thus labelled and set apart by the nature of his psychic constitution and by the insistence of the normal man that he, the shaman, was peculiar. But another force of even more compulsive urgency was to make for his separation from the ordinary world, namely, the demands imposed upon him by the older shamans who had selected him as temperamentally qualified and who controlled the conditions of his initiation into their order. These demands were prevailingly dictated by economic-social considerations—the desire for wealth and the craving for power. Let us turn to them.

We must remember, at the outset, that a definite correlation exists between the simpler societies organized on a non-agricultural basis and the extent to which, in such civilizations, neurotic-epileptoid individuals predominate among the medicine-men. The reason for this fact is purely economic. The competition for this position is there not so intense. The rewards are, after all, not very great. As a result very few men and women of the more matter-of-fact and normal type are attracted to it in contrast to what is the case in the more complex agricultural and pastoral communities. The neurotic individuals were thus in fairly complete control of the selection of new aspirants to their ranks, a fact clearly expressed by three things: the trials and ordeals through which the novices were made to pass, such as fasting, exposure, and self-castigation; the strong insistence on the adoption of specific methods of approach to the supernatural; and the new status into which the applicant was to be initiated. The first two represent conscious articulations and generalizations of compulsions to which the more pronounced neurotic-epileptoid individuals among the shamans are subject. They are part and parcel of their behaviour pattern.

The necessity of suffering, we cannot too strongly insist, was not a theory developed by the shaman in order to describe and authenticate the contact between man and the supernatural world. Pain and suffering were concrete facts imposed upon him by the very nature of his physical-mental constitution. It was the expression of a conflict within himself, the splitting off of an unconscious state from a conscious one and its subsequent reintegration on a new level of awareness. This synthesis was then projected outward and re-enacted before the world as the drama of man's perpetual struggle for security, a security to which he attains by delving into the unknown and by becoming as one with the hidden and the mysterious.

Under these conditions it is not difficult to understand how a trance or an epileptic seizure should have come to be interpreted as a type of temporary death and rebirth. This the ordinary man would likewise understand, for his experience had taught him certain contrasts, such as the waking condition as opposed to sleep and its attendant dreams, health as opposed to sickness and its accompanying delirium. He knew that these meant temporary separation from and a new re-entry into the world, thus offering a fruitful analogue to the trance of the shaman. And this psychological awareness was further reinforced by those transition states, physical and social-economic, which we have already discussed at some length in the preceding chapter. The neurotic behaviour, and the contents of the neurotic-epileptoid consciousness, of the shaman thus became representative of the world which the normal man accepted because he himself was conscious of these contrasts in his own life. Such behaviour corresponded to a world that was dramatically articulated for him by special individuals with a specific profession of vital concern to the ordinary man and with specific qualifications which the layman recognized as valid.

No number of general statements, however, will enable the reader to understand the neurotic-epileptoid mentality we have been discussing. That can be obtained only through concrete illustrations of the nature of the shaman's initiation into his craft and of his method of functioning. In this chapter I shall deal with the initiation first and then give a number of examples in order to show both the universality and the persistence of certain neurotic-epileptoid features in even the most complicated civilizations where the priest has become a figure of an entirely different order from the simple magician or shaman. They also serve to indicate the nature of the economic advantages possessed by the religious leaders over the laymen in their struggle for security. I am giving them in considerable detail and have chosen them with great care, so that they cover practically every geographic region of the world and represent the most varied forms of civilization, from a clanless fishing-hunting and a non-agricultural clan community, to an agricultural community with a clan organization associated with a monarchy and an agricultural society that possesses no clans but with the most rigorous of caste distinctions. The tribes selected are the Eskimo of Arctic North America [2], the Arunta of Central Australia [3], the Winnebago of Wisconsin [4], the New Malekula of the Hebrides in Melanesia [5], the Mentawei of the Dutch East Indies [6], the Amazulu of South Africa [7], the Ashanti of West Africa [8], and the Tahitians of

Polynesia.[9] With the exception of the Arunta, they represent accounts given by native priests and which were recorded verbatim. I am beginning with the Eskimo although their social and economic organization is far more complex than that of the Arunta, because the neurotic-epileptoid formula is there found so clearly and fully expressed.

I

Initiation of an Eskimo Shaman

When I was to be a shaman, I chose suffering through the two things that are most dangerous to us humans, suffering through hunger and suffering through cold. First I hungered five days and was then allowed to drink a mouthful of warm water. The old ones say that only if the water is warm will Pinga and Hila notice the novice and help him. Thereafter I went hungry another fifteen days, and again was given a mouthful of warm water. After that I hungered for ten days, and then could begin to eat though it only had to be the sort of food on which there is never any taboo, preferably fleshy meat, and never intestines, head, heart, or other entrails nor meat that had been touched by wolf or wolverine while it lay in a cache. I was to keep this diet for five months, and then the next five months might eat everything; but after that I was again forced to eat the meat diet that is prescribed for all those who must do penance in order to become clean. The old ones attached great importance to the food that the would-be shaman might eat. Thus a novice who wished to possess the ability to kill had never to eat [a specific kind of] salmon. If they eat it, they will, instead of killing others, kill themselves.

My instructor was my wife's father, Perqanaq. Perqanaq built a small snow hut at the place where I was to be, this snow hut being no bigger than that I could just get under cover and sit down. I was given no sleeping skin to protect me against the cold; only a little piece of caribou skin to sit upon. There I was shut in. The snow hut in which I sat was built far from the trails of men and when Perqanaq had found the spot where he thought it ought to be built, he stopped the little sledge at a distance and there I had to remain seated until the snow hut was ready. Not even I, who was after all the one to have to stay there, might set my footprints in the vicinity of the hut and old Perqanaq had to carry me from the sledge over to the hut so that I could crawl in. As soon as I had become alone Perqanaq enjoined me to think of one single thing and that was to draw Pinga's attention to the fact that there I sat and wished to be a shaman. Pinga should own me.

My novitiate took place in the middle of the coldest winter and I, who never got anything to warm me and must not move, was very cold, and it was so tiring having to sit without daring to lie down, that sometimes it was as if I died a little. Only towards the end of the thirty days did a helping spirit come to me, a lovely and beautiful helping spirit, whom I had never thought of. It was a white woman. She came to me whilst I had collapsed, exhausted, and was sleeping. But still I saw her lifelike hovering over me, and from that day I could not close my eyes or dream without seeing her. There is this remarkable thing about my helping spirit, that I have never seen her while awake, but only in dreams. She came to me from Pinga and was a sign that Pinga had now noticed me and would give me powers that would make me a shaman.

When a new moon was lighted and had the same size as the one that had shone for us when we left the village, Perqanaq came again with his little sledge and stopped a long way from the snow hut. But by this time I was not very much alive any more and had not the strength to rise. In fact I could not stand on my feet. Perqanaq pulled me out of the hut and carried me down to the sledge and dragged me home in the same manner as he had dragged me to Kingarjuit. I was now so completely emaciated that the veins on my hands and body and feet had quite disappeared. For a long time I might only eat very little in order to again get my intestines extended, and later came the diet that was to help cleanse my body.

For a whole year I was not to lie with my wife, who, however, had to make my food. For a whole year I had to have my own little cooking pot and my own meat dish; no one else was allowed to eat of what had been cooked for me.

Later, when I had quite become myself again, I understood that I had become the shaman of my village, and it did happen that my neighbours or people from a long distance away called me to heal a sick person or to "inspect a course" if they were going to travel. When this happened, the people of my village were called together and I told them what I had been asked to do. Then I left the tent or snow house and went out into solitude, away from the dwellings of man. But those who remained behind had to sing continuously, just to keep themselves happy and lively.

These days of "seeking for knowledge" are very tiring, for one must walk all the time, no matter what the weather is like and only rest in short snatches. I am usually quite done up, tired, not only in body but also in head, when I have found what I sought.

II

Initiation of an Arunta Medicine-Man *

When a person is about to become a medicine-man the evil spirits seize upon a particular individual who happens to be foot-loose and deprive him of his senses so that he runs about like one crazy and can rest neither by day nor night. The evil spirit throws stones at him which enter every part of his body. These magical stones are about the size of a pea and have different colours. Finally the evil spirit directs the man to the western entrance of his home and there he is repeatedly beaten until he falls unconscious to the ground. While in this condition a *kangar* or leg-bone is forced into his occiput and *ngankara* stones are placed in his shoulders, his hips, and his stomach.

At dawn two evil spirits bring him back to his camp. He is still unconscious and as they approach his home they burst out into mocking laughter so that it can be heard by his fellowmen. Two older medicine-men immediately appear, embrace him, and drive away the evil spirits.

* I have paraphrased this account.—P.R.

They then conduct him to his dwelling where he recognizes no one. They insert *ngankara* stones into his ears so that he may regain his hearing. He is so ill and exhausted however that he sleeps day after day and becomes perceptibly thinner. The two old medicine-men now build him a separate hut, give him some water to drink and a little soft meat to eat, and carry him into the hut. Here they make him stand up and paint him appropriately. When this is finished they go hunting and upon their return singe their booty over a fire and rub the hairs of the animal over the body of the novice. Then they roast the animal and give the novice the roasted intestines and liver.

After the meal they preach to him as follows: "Never lie down or kneel when you wish to drink but always use a small receptacle. Never eat any of the hard parts of an animal, but always such soft parts as the liver, the lungs, the heart, the intestines, etc. If you do eat a little of the hard meat always devour it half-cooked. Never eat any fat. Use it only for rubbing your body. You must pay your debts to the older medicine-men by bringing them meat." If he were to disobey, the magical stones in his body would cut his flesh and he would lose his skill as a practitioner.

Then one of the older medicine-men pierces the index finger of the novice with a pointed magical wand. By this operation he will be enabled to drive out the objects that are causing illness in his future patients. The novice must then place his finger in a plate and keep it there till the next morning. The next day all the old men of the neighbourhood gather together and the old medicine-man seizes the tongue of the novice and cuts a hole in it with a sharp stone. This will enable him to suck out the evil magical powers to be found in the bodies of his future patients. The young novice has now become a medicine-man and he is enjoined to observe silence.

The final act of the initiation consists in the interposition between the older medicine-man and the younger one of a bread which has been baked in ashes. The former sticks the finger of his right hand in that part of the bread where there is still to be found a raw portion. He then squirts a substance called *urbanama* upon his young colleague. The other medicine-men present thereupon sit in a circle around the bread and, with heads close together, sprinkle it upon the new magician. When the bread is used up, for it sticks to the fingers of the sprinklers, their young colleague is freed from his pledge of silence and the ceremony is over.

III

Initiation of a Winnebago Medicine-Man

I came from above and I am holy. This is my second life on earth. Many years before my present existence I lived on this earth. At that time everyone seemed to be on the warpath. Once when I was on the warpath I was killed. It seemed to me, however, as if I had merely stumbled. I rose and went right ahead until I reached my home. At home I found my wife and children but they would not look at me. Then I spoke to my wife but she seemed to be quite unaware of my presence. "What can be the matter," I thought to myself, "that they pay no attention to me and that they do not even answer when I speak to them?" All at once it occurred to me that I might in reality be dead. So I immediately started out for the place where I had presumably been killed and surely enough, there I saw my body. Then I knew positively that I had been killed. I tried to return to the place where I had lived as a human being but for four years I was unsuccessful.

At one time I became transformed into a fish. At another time I became transformed into a little bird. At another time I became a buffalo. From my buffalo existence I was permitted to go to my higher spirit-home, from which I had originally come. The one in charge of that spirit-home is my grandfather. I asked him for permission to return to earth again. At first he refused, but then after I had asked him for the fourth time, he consented. He said to me: "Grandson, you had better fast before you go and if any of the spirits take pity on you, you may go and live in peace upon earth." So I fasted for four years and all the spirits above, even to the fourth heaven, approved of my coming. They blessed me. They told me that I would never fail in anything that I wished to do. Then they decided to make a trial of my powers. They placed an invulnerable spirit grizzly bear at one end of the lodge and sang the songs that I was to use when I returned to earth. Then I walked around the lodge holding a live coal in the palm of my hand and danced around the fireplace saying *wahi*—! and striking the hand containing the coal with my other. The invulnerable bear fell forward prone upon the ground and a black substance flowed from his mouth. Then they said to me: "You have killed him. Even so great a spirit as this you have been able to kill. Indeed, nothing will ever be able to cross your path." Then they took the "bear" I had killed and cut him into small pieces with a knife, piled these in the centre of the lodge, and covered them with some dark material. "Now," they said, "you must again try your powers." I asked them for the articles that I would have to use and they gave me a flute and a gourd. Then I made myself holy. I walked around the object that lay piled up in the centre of the lodge and breathed upon it. Four times I did this and then the spirit grizzly bear got up and walked away in the shape of a human being. "It is good," they said. "He has restored him to life again. Surely he is holy." After a while they said to me again: "Just as you have done here, so will you do below. Whenever you wish to, you will be able to kill a person or restore him to life."

Then they placed a black stone in the shaman's lodge that stood above. There again they made a trial of my powers. I blew four times on the stone and I blew a hole through it. For that reason, if any person has a pain and he lets me blow upon it, I can blow it away. It makes no difference what kind of a pain it is. My breath was made holy by the spirits.

The spirits on the earth and those under the earth also gave me a trial of my powers. They placed an old rotten log before me. I breathed upon it four times, and spat water upon it and it got up in the shape of a human being and walked away.

My ability to spit water upon the people whom I am treating I received from an eel, from the chief among the eels, one who lives in the centre and in the deepest part of the ocean. Whenever I spit water it is inexhaustible because it comes from him, the eel.

When I came upon this earth I entered a lodge and there I was born again. As I have said, I thought that I was entering a lodge, but in reality I was entering my mother's womb. Even in my prenatal existence I never lost consciousness. Then I grew up and fasted again and again, and all those spirits who had blessed me before sent me their blessings again. I can dictate to all the spirits that exist. Whatever I say will come to pass. The tobacco you [the patients] offer me is not to be used by myself. It is really intended for the spirits.

IV

Initiation of a Malekula Medicine-Man

There was a Bwili of Lol-narong, whose sister's son came to him and said: "I want you to give me something." The Bwili said: "Have you fulfilled the conditions?" "Yes, I have fulfilled them." Again he said: "You have not been lying with a woman?" and his nephew said: "No." So the Bwili said: "All right."

Then he said to his nephew: "Come here. Lie down on this leaf," and the youth lay down on it. Then the Bwili made himself a bamboo knife and cutting off one of the young man's arms, placed it on two of the leaves. And he laughed at his nephew and the youth laughed back. Then he cut off the other arm and placed it on the leaves beside the first. And he came back and they both laughed again. Then he cut off his leg from the thigh and laid it alongside the arms. And he came and laughed and the youth laughed too. Then he cut off the other leg and laid it beside the first. And he came back and laughed, and saw that his nephew was still laughing. Lastly, he cut off the head, held it out before him. And he laughed, and the head laughed, too.

Then he put the head back in its place and took the arms and legs that he had taken off and put them all back in their places. And he covered the youth completely with the red *roware* leaves. Then he called to his own son and said: "Watch this boy and see what happens to him today."

And the Bwili went a short way off, stood still and suddenly said "*ko*" and, becoming a fowl, he sprang into the air and, flying back, alighted upon his nephew. But the boy did not move. So he flew away again and saying "*ko*" for the second time, resumed his proper form and coming back he said to his son: "You saw a fowl fly in and alight on the boy. Did the boy do anything?" And the son said: "No, he did nothing." "Very well," said his father, "stay here, and keep on watching."

He went away again and, saying "*ko*," became a fowl once more, and flew in and alighted on his nephew. And the boy shook. Then he flew away and returning in his own person said: "Did you see that fowl fly in again? Did the boy do anything?" and the son said: "Yes; he shook violently." "Good," said the Bwili, "stay here and keep on watching."

Again he went and turned himself into a fowl and alighted on his nephew. And the youth raised himself. And when the Bwili had flown away and returned in his proper form he found his nephew standing on his feet. And he laughed at him and the youth laughed, too.

Then he said: "Come here," and the youth came. And he said: "Do this." And they made as if clearing their throats, and immediately the nephew became a pig and the Bwili a sow, his mother. And they both went to the nephew's father's house where the Bwili lay down and the nephew drank of her milk. And the nephew's mother called out to her husband: "Come and look at this lovely sow with her young. We ought to have one like that." And they stood admiring it.

And when they had gone back into the house, the Bwili and his nephew grunted again and straightway became fowls. And the mother came out and saw the fowls and said: "Look at these splendid birds." And the father said: "See how plump they are. I must feed up my fowls so that they may get like that." Then he fetched his bow and arrows and drew a bolt at the birds but missed. And they lured him on, hopping out of sight and returning, so that the mother again called out: "Look, they are back again," and he shot once more and missed.

At last the fowls returned to the Bwili's house, and the Bwili said to his nephew: "Tomorrow you must go home." So next morning the new initiate went home in his own person and said: "Mother, have you seen one of my uncle's pigs, a sow with one of its young?" "You've come too late," she said. "They were here yesterday but have gone away now. If you had come yesterday you would have seen them." Then he asked: "Did you see two fowls belonging to him, too?" And she said: "Yes, they were here, too. Why didn't you come yesterday?" "Oh," he said, "we were looking for them elsewhere yesterday but could not find them. That's why I have come here to-day."

That night the nephew slept at home and heard his father say to his mother: "Tomorrow we will go and cut *wulu-wawa* [the aerial roots of the *wawa* tree]." So next morning he followed them to see in what direction they were going and, taking another route, slipped ahead in front of them and turned himself into a goodly *wawa* tree. When his mother came to the tree and saw what a good one it was she said: "Here is a splendid tree. I'll cut the roots of this one." But when she took hold of a root and tried to cut it with her knife, it jumped aside, so that she called to her husband and said: "Come and look at this tree. I can't cut it." And her husband tried to cut it but he missed, as she had done. Now he knew of the Bwili's power and said: "I think it's your brother who is playing a trick on us." He did not suspect his son. But the mother was thinking things out, and on the way home she said: "This was not my brother; it was my son. Why has he been staying all this time with my brother? He's been there seven days now."

And when they got home the son was there. And now his mother was angry with him and said: "What were you doing all the seven days that you were with your uncle?" "Nothing special," he said. "Oh," she replied, "do you think I'm a fool? You have deceived me three times now. First you pretended you were a pig, then a fowl, and now you've been pretending to be a *wawa* tree and making me miss it all the time. Don't deceive me any more. Tell me about it." And he said: "Yes, it was me."

V

Initiation of a Mentawei Medicine-Man

A man or woman may be made a seer by being bodily abducted by the spirits. According to the story of Sitakigagailau, the youth was taken up to heaven by the sky-spirits and given a beautiful body such as theirs. When he returned to earth he was a seer and the sky-spirits served him in his cures. In return he gave sacrifice to the sky-spirits at the time of *punen* [religious ceremony] held for healing.

The usual manner, however, in which boys and girls become seers is by being summoned through sickness, dreams, or temporary insanity. The sickness or dreams are sent by the sky-spirits or the jungle-spirits. Malaria is the usual form of sickness. The dreamer may imagine that he ascends to heaven or that he goes to the woods looking for monkeys. In either case, dreams or sickness, there is a temporary loss of soul. Then a professional seer is summoned to make the sick boy or girl well.

When the seer enters the house, he first sings before the house altar. The people in the house only hear the singing of the seer but the doctor is really in conversation with the spirits of the altar. He is trying to find out the cause of the sickness. Then the seer says to the youth: "Boy (or girl), what have you eaten, what have you planted, what have you done to make you sick? What have you done which was displeasing to our fathers, the wood-spirits, and to those in heaven? You must stop all word and stop eating things which are taboo. You must not eat bad meat [squirrels and birds]."

After the cure is at an end the boy recovers. If he is slow in recovering his health, however, and the spirits oppress him again, the father becomes uneasy. He says to the boy: "Boy, why is your illness not at an end? You had better get married; then your manner of life will be improved upon. That will put an end to your incorrect eating and your sins."

In the meantime the seer comes repeating his visits, questioning the spirits of the altar. "Spirits of the altar, what has made your father [the boy] sick? Speak, do not conceal anything."

The spirits of the altar reply: "Yes, seer, you wish to find out what the sins of my father are. He has stopped eating forbidden food. Yet the spirits of the lower heaven wish that he acquire magical power. If my father delays in acquiring the power the spirits of the lower heaven will bring him madness from the sky."

Then the boy promises to become a seer, saying: "You, spirits of the woods, and you, spirits of the lower heaven, you make strong my body. I will at once acquire magical power. I wish it." At once a seer is summoned to give the youth his power.

As soon as the instructor arrives he goes to the woods in order to gather magical herbs. These are for the purpose of purification, of casting off all that is evil from the boy. The instructor returns with the herbs and rolls them up. Then the instructor charms the plants: "We will make many sacrifices to you, spirits of the talisman. You, spirits of the *umbau* plant, throw off all that your father has incorrectly eaten. Drive off what he has eaten, what he has planted. Fall off, spirits of the food, spirits of what he has planted!" Finally the instructor throws the talisman into the river.

After all bad influence has been washed away with the evil plants named, the instructor gathers plants bearing good influence. These he charms: "We will make many sacrifices for you, spirits of the talisman, so that by your magic he [the pupil] will have clear eyes, will have changed eyes. Soon he will see with his eyes our fathers and our mothers, the spirits of the lower heaven." Then the pupil takes home his talisman and sticks it in the wall of his house. It is through this talisman that the pupil will later talk with his guardian spirits, those of the lower heavens.

Then the instructor washes the hair of the youth and the two go into the woods in order to search for herbs which will give the boy "seeing eyes." While they are gathering the plants, the instructor sings to them: "Spirits of the talisman, reveal yourselves. Make clear the eyes of the boy that he may see the spirits." The talisman replies: "Here is your magic power. If you wish to make clear the eyes of the boy, take this and that plant." The instructor and the youth gather the required plants and then go home.

When they arrive at the house of the instructor, the latter takes a cup into which the required spirits are to be summoned. The instructor charms: "Let your eyes be clear, let our eyes be clear, so that we may see our fathers and mothers of the lower heaven." While the instructor sings, the two keep ringing their bells. After the invocation, the instructor rubs the herbs on the eyes of the boy. For three days and nights the two men sit opposite each other, singing and ringing their bells. Until the eyes of the boy are clear, neither of the two men obtains any sleep. At the end of the three days the two again go to the woods and obtain more herbs which they place in a half-coconut. The purpose of the herbs is to make the bodies of the spirits shiny and beautiful, so that they will not be ashamed to reveal themselves to the boy. The instructor places the half-coconut between himself and the pupil and charms: "Here, make yourself shine for your father, my children [the wood-spirits]. Wood-spirits, you are the owner. Shine in his eyes, so that your bodies are visible to him; do not conceal your bodies from him." This clears the eyes of the boy a little. In another two days, since neither the heaven-spirits nor the wood-spirits have appeared as yet, the two men gather more herbs. If at the end of seven days the boy sees the wood-spirits the ceremony is at an end. Otherwise the entire seven-day ceremony must be repeated.

The next thing to be done is the making of the new seer's outfit. Nine days are taken up in the preparation of the outfit. Then the instructor gives the final charms to his pupil. He first asks: "Are your eyes clear now, so that you can see your fathers, your elder and younger brothers [the spirits]?" "Yes, I see them clearly," replies the boy. The instructor charms: "Boy! I am here when you are in need, for I made you. You will now be able to give medicine to the people of Mentawei with cold hands. You will now have seeing eyes to see the wood-spirits, hearing ears to hear the words of the spirits to whom we sacrifice at the altar. May your magic power secure you long life, may it enable you to visit continually the villages of men and to cure the sick." The instructor now places the headdress on the boy, who charms: "I take this headdress as decoration so that I have magic power, that I have power in the villages of the strangers. The people of the village will look on; the people of the villages I visit will look on; the wood-spirits will look on; the spirits of heaven will look on; the spirits of the sea will look on; the spirits under the ground of the village will look on; the poles of the village will look on; all the children of the *uma* [division of village] will look on. May I derive magic power from the seers of the other villages, so that I may question the altars of other villages, that I may join my singing with that of other seers who are also powerful. May my spirits rule over other villages, so that when I use my headdress as a means of knowing what to do I will be proficient in curing. I charm myself so that I be strong in body, that my magic power be enduring, that I have long life. Amen [*bulatnia*, may it be correct]."

Then the instructor places the breast band, the arm bands, and a leaf-tail on the youth, and the magical outfit is complete. After this the instructor blinds the eyes of the initiate so that he is unable to see for two or three days. This is done so that the people will also be blind when the seer plays his tricks on them. The seer puts ginger juice in both eyes of the candidate and charms: "Red *laiga* flower, make clear his eyes; may the faces of the spirits shine that he may see them. May the eyes of the people be blinded by this charm."

Next the instructor takes a bamboo container of a hand's length and open at both ends. He blows into both ears of the candidate, charming: "I blow into your ears, my child, so that you will be able to hear the words of the wood-spirits, and the speech of the altar. I cause you to have hearing ears, seeing eyes, and cold hands. I cause you to have magic power. I enable you to visit as a seer."

VI

Initiation of an Amazulu Diviner

The condition of a man who is about to be a diviner is this: At first he is apparently robust; but in process of time he begins to be delicate, not having any real disease. . . . He begins to be particular about food, and abstains from some kinds, and requests his friends not to give him that food, because it makes him ill. He habitually avoids certain kinds of food, choosing what he likes, and he does not eat much of that; he is continually complaining of pains in different parts of his body. And he tells them that he has dreamt that he is being carried away by a river. He dreams of many things, and his body is muddled and he becomes a house of dreams. And he dreams constantly of many things, and on awaking says to his friends: "My body is muddled to-day; I dreamt many men were killing me; I escaped I know not how. And on waking, one part of my body felt different from other parts; it was no longer alike all over." At last the man is very ill, and they go to the diviners to inquire.

The diviners do not at once see that he is about to have a soft head. It is difficult for them to see the truth; they continually talk nonsense, and make false statements, until all the man's cattle are devoured at their command. . . .

So the people readily assent to the diviners' word, thinking that they know. At length all the man's property is expended, he being still ill; and they no longer know what to do, for he has no more cattle, and his friends help in such things as he needs.

At length [after all his property is expended] a diviner comes and says that all the others are wrong. He says: "I know that you come here to me because you have been unable to do anything for the man, and have no longer the heart to believe that any diviner can help you. But, my friends, the other diviners have gone astray. As for the man, he is possessed by the *itongo*. There is nothing else. Your people move in him. They are divided into two parties; some say: 'No, we do not wish that our child should be injured.' It is for that reason and no other that he does not get well. If you bar the way against the *itongo*, you will be killing him. For he will not be a diviner; neither will he ever be a man again; he will be what he is now. If he is not ill, he will be delicate, and become a fool, and be unable to understand anything. I tell you you will kill him by using medicines. Just leave him alone, and look to the end to which the disease points. Do you not see that on the day he has not taken medicine, he just takes a mouthful of food? Do not give him any more medicines. He will not die of the sickness, for he will have what is good given to him."

So the man may be ill two years without getting better; perhaps even longer than that. He may leave the house for a few days, and the people begin to think he will get well. But no, he is confined to the house again. This continues until his hair falls off. And his body is dry and scurfy; and he does not like to anoint himself. People wonder at the progress of the disease. But his head begins to give signs of what is about to happen. He shows that he is about to be a diviner by yawning again and again, and by sneezing again and again. And men say: "No! Truly it seems as though this man was about to be possessed by a spirit." This is also apparent from his being very fond of snuff.

After that he is ill; he has slight convulsions, and has water poured on him, and they cease for a time. He habitually sheds tears, at first slight, and at last he weeps aloud; in the middle of the night, when the people are asleep, he is heard making a noise, and wakes the people by singing; he has composed a song, and men and women awake and go to sing in concert with him. . . .

In this state of things they daily expect his death. He is now but skin and bones and they think that tomorrow's sun will not leave him alive. The people wonder when they hear him singing and they strike their hands in concert. They then begin to take courage, saying: "Yes, now we see that it is the head."

Therefore whilst he is undergoing this initiation the people of the village are troubled by want of sleep, for a man who is beginning to be an *inyanga* causes great trouble, he does not sleep but works constantly with his brain; his sleep is merely by snatches and he wakes up sing-ing many songs. And people who are near quit their villages by night when they hear him singing aloud, and go to sing in concert. Perhaps he sings till the morning, no one having slept. The people of the vil-lage smite their hands in concert till they are sore. And then he leaps about the house like a frog; the house becomes too small for him; he goes out, leaping and singing, and shaking like a reed in the water, and dripping with perspiration.

At that time many cattle are eaten. The people encourage his be-coming an *inyanga;* they employ means for making the *itongo* white, that it may make his divinations very clear. At length another ancient *inyanga* of celebrity is pointed out to him. At night, whilst asleep, he is commanded by the *itongo,* who says to him: "Go to so-and-so; go to him and he will churn for you *emetic-ubulawo,* that you may be an *inyanga* altogether." Then he is quiet for a few days, having gone to the *inyanga* to have *ubulawo* churned for him; and he comes back quite another man, being now cleansed and an *inyanga* indeed.

And if he is to have familiar spirits, there is continually a voice saying to him: "You will not speak with the people; they will be told by us everything they come to inquire about." And he continually tells the people his dreams, saying: "There are people who tell me at night that they will speak for themselves to those who come to inquire." At last all this turns out to be true. When he has begun to divine at length his power entirely ceases, and he hears the spirits who speak by whistlings, and he answers them as he would answer a man. He causes them to speak by asking them questions. If he does not understand what they say, they make him understand everything they see.

VII

Initiation of an Ashanti Priest

The majority of priests and priestesses insist that they first adopted their profession because they suddenly discovered that they were subject to possession by some spirit influence. As a rule this realization comes upon them unawares, either while engaged in the ordinary business of life or while attending some religious ceremony. They hear the voice of some god or fall down in a fit or, it may be, go into a trance. Some fully qualified priest is then called in to interpret the phenomenon and he comes to the conclusion that a particular spirit or god desires to "marry" the afflicted person. It is then left to the decision of the latter. If he consents, he enters the service of some fullfledged priest of the particular god whose spirit he has been told manifested itself in him.

The novitiate lasts three years, during which the neophyte resides with his new master. If married, he leaves his wife, with whom he may no longer cohabit until his training is over. There are three divisions to the training, each lasting a year. The first year is occupied in ceremonial ablution, "bathing with medicine." The officiating priest gathers the leaves of certain plants in order, as he says, "to strengthen his ankles" [for dancing] and "to cause his god to stay with him." He must wash in a decoction made from these leaves for seven days. Then the leaves of other plants are mixed with white clay and are rubbed upon his eyes so "that he may see his god daily." If the spirit of possession will not manifest itself to him the priest takes the leaves of still other plants and presses them upon the novice's eyes, knee-joints, and soles, "when the spirit will return whence it had gone."

For a novice who cannot hear his god's voice, certain leaves are put under his pillow. After this the officiating priest collects leaves from any plant growing over a grave in the so-called "thicket of the ghosts" and brings them to the village where they are placed in a pot. Eggs and a fowl are then sacrificed and the pot containing them is placed upon the grave from which the leaves had been removed. The novice is then ordered to go alone in the middle of the night to "the thicket of the ghosts" and bathe himself with the medicine contained in the pot. The ghosts will beat him and he can be heard screaming, but he must bathe nevertheless.

These and other lustrations which he must practise are all intended to bring "the spirit of possession" upon the pupil. The bathing in the cemetery has for its object the establishment of contact with the spirits of dead men. He bathes together with these spirits using various plants and roots and then "the spirit of possession" comes upon him, little by little. He can be seen trembling.

Beside the taboo of sexual intercourse the novice must first observe the taboos of his own god and, secondly, those of the new god whose priest he is striving to become. In this particular instance, in addition, he is prohibited from tapping palm-wine, setting fish-traps, plucking palm-nuts, and roaming about other people's homes.

Throughout all this time, he lives with the priest, helps him on his farm, and, at night, sleeps in the temple beside the shrine of the god whose service he has entered. The old priest, who is training him, keeps him under constant observation and, should he not prove obedi-ent and attentive to instruction, his family is informed that the novice is not likely to make a good priest and his training ceases.

The training during the second year is somewhat similar to that for the first except that he is now given various fetishes to wear and taught the taboos peculiar to each fetish, but he is not as yet taught how to make them or energize them. He is permitted to bathe in water without medicine in it and to use a sponge. He is admonished to remember a number of things: not to drink any alcohol; not to gossip; not to quarrel or fight; never to adjure his god to kill anyone; never to attend the king's court unless summoned; not to go out at night and join other men; and to salute his elders by bending the right knee and touching the ground with the right hand.

During the third year the novice is taught water-gazing; divining; how to impregnate charms with various spirits; how to hear the voices of the trees and the stream; what trees he should salute and in what manner; and what animals have a revengeful spirit more to be feared than others.

The novice is taught what lies within the water in the following manner. Water is freshly drawn from a stream and this is energized by an incantation of the priest as the novice kneels beside a pot containing palm-wine, palm-oil, seven eggs, and the blood, intestines, neck, and legs of a fowl:

Ye gods, come and accept this wine and drink.
Ye ghosts, come and accept this wine and drink.
Trees and lianae, come and accept this wine and drink.
Supreme Being, who alone is great, it was you who begot me, come and accept this wine and drink.
Spirit of the earth, come and accept this wine and drink.
Spirit of pools, come and accept this wine and drink.

Stand behind me with a standing, and let me be possessed with a good possession.
Do not take water and retain it in your mouth when you speak to me (but address me clearly).
If anyone is sick, let me be able to tend him.
When I become possessed and prophesy for a chief, grant that what I have to tell him may not be bad.
Do not let me become impotent.

Do not let my eyes become covered over.
Do not let my ears become closed up.
Do not let my penis make a slave of my neck.

After that a number of new ingredients are thrown into the pot:
an Ashanti weight, a neolith, several seeds of the *abrus precatorius,*
several small white pebbles, a red bead called the horse's urine, a bone
of a sheep that had been sacrificed to one's particular local god, a special bead called *akomen,* a cowrie, a miniature hoe, and an *ate* seed.
The pot is then set upon a head-rest and the novice is asked to look into
it. He may see the faces of his ancestors on the surface of the water, or
again, he may see his god, that is, the water may become disturbed.
For a proverb says: "No priest may look upon the face of his god and
live." He then takes a wooden spoon, stirs the contents of the pot, and
picks out something with the spoon. Thereupon he is taught the symbolical meaning of the objects he has put in. The *abrus precatorius,*
the *akomen* bead, and the horse's urine, for instance, signify "sorrow";
the Ashanti weight, "a debt"; the cowrie, "ridicule"; the *ate* seed,
"weeping"; the neolith, "that a groove will be dug"; the miniature
hoe, "death"; the leg of the fowl, "that a path is clear which you
should follow," and so on. The water is regarded as the god's wife.
The novice will be unable, for many weeks after, to look into running
water without seeing the faces of the ghosts of his ancestors.

The last phase of his initiation is now at hand. He is told when approaching certain trees to make a deep obeisance and say: "Good
morning, grandparent, stand behind me with a good standing," and
he is taught how to read omens from the colour of a fowl's kidneys.

At the end of the third year he enters into the status of full priest.
This occurs after the following rite has been performed. A pot is set
near some logs that have been placed outside the old priest's house.
After dark, drummers and singers assemble and the logs are lit, the
fire being kindled with a flint and steel. The new priest is dressed in a
palm-fibre kilt with all his charms upon him. His hair is then cut and
put into a pot and the old priest examines the new priest's head in order
to take away any bad "spirits of possession," for it is these, placed there

by certain fairies, that are supposed to cause a priest to do wrong. The new priest will dance all night to the accompaniment of the drums and of singing. Early the next morning this pot is placed on the head of some young boy and he is told to run off with it wherever he wishes and to place it, inverted, on the ground. Finally the new priest will "cut" a sheep for his god and pray:

"God so-and-so, accept this sheep and eat; today you have completed marriage with me; this is a sheep from my hands, stand at my back with good standing."

VIII

Initiation of a Tahitian Priest

The men set apart for the priesthood were able-bodied and most of them were tall. They were free from personal defects as the gods were supposed to reject a man with a blemish, such as having a humpback, bald head, blind eye, or eyes that squinted. They must also be deft of hand and sure-footed, so as not to be awkward in the service of the gods.

After becoming an adept in all the knowledge of the land, a candidate for the priesthood withdrew from his family and people to go through his novitiate with the priests. There he learned all the prayers and mystic rites, communing with the gods in solitude, often at night, and sometimes going down into dark caverns to hold intercourse with the gods and to pray, and thus become immune to contact with good and evil spirits.

He learned to recite without hesitancy the following subjects: temple (*marae*) prayers; religious and political speeches for the public; war songs and enchantments with the *ti* leaf; the manner to sue for peace, and to cut short a prayer in emergencies; invocation to inspire idols or other objects with the dignity of the gods; invocation for tying prisoners in sennit; disenchantment from witchcraft or the black art; night invocation; fishing invocation.

Night invocations were taught in the dark or moonlight stillness upon the hills in the woods and upon the seashore, where the novice learned to observe omens and signs in the sky and upon the earth where he walked: the fall of meteors, the flight of clouds, the cry of birds and insects. The closing invocation was:

"O host of the gods! The prayer must close. Send obscurity out and let light come in as the flow of the freshet. Let it move and run, let it shake out to fill tightly; let it be means of accomplishing much.

"Give me the gift of prayer; let me become a herald, an orator, in one night, O gods! Fly to the rising sun; with the sun that is rising, is life, O gods!"

When the novice had acquired proficiency in his recitations, he was required to appear before the fraternity called *autahua* to display his eloquence and if he broke down in any part of his speech he had to take up his lesson again and reappear later for examination. Upon graduating with honours, he was received by the body of priests as an *utupa's* [lips-inured], and then he was ready for inauguration, called *amo-o-upu* [forerunner-of-prayers]. This consisted of a good feast prepared by his family, for the priests exclusively, on the temple ground. Of it they solemnly partook after placing an appropriate share upon the altars for the gods. Then the new priest was established permanently as a member of the fraternity. If anyone questioned his right to his title he would proudly answer:

"I am no beggar; I am no eater of scraps; an invoker from Ta-ere [the god and source of all knowledge] am I.

"Bark have I taken to the teachers; fish have I chopped up for the teachers; finely braided clothes have I taken to the teachers; mats have I taken to the teachers; fruit batter have I pounded for the teachers; and family pigs have I taken to the teachers."

Then he would enumerate the schools he had attended, and the famous teachers and priests who had taught him, which always secured him his proper standing.

The examples of initiation we have just given will have made it clear to the reader that the basic qualification for the shaman and medicine-man in the more simply organized groups like the Eskimo and the Arunta is that he belong to the neurotic-epileptoid type. It is likewise clear that, as we approach tribes with a more complex form of economic organization, these qualifications, while they are still present, become secondary to new ones. For this we have already given the explanation, namely that, as the emoluments of office increased, many people who were quite normal were attracted to the priesthood. The pattern of behaviour, however, had by that time become fixed and the non-neurotic shaman had to accept the formulation which owed its origin and its initial development to his neurotic predecessors and colleagues. This formulation, as the examples given indicate, consisted of three parts: first, the description of his neurotic temperament and of his actual suffering and trance; second, the description of his enforced isolation, physical and spiritual, from the rest of the group; and, third, the detailed description of what might best be called an obsessive identification with his goal. From the first arose the theory of the nature of the ordeal through which he must pass; from the second the insistence upon taboos and purifications; and from the third the theory either that he was possessed of the goal or that he was possessed by the goal, in other words, all that is connoted by the concept of spirit-possession.

What was thus originally due to psychical necessity became the prescribed and mechanical formulae to be employed by anyone who desired to enter the priestly profession or for any successful approach to the supernatural. In other words, some of the basic problems of religion were to be envisaged, for good or evil, in terms derived from a very special and manifestly non-normal experience.

The opportunities this left for internal and external conflict can well be imagined, particularly when we bear in mind that primitive religion is primarily concerned with the maintenance of the life-values of man and is rigorously circumscribed by the insistent economic demands of the community at large. In the evolution of the religious thinker from magician to priest these conflicts assumed different forms and took on a different protective colouring in response to the conditions to which they were compelled to adjust themselves. As long, however, as religion was largely in the hands of neurotic-epileptoid individuals, those aspects of religion especially congenial to their type of thinking remained predominant. For reasons we have already pointed out in a previous chapter, magical rites and observances received a voluminous and loving elaboration at their hands. We shall have to return to both again, but before we do so we must attempt to sketch the nature of the functions of the medicine-man and shaman and the changes to which they were subjected.

7

From Magicians to Priests:
Their Function

IN the preceding chapter we discussed the personality of the
shaman and medicine-man as it bore directly on their own
description and on the analysis of the acquisition of their powers
and the ideals and objectives they seemingly had in view. This
personality will emerge even more clearly when we examine
more precisely the manner in which the shamans worked and the
purposes for which the ordinary man employed them. Both are
so inextricably intertwined that it will not always be possible to
treat them apart.

The manner in which the medicine-man worked represented a
simple extension to another individual of the analysis which the
shaman had made of himself and of the various mental phases
through which he had passed. The formula, we saw, was clearcut—suffering, isolation, a trance or its symbolical equivalent,
and then a new normalcy and reintegration. The primary and
constantly recurring ills of life everyone recognized. They were
sickness and economic insecurity. An individual could, at least,
comprehend the latter and, to some degree, attack it unaided, but
he stood bewildered and he was powerless in the presence of a
disease with which he was suddenly stricken. Here he needed
the help of another person, someone specially qualified. So we
find that the shaman was first and foremost a physician and a
curer. His neurotic-epileptoid constitution came to his aid here,
for was he not, in a sense, periodically ill? He differed from the
generality of mankind, however, not only because he possessed

such a special and diseased mentality but because he was at the same time endowed with the power to cure himself.

In the early days, so an old Eskimo told Rasmussen, there were no shamans. Only sickness existed and it was the fear of sickness and suffering that led to the development of the first official shaman. Human beings, so he insisted, have always been afraid of sickness. Let us accept the old Eskimo's challenge and ask what the powers within himself and outside himself were that the shaman and medicine-man believed necessary to effect a cure? In no instance, certainly not in the simpler tribes, was the cure effected by some miraculous power supposed to inhere within himself or acquired by the shaman from the mere act of his initiation. The gift to heal was always derivative. Here again our old Eskimo shaman comes to our help and tells us the nature and limitations of his profession with admirable clarity.

It is not enough [he insists] for a shaman to be able to escape both from himself and from his surroundings. It is not enough that, having the soul removed from his eyes, brain, and entrails, he is able to withdraw the spirit from his body and thus undertake the "great flights" through space and through the sea; nor is it enough that by means of his power he abolishes all distance, and can see all things, however far away. For he will be incapable of maintaining these faculties unless he have the support of helping and answering spirits. . . . But he must procure these helping spirits for himself; he must meet them in person. He cannot even choose for himself what sort he will have. They come to him of their own accord, strong and powerful.[1]

Such a theory in no way contradicts the very common belief that disease comes from the evil machinations of other individuals, for this evil power, in its turn, is always supposed to have been derived from some spirit or deity.

The diagnosis and the treatment of disease are thus, from the very beginnings, intimately linked up with the development of the belief in spirits and in spirits who, as the Eskimo so well put it, "exist to be questioned." For the evolution of objective thought, for the freeing of the individual from the thraldom of his subjectivistic obsession, both these functions of the medicine-man are of fundamental significance. The theory of the shaman, on the other hand, that the cure is rooted in a formula which is the projection of a neurotic-epileptoid mind contravenes this objectivity, definitely plays into the hands of this subjectivistic obsession again, and makes for the persistence of magic often in a crude and undiluted form. The conflict that thus arose was not helped by the injection into it of the practical and indisputable fact that herbs, the inducement of sweating, and the use of purgatives were also effective in the treatment of diseases.

But here, again, as in the case of initiation, it is only by examples that we can really clarify and prove the points we have made. Those I shall now give have been selected to show specifically, first, how certain aspects of the personal problem of the shaman have become transformed into generalized formulae which have crystallized in different fashions in different tribes and, secondly, how the shaman has attempted to weld together into a consistent whole all the conflicting elements which enter into this, one of the most difficult and persistent of all human crises. I shall begin with an Eskimo example, where the disease is regarded as self-caused, in the sense of its being due to the breaking of a taboo. The spirits play a very secondary and unimportant role. They are simply asked what taboos have been broken and who has broken them and they must answer. Even this role, in our example to be given, is somewhat rhetorical, for after the introductory request made to the spirit, he is no more questioned and it is the patient herself who answers. The Eskimo example follows [2]:

A woman named Nanoraq, the wife of Makik, lay very ill, with pains all over her body. The patient, who was so ill that she could hardly stand upright, was placed on the bench. All the inhabitants of the village were summoned and Angutingmarik inquired of his spirits as to the cause of the disease. The shaman walked slowly up and down the floor for a long time, swinging his arms backwards and forwards with mittens on, talking in groans and signs, in varying tones, sometimes breathing deeply as if under extreme pressure. He says:

"If it is you, who are Aksharquarnilik, I ask you, my helping spirit, whence comes the sickness from which this person is suffering? Is it due to something I have eaten in defiance of taboo, lately or long since? Or is it due to the one who is wont to lie beside me, to my wife? Or is it brought about by the sick woman herself? Is she herself the cause of the disease?"

The patient answers: "The sickness is due to my own fault. I have but ill fulfilled my duties. My thoughts have been bad and my actions evil."

The shaman: "I espy something dark beside the house. Is it perhaps a piece of a marrow-bone or just a bit of boiled meat, standing upright, or is it something that has been split with a chisel? That is the cause. She has split a meat-bone which she ought not to have touched."

The audience: "Let her be released from her offence! *Tauva!*"

The shaman: "She is not released from her evil. It is dangerous. It is matter for anxiety. Helping spirit, say what it is that plagues her. Is it due to me or to herself?"

Angutingmarik listens, in breathless silence, and then speaking as if he had with difficulty elicited the information from his helping spirit, he says: "She is not yet released. I see a woman over in your direction, towards my audience, a woman who seems to be asking for something. A light shines out in front of her. It is as if she was asking for something with her eyes, and in front of her is something that looks like a hollow. What is it? What is it? Is it that, I wonder, which causes her to fall over on her face, stumble right into sickness, into peril of death? Can it indeed be something which will not be taken from her? Will she not be released from it? I still see before me a woman with entreating eyes, with sorrowful eyes, and she has with her a walrus tusk in which grooves have been cut."

Listeners: "Oh, is that all? It is a harpoon head that she has worked at, cutting grooves in it at a time when she ought not to touch anything made from parts of an animal. If that is all, let her be released."

Shaman: "Now this evil is removed, but in its place there appears something else; hair combings and sinew thread."

The patient: "Oh, I did comb my hair once when, after giving birth to a child, I ought not to have combed my hair; and I hid away the combings that none might see."

Listeners: "Oh, such a trifling thing; let her be released."

Shaman: "Return to life. I see you now returning in good health among the living, and you, being yourself a shaman, have your helping spirits in attendance. Name but one more instance of forbidden food, all the men you have lain with though you were unclean, all the food you have swallowed, old and new offences, forbidden occupations exercised or was it a lamp that you borrowed?"

Patient: "Alas, yes, I did borrow the lamp of one dead. I have used a lamp that had belonged to a dead person."

Listeners: "Even though it be so, let it be removed. Let all evils be driven far away, that she may get well."

Here the shaman ended his exorcisms, which had taken place early in the morning, and were now repeated at noon and later, when evening had come. The patient was by that time so exhausted that she could hardly sit upright, and the listeners left the house believing that all the sins and offences now confessed had taken the sting out of her illness, so that she would now soon be well again.

Among the Mentawei of Indonesia, a clanless community with a simple agricultural economy, the spirits play the same subsidiary role as among the Eskimo. They are still essentially listeners who obey the behests of the shaman or priest. As among the Eskimo they tell the priest what has caused the illness of the patient. No more than the Eskimo spirits are they held responsible for it nor can they cure it. That is accomplished by medicines designed to extract the disease-bearing object from the body of the patient. All the spirits can do, and all they are expected to do, is to help the priest. They give him his diploma at initiation, during which they bestow upon the future priest the magic power of the seer. The officiating priest implores the spirits:

Let this, our child, be blessed by you with long life and a strong body.
Reveal to him the faults of the people of our household, reveal to him
that which you wish done. Here is your meat, O wood-spirits, the livers
of pigs. May you create the magic power of this, our child. He is your
father. And you, spirits and owners of the household, bless him and
give him seeing eyes. Bless him and let his ears, which have been blown
into, be hearing ones. Bless him with cold hands, bless him with hands
of magic power, bless him with hands that can extract poison, bless
him that his magic power be potent. Be with him when he doctors, be
with him when he gathers herbs, be with him when he sings, be with
him when he makes his medicine.[3]

The situation becomes markedly different the moment we turn
to a typical clan organization with an agricultural economy, as
among the Winnebago. The connexion between the spirits and
the curing of the patient is much closer and the spirits are directly
addressed throughout the treatment. Take, for instance, the following invocation of the priest-doctor before he begins his treatment [4]:

"Spirits, a person is sick and he offers me tobacco. I am on earth to
accept it and try to cure him.

"You will live [this is addressed to the patient], so help yourself as
much as you can and try to make yourself strong. Now as I offer this
tobacco to the spirits, you must listen and if you know that I am telling
the truth, you will be strengthened by it.

"*Haho!* Here is the tobacco, Fire. You promised me that if I offered you tobacco you would grant me whatever request I made. Now
I am placing tobacco on your head as you told me to do when I fasted
for four days and you blessed me. I am sending you the plea of a human being who is ill. He wishes to live. This tobacco is for you and I
pray that the one who is ill be restored to health within four days. . . .

"To you, the Chief of the Eels, you who live in the centre of the
ocean, I offer tobacco. You blessed me with your power of breathing
and with your inexhaustible supply of water. You told me that I could
use all the water in the ocean. A person has come to me and asked me

for life. When I spit upon the patient may the power of my saliva be the same as yours. Therefore I offer you tobacco.

"To you, the Turtle, you who are in charge of a shaman lodge, you who blessed me after I had fasted seven days and carried my spirit to your home where I found many birds of prey, I offer tobacco. You told me that should, at any time, a human being have a pain I would be able to drive it out of him. For that reason you called me One-Who-Drives-Out-Pains. Now before me is a person with a bad pain and I wish to take it out of him. That is what the spirits told me when they blessed me before I came down to earth. Therefore I am going to heal him.

"To you, who are in charge of the snake lodge, you who are perfectly white, Rattlesnake, do I pray. You blessed me with your rattles to wrap around my gourd and you told me after I had fasted for four days that you could help me. You said that I would never fail in anything that I attempted. So now, when I offer you tobacco and shake my gourd, may my patient live and may life be opened to him.

"I greet you, too, Night-Spirits. You blessed me after I had fasted for nine days and you took my spirit to your village which lies in the east, where you gave me the flutes which you told me were holy. You made my flute holy likewise. For these I ask you now, for you know that I am speaking the truth. A sick person has come to me and has asked me to cure him; and because I want him to live I am speaking to you.

"To you, grandmother, the Earth, I too offer tobacco. You said that I could use all the best herbs that grow upon you and that I would always be able to effect cures with them. Those herbs I ask of you now and I ask you to help me cure this sick person. Make my medicine be powerful, grandmother. . . .

"I offer tobacco to all of you who have blessed me."

Then the shaman blew upon his flute, breathed upon the sick man and sang four times. Then he walked around the lodge and spat water upon the patient. After this he sang four times and stopped. The spirits were now to let him know whether the patient was to live or die.

It is interesting to see how this intervention of the spirits in the curing of disease increases as the social-economic organization of the tribe becomes more complex and the religious formulations become more clarified and systematized. For instance, among the Tinguian, a Malayan tribe of the Philippines, a clanless community with a highly developed agricultural economy, the spirits participate directly. Cole [5] has given an excellent account of the extent to which they take part:

A woman of Lagangilang was ill with dysentery; and a medium, in this instance a man, was instructed to make *Dawak*. He began summoning the spirits by striking a dish with his head-axe. Soon he covered his face with his hands, began to sway to and fro, and to chant unintelligible words. Suddenly he stopped and announced that he was the spirit *Labotan,* and that it was his wish that blood and rice be placed on a head-axe and be laid on the woman's abdomen. Next he ordered that they should feed some rice to the small pig which lay bound on the floor. "If he eats, this is the right ceremony, and you will get well," he said. The pig refused the food and after expressing regret that he was unable to help, the spirit departed to be succeeded by *Binongon*. He at once directed that the pig be killed and the palpitating heart be put on the woman's stomach, and be then pressed against each person in the room as a protection against illness. At first he refused to drink the liquor which was offered to him for it was new and raw; but when he learned that no other could be obtained, he drank and then addressed the patient. "You ate something forbidden. It is easy to cure you if the spirits have made you ill; but if someone is practising magic, perhaps you will die." With this cheering message the spirit departed and *Ayaonwan* appeared. He directed an old woman to feed rice and water to the patient, and then, without further advice, he said: "The other spirits do not like me very well so I cannot go to their places. I went to their places but they said many bad words to me. I offered them *basi* but they did not wish to take; so I asked the way and they showed me to the other spirits' place. I was poor, and had nothing to eat for noon or night. When I was on the road, I met many long snakes and I had to push them apart so I could walk. And I met many eels and asked of them the road; but the eels bit me and took me into their stomachs, and carried me to *Luluaganan*, to the well there. Then I died. The people who go to the well say: 'Why is *Ayaonwan* dead? We have a bad odour now.' And the eels say: 'Whose son is this?' and they rubbed my dead spirit and I received life again. Then I took blood and rice with me to the sky, to the other eels, to make *Sayang*. The eels gave me gold for my wrists; the monkeys gave me gold for my teeth and hair; the wild pig gave me bracelets. There is much more I can tell you, but now I must go." The spirit departed, and a new one was summoned. This spirit took the spear in his hand and after chanting about the illness of the woman, he drank *basi* out of a dish, sitting on the head-axe. Then, singing again, he dipped the spear in the oil and allowed it to fall, drop by drop, on the stomach of the sick woman. Later he touched the heads of all present with the spear, saying: "You will not be sick any more," and departed.

There are times, however, when all appeal to magic and to the gods is eliminated and the medicine-man becomes a simple lay physician. As such he is depicted in the following interesting account about a certain Tiurai, a Tahitian practitioner [6]:

A young man of Raiatea had for a number of weeks been suffering from a disease of the throat.

All the remedies of the district were tried in vain, even the famous "*tahua*" were consulted. The disease got worse and finally the parents of the young man decided to take him to Tahiti, to see Tiurai.

When they arrived at the home of the medicine-man, the young man, whose throat was highly inflamed and whose jaw had become stiff and rigid, was hardly able to utter a word.

His old father who accompanied him explained to Tiurai that the illness had begun more than a month ago and that the inflammation had during the last few days become such that the young man had not been able to eat and that it had just been possible for him to swallow a little coconut milk.

Tiurai, who was listening without uttering a word, now signalled the young man to approach and told him to open his mouth; but the pain was so great that he could not even pry free his teeth.

"Get on your knees!" shouted Tiurai. The young man, looking around cautiously, obeyed slowly and trembling; his slightest movement caused the most painful twinges of pain in his throat.

Seeing his hesitation Tiurai again shouted and more loudly: "I tell you to get on your knees and put your hands on the ground in front of you. Then walk on all fours as if you were a pig."

Tiurai continued: "Now run just as if you were a pig pursued by a pack of dogs; run!"

The young man obeyed again although the pain was almost insupportable.

The young man finally came breathless to a bunch of bananas but he was too weak to obey the last order given him and he stopped short begging Tiurai for better treatment.

"Bite this banana," shouted Tiurai. "I tell you to bite and tear this fruit with your teeth!"

In terror the young man obeyed and groaned deeply. But the energy that had been required to force open his mouth had broken the abscess in his throat and one could see the white and yellow pus flowing freely from between his teeth.

Tiurai, softening his tone of command, now said: "Bend your head and lift up your rump," and the patient obeyed docilely for he felt much better already.

Still seated on a coral block from which he had not budged all this time, Tiurai now turned to the father of the boy and said: "Take one of these fresh coconuts"—he showed him a package that had been brought in a little while before—"open it and take it to your son so that he can rinse his mouth with the water."

The old man, quite excited and amazed, obeyed and carried a coconut to his son, holding it in such a manner that he could wash his mouth.

"Now," continued Tiurai, "break open another coconut and let your son gargle his throat with it."

The old man obeyed again and Tiurai now ordered the young man to stand up and then gargle his throat.

"Now you may go," he said, "and in a few days neither of you will even be able to remember that one of you had been sick.

"My son," added Tiurai, addressing the young man, "gargle your mouth with this coconut milk at least three times a day and even oftener if you wish to."

When Tiurai was subsequently asked why he had staged this whole scene he answered as follows: "It should be clear enough to you. In order to treat my compatriots, it is necessary to represent the simplest things as though they were the most complicated and it is only by the successful outcome of a treatment that they realize that I was right. If I had explained to the old man and to his son all that I was going to do beforehand, it would have been just a waste of time. And that makes me think of Michaela who told me the story of the egg and the white man who first landed in America. When he had caused the egg to stand up and those around him said that they had always known that an egg could be made to stand up in that way, he answered and said: 'True enough, but one must think of it.' I saw at once that this boy was suffering acutely and by the outline of the swelling of his neck, I realized that it was an abscess in his throat. I would never have been able to cut open this abscess with my knife for the patient could not open his jaws. In ordering him to put a banana between his teeth, I knew very well that the abscess, if it was on the point of breaking, would open of itself and would empty its contents into the mouth and I, accordingly, had him lower his head so that the pus would not enter his stomach. The coconut milk with which he was to wash his wound is the purest liquid that can be found for it is naturally sterilized. As you saw I did not have to touch him and the patient left completely satisfied and convinced that I was a great man, whereas all that I did, anyone else with good sense could have done just as well."

Surely I do not have to add that the whole theory of the shaman-priest from prehistoric times to the present day is contained in such a sentence as this: "*It is necessary to represent the simplest things as though they were the most complicated and it is only by the successful outcome of a treatment that they [the people] realize that I was right.*" It definitely confirms the thesis I advanced in a previous chapter, that the initial and primary task of the shaman-priest is to emphasize and magnify the obstacles that stand between man and his natural and realistic adjustment to the outside world. It is through the excellence and effectiveness of the "technique of obstacles" that he made his living and retained his hold upon the imagination of the people. Nor does this necessarily imply that he was an impostor, a dupe, or an individual with only mercenary motives. Granted his temperament and its contrast to that of the layman, he could have been both sincere and altruistic. If he frequently was not, that was because the profession as such and its enmeshment in the economic set-up made this impossible.

Let me now give two final examples, one from the highly complex African civilization of the Amazulu and the other from the Zande, in both of which we find the typical and well-known African scepticism and realism illustrated with all its force:

Consulting a Diviner among the Amazulu [7]

If a man is ill, the people go to a diviner, to inquire of him. He says the man is suffering from disease. Or perhaps he says, he is injured by someone who is a sorcerer. They go home, not knowing the man who practises sorcery.

But others dispute, saying: "No! The diviner lies; that man is not a sorcerer." Others say, he speaks the truth. At length the man hears that the diviner has pointed him out as a sorcerer. He is angry, leaves the place and goes to be a dependant among other people. But some people believe in what the diviner says. Others do not believe.

If a man is ill they go to inquire of the diviner. He says: "The man is made ill by the *idhlozi.* Let them eat an ox; the man will get well if they eat an ox." They eat an ox. They worship the *amatongo,* and kill it.

When they have eaten all the flesh and the man does not get well but is constantly ill until he dies, some say: "The diviner lies." Others say: "He was called by the *amatongo;* a diviner cannot conquer the *amatongo.*"

When he is dead, they go to inquire of the diviner. He says: "He has been called by the *amatongo;* they wish him to die and go and live with them." And yet people do not cease to inquire of the diviner. Sometimes they say, the diviner is true; sometimes they say, he is false. For when a man is ill they will inquire of a diviner; and the diviner says, if they kill an ox the man will get well. They kill an ox, and the man gets well; and then they believe in the diviner's word. And yet forsooth the man would have got well after a time. But the people believe he has been saved by the *amatongo.*

When a man is ill, they call doctors to see him; they treat him, and when he gets well they demand cattle, telling him he must pay because they have cured him. He pays and after he has paid, he is ill again, and goes to the same doctor whom he has paid. He treats him but does not remove the disease; and tells him, it masters him. And the sick man asks his ox to be sent back that he may go to other doctors. They go to others. They treat him. Perhaps they cure the disease [and] then the first doctor feels hurt and says that the sick man was cured by him. But they have paid the man that gave him physic last.

When a doctor treats a sick person, he kills an ox, and cuts away the tendons of the legs, mixes them with medicines and chars them till they are dry. When they are dry they are powdered, the sick man is scarified and the medicines are rubbed into the scarifications. The gall is poured on him that the *amatongo* may come and see him and lick him, that he may get well.

Men go to the diviner that he may tell them what they wish to know. They merely go to him. On their arrival they do not tell him for what purpose they have come. They are silent. But he tells them they have come on some matter of importance. They assent by striking the ground. If they strike vehemently, they do so because they hear the diviner mention things which they know and about which they have come to him. If he mentions things unknown to them, they strike the ground slightly. If he mentions the very things they know, they strike vehemently.

How the Zande Witch Doctor Badobo Cures His Patients [8]

Badobo told me that, before I commenced to treat a patient, I was to cut a piece of *togoro ranga* and shape it with a knife until it was like an object of witchcraft. I was to conceal this between my fingers, or alternatively, to put it under my nail. He said I was to sit still and do nothing and let some layman prepare the poultice, and when he handed it to me I was to take it from him quickly and squeeze it between my fingers so as cunningly to insert into it the little object from under my finger nail; to see that it was well set in the poultice and then to place it on the affected part of my patient.

First I should have rubbed some *mbiro* medicine across the mouth of my patient and afterwards I should have taken a mouthful of water and, after having gargled it, blown it out. I was then to begin to massage the patient and, having done this, to remove the poultice and, holding it in my hand, to search it until I discovered an object of witchcraft in it. When I found it, I was to show it to the onlookers so that they might see it and say: "Heu! Well, I never! So that's the thing from which he was dying!"

A man will perform this act of surgery with one object about three times. When he has removed it from the poultice he will go and place it on the stump of a tree near by and will warn everyone not to touch it because it is a thing connected with witchcraft. Then he will take it again and hide it once more under his nail, and for a second time will perform a surgical operation with it. A man who is good at cheating will make use of the same object about three times.

Thus they said to me about it: "They go to treat a sick patient and deceive him saying that they have taken an object of witchcraft from his body, whereas they have not taken it at all but, on the other hand, they have put *mbiro* into the sick man's mouth and cut his skin at the part of the body where he is in pain and have rubbed their *mbiro* across the cut." When the man has recovered, people say that indeed the witch-doctors are skilful healers whereas it is the *mbiro* which really cures people and it is on account of *mbiro* that people recover when they are treated by witch-doctors. The people think that healing is brought about by the extraction of objects and only the witch-doctors know that it is the *mbiro* which heals people. The people themselves do not learn the truth because only witch-doctors know it and they keep it a secret. They do not spread their knowledge abroad but tell it only to those who have first eaten their medicines, because their treatment is very deceitful.

With regard to their use of a spider, they cut off its head and with the aid of a small stick they fill its decapitated body with red juices which they have extracted by making an incision into a *bakuli* tree. When the spider is full of this red juice they put it in between their fingers and later insert it in the poultice when treating a patient. After massaging the patient for a time they remove the poultice and discover in it this spider and show it to him, saying: "Heu! Look at the spider from which you were dying." They also show the spider to the onlookers, saying: "Heu! Look at the sick man's blood in the stomach of the spider." They press the stomach of the spider between their fingers and, with a pop, squeeze out the juice of the *bakuli* tree. However, it is the juice of the *bakuli* tree and not the blood of the sick man; it is the juice of the *bakuli* tree with which witch-doctors deceive people.

There are insects which propagate in a kind of hollow grass (*mbepe*) and give birth to young like grubs (*agbile*). A witch-doctor opens up this hollow grass and removes them and goes and digs a little hole, having hid them first in his horn. He sticks one horn in the ground here and another one there, with the hole in between them.

The witch-doctor gazes fixedly at the sick man while he empties the grubs into the little hole and then quickly replaces the horn again in the ground; and he takes a *kpoyo* poultice and puts it on top of these grubs. He then says to the sick man: "Come and lie down," and he comes and lies down on his stomach over the hole. Then the witch-doctor takes a draught of water and blows it out and afterwards begins to massage the patient and massages him for a long time. When he has finished he says to him: "Now get up." He then scoops up in his hand water and *kpoyo*, searches it and finds grubs in it and says to the sick man: "Heu! That illness from which you are dying, here it is, these *akirima*." The patient is amazed at what he sees. The witch-doctor then takes his knife and makes a few transverse cuts across his patient's stomach, and takes his horn and sticks it into the ground in front of him. He afterwards takes his patient's hands and puts them on the edge of the horn and rubs them down with *mbiro* medicine (he takes both the patient's hands in both his hands). The patient grips the horn and then is told to leave go of it, and the witch-doctor places his foot on the sick man's foot and raises the sick man's arms and jerks them sharply down and tells him: "Run and put your foot against a tree-stem." The patient runs a little way and puts his foot against a tree-stem and the *akirima* cleave to the tree.

Witch-doctors take the gut of a small rat called *ndakatakpwoli* and they cut it down to a little short thing which they dry in the sun. Somebody afterwards summons a witch-doctor to dance in order that he may produce *abise*. *Abise* is the *likikpwa* of a man which witches have removed from his body and have hidden in order that he may die. They say: "Let us summon a witch-doctor to come and dance and discover the *likikpwa*." Now when the witch-doctor has heard that he is to come and dance and produce *likikpwa* of the man from whom witches have removed it and hidden it, he takes his rat's gut and hides it in the palm of his hand behind the handles of his hand-bells. He dances for a long time and arranges the gut in his hand. He then collects the people whose *likikpwa* has been hidden by witches. He places them on the ground in the open and dances round and round them. He pulls the nose of one of them. He then orders a hole to be dug in the centre of the homestead so that he can take the *likikpwa* from it. When the hole is finished the witch-doctor takes those persons whose *likikpwa* has been removed and makes them sit down, one by one, over the hole. Here he thumps them on one knee and then on the other and he strikes them with the flat of his hand on the top of their heads and on their backs. But the truth is that the *likikpwa* is really in the palm of the witch-doctor the whole time. He then says to the man whose spirit (*mbisimo*) has been hidden by witches: "Get up from over the hole." (He has been sitting with his legs over the hole and he now raises both feet and swings them to one side.) The witch-doctor drops suddenly to the ground at the mouth of the hole and lets his hands, still gripping the hand-bells, wander over the bottom of the hole and suddenly exclaims that he has found the *likikpwa*. He says: "Look! Witchcraft has hidden the *likikpwa* of this man. Look! Here it is!" People are amazed and say: "Phew! This witch-doctor is a wonder for he has discovered the *likikpwa* of this man which witches have removed and hidden." Whereas in truth it is the gut of a rat which he has used to deceive them by hiding it in his hand when he was dancing.

The foregoing examples give us an insight into the curious blend of magic and religion so common in the treatment of disease. The religious thinker is here still largely under the sway of the magical mentality. The two functions of magician and priest are still prevailingly exercised by one man even where a fairly marked separation of these functions exists for other aspects of culture. One thing is, however, clear, that the better organized the medicine-men are the more prominent the strictly religious ingredients become. The spirits and deities prove to be in origin the specific constructs of the shamans and the priests by the manner in which, at the beginning, they are represented as concerning themselves primarily with the welfare of their creators.

Magic is thus relegated to the background and its practice becomes, after a while, unaristocratic and proletarian. Yet even the fully developed priest of a complex civilization cannot discard it entirely, for he would lose his support if he did. Recognizing this he accordingly attempts to organize the magical practices and rites and yet, at the same time, to keep the whole domain of magic distinct from religion. This is a task in which, of course, he was never successful except in those relatively few cases where the priests developed into a group apart and separate from the rest of the population. But even in these instances, true religion and religious speculation remain essentially the special preoccupation of the artist-thinkers among the priesthood. Both are reserved for the major problems of life. The minor problems and the ordinary and casual events of life are still delivered up completely to magic. Obviously this must be so. Yet just as, among ourselves, a physician who is a specialist will, at times, condescend to treat an ordinary case of cold in the head, so will a medicine-man or priest who concerns himself exclusively with religion proper, on occasion, condescend to practise simple magic.

Under these circumstances we should not be surprised that even in complex agricultural societies the securing of the goods of the world is completely saturated with magic. Earthly goods are obtained by the use of magic, and normal success and normal health are obtained and interfered with by the use of magic. We need not give examples. They will occur to everyone. What we desire to stress, above all, is that, no matter how complicated the social-economic structure of the tribe is, no matter how spiritualized is the religion that a given priesthood may have elaborated, the everyday affairs of man are still dominated by magic. If, for instance, among the Zande of the Sudan, a blight seizes the ground-nut crop, it is *mangu* (witchcraft); if the bush is burnt vainly in pursuit of game, it is *mangu;* if women laboriously ladle out water from a pool and are rewarded by but a few small fish, it is *mangu;* if termites do not rise where they are due and a cold night is wasted in waiting for their flight, it is *mangu;* if a wife shows herself sulky and unresponsive to her husband, it is *mangu;* if a chief is cold and distant to a subject, it is *mangu;* and if a magical rite fails to achieve its purpose, it is *mangu.* How closely it can be bound up with specifically economic aspects comes out neatly, on the other hand, among the Bukaua of former German New Guinea. There we find a pig magic which has the following as its objective: that the pigs of the various owners who are to bring them to the market should not die, that they bring good prices, and that the market transactions take place in an atmosphere of quiet and amity.

Where the population of a given tribe is small, as is almost always the case in the non-agricultural civilizations, the functions of the shaman and medicine-man are very generalized. This does not imply that the shamans are not frequently specifically organized but that the kind of organization is quite different in type from that prevailing in highly populated areas with marked class and caste distinctions, such as in Africa, Oceania, and a few parts of North America, not to mention the ancient cultures of Mexico and Peru. Among the latter, we find not only an elaborate differentiation but a perplexing hierarchy of rank and the reflection of rigid class and caste demarcations. We are dealing here with an organization of religion and religious ritual strictly comparable to that of civilized people. Really to understand its nature would require a lengthy exposition which is obviously out of the question in a work of this kind. I have deemed it best, consequently, to illustrate this complexity of organization and multiplicity of functions in terms of two civilizations, the Maori of New Zealand and the Ewe of West Africa, and, even to these, we can but give passing mention.

Among the Maori an elaborate training was required for the priesthood. The priest had to learn the contents of "the three baskets of knowledge," as they were called—the first containing the knowledge of peace, of goodness, and of love; the second containing the prayers, incantations, and rituals used by mankind; and the third containing the knowledge of the wars of mankind, of agriculture, of woodwork, stonework, earthwork, in fact, of all things pertaining to earthly life. Since, in addition, the priest had to be conversant with divination, second sight, the technique of exorcism and of placation of the spirits, it is not strange that we should encounter a definite hierarchy of religious functionaries: *ahurewa,* a first-grade priest; *taua,* a high-class priest; *pukenga,* an instructor of occult matters; *tuanopaki,* an acolyte; *puri,* a wizard; *tauira,* a junior priest; *matakite,* a seer; *makutu,* a wizard; *kehua,* a lower-class shaman; and *kokatangi,* an astronomical expert. The closely affiliated Tahitians had eight classifications: the great-author or high priest, author-of-prayer or priest, author-of-medicine or doctor, author-of-temples or director of temple buildings, author-of-houses or planner and builder of houses, author-of-canoes or adept in canoe-building, and author-of-fishing or authority on fishing seasons.

Complicated as is the religious organization in Polynesia it is relatively simple compared to that which we find in the amazing civilizations of the west coast of Africa. This intricate organization was necessitated by the large number of cults existing there, the multiple interconnexions between the religious and the civil authorities, and the marked historical transformations to which the cultures of this part of the world have been subjected for the last five hundred years at least.

Let us take the Ewe for instance. There we have, first, the cult of the Supreme God and his immediate entourage; secondly, the cults of the gods of the soothsayers; third, the cult of the aboriginal spirits called *trowo;* and, lastly, the cult of the *trowo* who have been introduced from without. There are one hundred and twelve in the first group and twenty-five in the second. Finally there are the cult organizations connected with the secret societies and with magic, private and public. For all these cults innumerable priests and attendants are needed. I shall take as an example the cult of the Supreme Deity, *Mawu.*

A *Mawu* priest is appointed by the priest of the *trowo* cults. He is always selected from among the ranks of the wealthy and the honoured members of the group and is always a comparatively old man. He must go through an elaborate initiation. After he has been initiated and placed in charge of the cult, he must observe a number of taboos. He can eat no carrion, no snakes, no rats, no porcupine, no wildcats, and no monkeys. He must dress only in white and blue clothes. When he goes to a funeral, however, he is barred from wearing these. He can eat no food that has been cooked by a menstruating woman. Plates and cooking utensils have to be placed in a prescribed position when they are brought to his enclosure. He is strictly forbidden to use certain kinds of wood for his fireplace. He must perform specific rites, some daily, others weekly, and still others at undetermined times. For instance, as soon as he arises in the morning he must go to the sanctuary of the god, take water from the basin there, and wash his hands and face. Then he must take three swallows of it, expectorate, and, invoking the different names of the god, exclaim: "I seek no one's death. But if someone desires to kill me, then he himself will die." In the evening he must do the same.

On the market day of his clan, which is held every fourth day, he must stay at home, and he is not allowed to speak to anyone until he has performed certain rites. When these are over, he retires to his room and, pouring an offering of palm-wine on the ground, he prays to the god as follows: "I need meat and palm-wine. May people come to me today bringing them!" Every Saturday morning he paints himself with white ochre, clothes himself in a white dress, and binds a band around his forehead. These he must wear till evening. He is not permitted to go out on this day and must concern himself only with eating and drinking and conversations with other *Mawu* priests and the members of his family.

Apart from his primary function of attending to the innumerable duties of a priest of *Mawu,* he has the secondary function of curing disease and praying for sterile women.

However, there is no need to continue. The above example will not only indicate the very specific nature of the cult duties of the priest but will also serve to emphasize again how strange is the medley of economic-magical and strictly religious factors that enter into the worship of even a Supreme Deity.

But we must bring this discussion of the nature and the function of the medicine-man and priest to an end. It has been made clear that the formulations with which he operates and the techniques he uses are fundamentally rooted in the projections and behaviour of individuals carefully selected on the basis of their neurotic-epileptoid mental constitution and that, however normalized these, in the course of time, may have become through the influence of the more normal individuals who entered the profession, their origin in a neurotic mentality is still clearly patent. This is particularly true of that aspect of religion which we shall treat in the following chapter, the methods of approach to the supernatural.

8

The Approach to the Supernatural

THERE can be little question but that the neurotic-epileptoid shaman recognized the existence of his two personalities and the marked differences between them. But how was he to interpret the relation of that personality which emerged in a trance or a seizure to that of his normal self? Upon the answer to this question much of his approach to the supernatural depended, for the answer to this question indicated the specific form the supernatural was to assume and the immediacy of its relation to him. And this, in turn, affected the nature of his relationship, as a shaman or medicine-man, to the community at large. If the new ego was simply the continuation of his normal one, then he was merely a passive spectator of the strange scene that spread out before him in the hallucinatory world of his trance, and no difference in kind need be postulated between this and his normal dream experience. The suddenness and the compulsive nature of his transformation, the suffering it entailed, the accompanying catalepsy, all these seemed to set it off clearly from the somewhat analogous phenomena and experiences of sleep and dreams. Certainly in his trance state he was not wholly his own older self. Why then was it not possible that, temporarily at least, he was somebody else? There seemed to be ample physiological confirmation for such an interpretation. He had lost consciousness completely amidst great mental distress and upon awakening found himself utterly exhausted and possessed of the recollection of a most vivid experience beating upon his brain with an obsessive urgency to become articulated.

But if he was somebody else, who was this person? A number of answers were possible. He might, for instance, be the ghost of his dead self or the reincarnation of himself from a former existence or some reincarnated ancestor or, finally, he might be some being utterly unconnected with his normal self. To what extent, however? Since, upon coming out of his trance, he again became his normal self, the answer seemed to be obvious. He was all these—his ghost, a reincarnation from a former existence, a reincarnated ancestor, some totally different being—all of these, but only for a passing time. In other words, he was temporarily possessed by them. The moment he accepted this interpretation then some purpose could be discerned behind all his initial physical and mental suffering, behind his enforced isolation from the rest of his people, and behind those specific aspects of his experience in which it differed significantly and dramatically from his normal dream-life. They were all, he could assume, definitely connected with, and perhaps even conditioned by, the fact that he was possessed by a spirit. With this spirit, who was conceived to be partly outside and partly inside himself, he must consequently establish some type of objective relationship. And this he accordingly did by publicly re-enacting his specific personal experience, that of a man suffering from a particular mental affliction. His projections, his hallucinations, his journey through space and time, thus became a dramatic ritual and served as the prototype for all future concepts of the religious *road of perfection*.

With the examination of the relation of an individual to the spirit who had taken possession of a shaman, we must accordingly begin.[1] The actual moment of possession is conceived of either as taking place quietly and imperceptibly or as the result of a violent seizure by a spirit. Where the belief is found that everyone can become possessed, where ancestor worship, for instance, prevails, the former conception is by far the commoner although it also occurs in many regions where no ancestor worship exists. In all those areas, however, where shamanism proper is widespread —throughout Siberia and its contiguous territories in northern North America and, to a considerable extent, Malaysia and Me-

lanesia—violent seizure is dominant. Of the most vital importance for a correct understanding of this subject is the fact, however, that everywhere in the world it is the religious leader who
is so seized upon, one might almost say, preyed upon, whether
he is a shaman proper, a medicine-man, or a priest. Although not
the only way in which a spirit can enter him, it is a favourite one.
May we not see in this a simple projection, an objectification of
the actual seizure from which the neurotic-epileptoid shaman
suffers? When an Eskimo shaman cowers in inexplicable fear as
he seeks for a helping spirit, is it not the terror felt at what is
taking place within himself that is here reflected? The helping
spirit is pictured as literally attacking him in a violent and mysterious manner. The sea-ermine spirit, so he claims, dashes upon
him out of the sea and so suddenly and unexpectedly that defence
is out of the question. It slips into his sleeve and, running over
his naked body, fills him with such a shuddering horror that he
loses consciousness almost immediately.

Certainly this interpretation of the shaman's terror-formula
seems reasonable, and it is equally reasonable to assume that the
mentality of the neurotic shaman is indelibly impressed upon
many other details of the formulae that have been devised for
approaching the supernatural, in spite of all the changes, despite
all the amplifications, reinterpretations, and symbolic transfigura-
tions to which, in the course of time, they have been transformed
by his more normal colleagues.

Part of the task awaiting the shaman in his capacity as a religious formulator now becomes clear. He must analyse, first of
all, his preparation for the approach to the supernatural; he must
endow each of the constituent elements of this preparation with
a definite individuality and introduce a specific sequence into the
order of their appearance; he must then establish a series of
gradations indicative of the relationship between him and the
spirit; and he must finally clarify the precise nature of the relationship existing between him and the community he is to serve.
Then this must all be systematized.

We have already pointed out that his earliest function, and one he was never to lose, was the curing of disease. He had, as the prototype for this, his own affliction and the manner in which it had been alleviated. In shamanism proper, certainly, this affliction was to bring him into direct connexion with the spirit that had possessed him. The theory which he developed was accordingly that he personally must suffer voluntarily so that his patient could be cured.

Out of such a theory the concept of a divine vicarious sacrifice should easily have developed theoretically. There are in fact numerous anticipations of it. But they never crystallized into the figure of a saviour until a new social and economic order had first led to a centralization of power in the hands of a priest-king, who then became deified. This took place, we know, in the ancient East, beginning in Egypt and Babylonia and then spreading to Palestine. It has recently been contended [2] with some justification that the annual feasts of the ancient civilizations of Egypt, Babylonia, and Palestine had a specific pattern and that this pattern contained the following elements:

(1) The dramatic representation of the death and resurrection of the God.
(2) The recitation or symbolic representation of the myth of creation.
(3) The ritual combat in which the triumph of the God over his enemies was depicted.
(4) The sacred marriage.
(5) The triumphal procession, in which the king played the part of the God followed by a train of lesser Gods or visiting deities.

The ritual drama of many primitive peoples contains most of these elements too, but the fateful synthesis that was to lead to the idea of a Saviour-Messiah and to the Christian Passion could have been arrived at only in a civilization built up on an utterly different economic and social basis from that which prevailed in primitive societies and only then where an ideology had become dominant which apotheosized earthly suffering and converted the home of the dead into a glorified crazy-quilt of wish fulfilments. When Freud likens religion to a neurosis, it is manifestly this he is thinking of. But religion is a neurosis only to this extent: that it perpetuates an interpretation contrived by a neurotic individual of man's relation to the world outside himself. If it is a neurosis, it is a laicized and normalized one. But let us return to our shaman-priest.

From the curing of the sick, this ritual of suffering was extended to embrace every other aspect of importance in life, to find its expression, finally, in the ordeal of fasting which we encounter practically everywhere in the primitive world.

The formula for religious fasting now becomes clear. The faster must have a purpose, and for this he must be prepared to inflict suffering upon himself. He must become either completely unconscious or semi-conscious and, in this condition, either journey to the land of spirits or be approached by the spirits at his fasting place. At times he may become identified with them. As this formula came more and more to be taken over by healthy-minded priests and realistic laymen, the original significance of the ordeal was lost. Suffering became an inherent attribute of the attitude to be assumed by a worshipper in the presence of a god and took on new interpretations, such as being a form of purification, a catharsis, a voluntary withdrawal from the workaday world in order to be able to return to it again with some divine warrant for continuing the journey through life on a higher level. And so, for the elect, it is quite conceivable that the original physiologically conditioned terror of the shaman became the *tremendum* of which the religious philosopher Otto speaks; that the desire for solitude and withdrawal from the world became his *mysterium;* and the hallucinatory experience of the trance, his *wholly-other,* the beatific vision of the mystics. It is this evolution we must now try to trace, from the *via hallucinatoria* through the *via purgativa* to end in the *via mystica.*

In those regions where shamanism proper flourishes the only requirement for the call is the proper tendency to neurotic ecstasy and trance. The shaman need be neither pure in mind nor humble in spirit. All that is demanded of him is that he suffer physically. Many youths among the Chukchee, for instance, prefer death to the call of the spirits, according to Bogoras. The physical hardships and the mental suffering are too intense. Bogoras states that the process of gathering inspiration is so painful to young shamans because of their mental struggle against the call, that they are sometimes said literally to sweat blood on the forehead and temples. And after they have accepted the call, the spirits demand from them the impossible, such as showing no signs of fatigue after having been made to dance violently for long periods of time. At other times the spirits "play" with them, as they euphemistically say.

Sternberg recounts his experience with a young Gilyak boy already possessed of two souls at the age of twelve and the son of a great shaman who had four. Once, on being suddenly awakened from his sleep, the young boy began throwing himself about and shouting as shamans are accustomed to do. When this was over, the boy's face looked worn and tired, and he afterwards informed Sternberg that, during the sleep which had preceded this outbreak, two helping spirits had appeared to him whom he recognized as his father's and they said to him: "We used to play with your father—let us play with you also."

The suffering of those Yakut shamans who have as their helping spirit a dog is even worse, for this spirit is believed to be insatiable. He gnaws the shaman's heart with his teeth and tears his body into pieces.[3] The whole purpose of the long and arduous initiation of the shaman in Siberia is to make the impact of the spirit upon him as light as possible. But this is never done by encouraging the practice of the contemplative life or by the inculcation of such virtues as humility and self-abnegation. Not that this did not occur. An Eskimo shaman who could insist that solitude and suffering open the human mind to true wisdom was, obviously, well acquainted with the life of contemplation and knew something of humility. But this was not an official requirement nor did a shaman gain in prestige by propounding such a view.

The stressing of personal and ethical qualifications for the proper approach to the supernatural was, however, the necessary preliminary to any reinterpretation of the hallucinatory vision of the neurotic shaman if it was to be made more acceptable and more palatable to the normal intelligence. But such qualifications would not be stressed except in a society that tolerated individual expression, such as, for instance, the democratic societies of so many parts of aboriginal North America, or among special individuals of highly stratified societies, like those of various parts of Africa and Polynesia. It is only in such a militantly individualistic civilization as that of the Sioux that a man would say: "In order to secure a fulfilment of his desire, a man must qualify himself to make his request," or that he would insist: "It is not fitting that a man should suddenly go out and make a request of Wakan tanka [the great spirit]," or, finally, that a man would stand weeping in the presence of the spirits while his heart "ached to its very depths" as did some Winnebago priests.* And it is clear that where the worshipper insisted upon subjective purification there, likewise, the figures of the gods would become purified and the vision of the journey to the land of the spirits would become coherent and be robbed of much of its terror.

As an illustration of the displacement of spirits conceived of as fear-inspiring and the substitution for them of the idea that they were kindly helpers, let me give the following account from the Winnebago [4]:

Near the place where we lived there were three lakes and a blackhawk's nest. Right near the tree where the nest was located, they built a lodge and our war-bundle was placed in it. There my elder brother and myself were to pass the night. It was said that if anyone

* Cf. pp. 19–20 and 33–34.

fasted at such a place for four nights he would be blessed with victory and the power to cure the sick. All the spirits would bless him.

We were told the following would happen to us. On the first night we would imagine ourselves surrounded by spirits whose whisperings we would hear outside of the lodge. The spirits would even whistle. I was told that I would be frightened and nervous and that if I still remained there, I would be molested by large monsters, fearful to look upon. Even the bravest man might well be frightened. Should I, however, manage to get through that night, I would then, on the following night, be molested by ghosts whom I could hear speaking outside. These ghosts would say things that might well cause me to run away. Towards morning, I was told, these ghosts would even take my blankets away from me. They would grab hold of me and drive me out of the lodge and not stop until the sun rose.

If I was able to endure a third night, then I would be addressed by the true spirits. They would bless me and say: "We bless you. We had really intended to turn you over to the monsters and bad spirits and that is why these approached you first. But you overcame them and now they will not be able to take you away. Now you may go home for we bless you with victory and long life; we bless you with the power of healing the sick. Nor shall you lack wealth. So go home and eat, for a large war-party is soon to fall upon you. As soon as the sun rises the war-whoops will be given so that if you do not go home now you will be killed."

Thus the spirits would speak to me. I was told that if I did not care to do the bidding of one particular spirit, then some other would address me and repeat very much the same thing. So the spirits would speak alternately until the break of day. Then, just before sunrise, a man wearing a warrior's costume would come and peep into the lodge. He would be a scout. I was told that when this happened, then I would surely believe that a war-party had come upon me. Soon another spirit would come and say: "Grandson, I have taken pity upon you and I will bless you with all the good things that the earth holds. Go home now for a war-party is about to rush upon you." If then I went home the war-whoops would be given just as the sun rose. The members of this war-party would give the whoop all at the same time. They would rush upon me and capture me and after *coup* had been counted me [i.e., after I had been struck] they would say: "Now, grandson, we have acted thus in order to teach you. Thus shall you act. You have completed your fasting."

Thus would the spirits talk to me, I was told. Now this war-party was really composed of spirits, spirits from the heaven and the earth. Indeed all the spirits that exist would be there. These would all bless me. I was also told that it would be a very difficult thing to obtain this particular blessing.

So there I fasted at the black-hawk's nest where a lodge had been built for me. The first night I stayed there I wondered when something would happen. But nothing took place. The second night, rather late in the night, my father came and opened the war-bundle and then, taking out a gourd, began to sing. I stood beside him without any clothing except my breech-clout and, holding tobacco in each hand, I uttered my cry to the spirits:

"O spirits, here humble in heart I stand beseeching you."

My father sang war-bundle songs and wept as he sang. I also wept as I uttered my cry to the spirits.

The contrast between this and the terror visions of those tribes where spirit-possession prevails is tremendous. Terror is still present, that is manifest, but it is associated with evil spirits and the faster is specifically warned against them. In another fasting experience it is implied that the faster who accepts the fictitious promises of the evil spirits is thereby indicating that he lacks the stamina and the real desire to wait for the blessings of the good and true spirits.

Just as the terror has been ameliorated and just as the faster and the deities appealed to have been purified, so, likewise, as the economic organization becomes more complex, does the vision which constitutes the core of the shaman's most significant trance experience, his journey to meet the spirits, become freed from the materialistic dross adhering to it. The contrast between the two emerges clearly if we compare the account of the journey of an Eskimo shaman to the dreaded *Takanakapsaluk* with that of his journey given by a Winnebago on the pages following. According to Rasmussen [5]:

When a shaman wishes to visit *Takanakapsaluk,* he must wear nothing but his *kamiks* and mittens. He sits for a while in silence and then begins to call upon his helping spirits saying: "The way is made open for me; the way is made open for me." And then, when they arrive and the earth opens under him, he has to struggle for a long time with hidden forces until he finally hears the cry: "Now the way is open." In his flight to the bottom of the sea he encounters many dangers. The most dreaded of these dangers are three large rolling stones incessantly churning about and between which he must pass. Then he comes to a broad, trodden path, the shaman's path, and following a coastline resembling that on earth, he comes to the house of the dreaded *Takanakapsaluk.* Outside the house one can hear the animals puffing and blowing. In the passage leading directly to the deity lies a ferocious dog gnawing at a bone and snarling. Only the most courageous shaman can pass him. And then he sees *Takanakapsaluk,* who is always angry. Her hair hangs down loose all over one side of her face, a tangled untidy mass hiding her eyes, so that she cannot see. It is the misdeeds and offences committed by men which gather in dirt and impurity over her body. All the foul emanations from the sins of mankind nearly suffocate her. He grabs *Takanakapsaluk* by one shoulder and turns her face toward the lamp and the animals, and strokes her hair, smoothing and combing it until she is calmer. And then speaks to her saying: "Those up above can no longer help the seals up by grasping their foreflippers." To which she responds in spirit language: "The secret miscarriages of the women and the breaches of taboo in eating boiled meat bar the way for the animals." Slowly the shaman appeases her and finally, in kindlier mood, she takes the animals and drops them on the floor. Water pours out from the pool and the animals disappear in the sea.

This is manifestly the vision of a disordered mind, a true *via hallucinatoria*. Yet it was possible, even in comparatively simple societies, for the select few to transform this journey into one with marked affiliations to the memorable journey of Dante, with its proper division into a *via purgativa*, a *via illuminativa*, and a *via unitiva* and then, with possibly a more profound understanding than the great Florentine possessed, to transfer it to this world so that the divine experience could become a preparation for the earthly experience and not the reverse. Even at the risk of tiring the reader, let me, in brief outline, describe this journey along the road of life to the road of spiritland and back to that of life again. It is in the terms of a Winnebago religious philosopher and it runs somewhat as follows [6]:

As you travel along the road of life do not doubt it. The first thing you will encounter on this journey is a ravine extending, on both sides, to the very ends of the world. In spite of its forbidding appearance, you must plunge right through it. The ravine signifies that you will lose a child and that, in your misery, thoughts of death will come to you. But if you get frightened and dwell upon your hardship too much this will be your grave.

Soon you will reach an impenetrable brushwood of stickers, thorns and weeds. These, too, you will surmount. The brushwood means that someone greatly beloved by you, will die. If you get frightened and dwell upon hardship too much, this too will be your grave.

Then, as you journey on, evil birds will continually din their noises into your ears and cast their excrement upon your body. You must disregard both. It is not proper to brush such excrement away. Not in such a manner can you prepare yourself for the real goods of life. This excrement is, after all, simply the evil gossip of jealous and petty people. Why should you get angry? It is better to contain yourself and hold your peace.

You will next come to an enormous fire encircling the earth and seemingly impossible to cross. Though it singe and scorch you, you must plunge through it. The fire signifies that your wife will die.

Here, too, you must not become discouraged but continue on. Finally you will come to tremendous perpendicular bluffs. These you must ascend and then you will find yourself safe on the other side. You will now be alone, for all your loved ones have died and you yourself will wonder why you cannot join them. Difficult as it is to continue yet you must persevere.

Thus ends the *via purgativa*. The *via illuminativa* is now to begin:

There are four hills which you must now ascend. At first you will find yourself in the rear of a long procession of men and women, but as you begin to ascend the third hill only a few will be in front of you and a vast number behind. Halfway up this hill you will have to rest and, as your eyes look ahead, you will see a reddish haze extending across the land. It is not the land, however, that is covered with a haze but you, for you are now an old man; your eyes have become dim and your hair grizzled.

Finally you will come to the fourth and last hill which you will be able to ascend only with the greatest difficulty. Now, old in years but full of knowledge and wisdom, you must be prepared to die.

Thus ends the *via illuminativa*. The *via unitiva* follows:

Having ascended the fourth hill you will see near you an oval lodge. This you must approach. There a man will ask you: "Grandson, how have you acted in life?" And you will answer: "I do not know." Thereupon he will say: "Grandson, but I know," and give you some food. After partaking of it you will, for a short time, become unconscious. Your body will die but you will proceed on in the spirit as if you had only stumbled. You have still some distance to go before you reach the presence of Earthmaker. You have first to ascend the tree-ladders which extend to heaven. They are slippery, dirty, worn down from incessant handling by those who have preceded you. Having ascended them you will come to the land where Earthmaker lives. There you will find many lodges and those of your relatives who, like you, have succeeded in passing through the various obstacles that bar the way from earth to heaven. In this land you will dwell for some time. It is a happy land. No bad clouds float over the sky; there is no night; there is no work and no one is ever in want. Then although you are a mature and grown-up person, you will be placed on the laps of all the people there. Now you are prepared to meet Earthmaker. Him you will see, face to face, and he will validate your return to the world of men.

And, like Dante, having wandered into a dark wood straightway to become lost, so our Winnebago sage emerges from the hidden road to see the stars again and come once more into the air of life.

9

The Conciliation and Propitiation of the Supernatural

THE type of approach to the supernatural and the methods adopted for the conciliation of the supernatural are both manifestly integral parts of the same phenomenon. The one conditions the other. They, in their turn, are determined by the specific concept of the supernatural encountered in a given area and the nature of its relations to the specific social-economic values. Both again depend to an appreciable degree upon the temperament of the individual and his status in a particular group. It is one of the faults vitiating many treatments of primitive religion that a subject of this magnitude and one possessing so many facets and ramifications has been described in the most generalized terms and as if it were basically and primarily concerned with the simplest wants of the most naïve mentalities. To speak of primitive man as conciliating and propitiating the supernatural as such is absurd and meaningless, and only indicates how lightly anthropologists have taken their task and the extent to which they still subscribe unconsciously to the theory that they are there dealing with a dead level of mentality.

We have pointed out repeatedly that the outstanding characteristic of true spirit-possession is what we have termed its violence. This holds for the shaman as well as for the spirit. In so immediate a relationship as this, it would be somewhat meaningless to say that the problem for the shaman is one of conciliation and propitiation as far as he himself is concerned. It would seem more accurate and more correct to say that it becomes one of adjustment, and this adjustment always remains an essential ac-

tivity of the official intermediary between man and the supernatural. The violence in the relation can then be understood. It
is the outward reflection of this conflict, in addition to its being
likewise an expression of the shaman's neurotic constitution. But
the shaman, the medicine-man, and the priest are also the official
intermediaries of normal people who have normal wants which
are to be brought to the attention of the spirits and deities. What,
psychologically considered, will be the approach to the supernatural under these circumstances, where the shaman must be
both passive and active? The answer must be that he will develop
one aspect of the subject at the expense of the other. The facts
at our disposal indicate rather definitely that the economic factors
determined his course and that he, in the main, chose to be an
intermediary between the spirits and the community. In consequence, the elaboration of the technique for the layman's intercourse with the spirits became the focal point of his interest, and
his own personal relationship to the spirits, however intricate he
made it, became of subsidiary importance.

Sociological and economic considerations reinforced the psychological ones if, in fact, they did not determine them. We
must never forget that it was as an intermediary for others, after
all, that the medicine-man made his living. The layman, it must
be remembered, was not primarily interested in the methods
employed for obtaining help and protection from the spirits even
if he was not altogether indifferent to them. All that he demanded was some tangible result from these methods. The task
of the medicine-man was consequently obvious. He must first
cement his relationship with his clients. Then, if he wished, he
could devote himself to speculation concerning his own relationship to the deity. These speculations not only brought him no
prestige but were likely, if pressed to the extreme, to be branded
as antisocial and dangerous. This does not necessarily mean, however, that no attention was paid to them. We have, in fact, ample
evidence to the contrary. But the intricate analysis which this
personal relationship of the medicine-man to the divine occa-

sionally received was not due to any real love of speculation as such but was, in large measure, simply part of the conflict among the medicine-men themselves for prestige and affluence. Some few there were who, like our mystics, would have preferred to bathe permanently in the effulgence of some divine splendour and in the contemplation of a beatific vision. For such egotism, however, there was, fortunately for the community, no room and no appreciation in primitive civilizations.

The primary function of the medicine-man here, accordingly, was to act as intermediator, just as his primary task was to develop a type of approach to the supernatural that would appeal to the layman and furnish him with explanations for success or failure that would be acceptable to him. Here it was that the profound gulf separating the religious from the non-religious temperaments immediately came to the surface. The religious man insisted, if not on subjective qualifications, at least on a specific type of behaviour; the non-religious man, on the other hand, asked simply for guarantees of objective success irrespective of the manner in which they were obtained, although he preferred methods similar to those to which he was accustomed. What these were we know: they were the methods used in ordinary human transactions and in magic. Human transactions implied gifts and their automatic repayment; magic implied constraint. The spirits were supposed to be at least as reasonable as human beings and to make the return gift a little more valuable than that which they received. That was the layman's formula.

The shaman-priest's formula was utterly different. It meant, we have seen, suffering and an arduous and painful initiation. Combining his formula with that of the layman the religious formulator arrived at a most satisfactory solution which did justice to all aspects of what, at first sight, seemed an insoluble conflict. The history of the methods of conciliating and propitiating the supernatural is the history of the fate that befell the various constituents of this composite formula. To trace it would require a work in itself, and I shall therefore limit myself to only a few of its aspects, such as the manner in which the relation of constraint was replaced by one of free exchange between independent parties to a contract; how out of gifts there developed true offerings and sacrifice; and how spells and incantations merged into prayers.

The problem of translating a constraint relationship into a free relationship is one in which, we can be certain, the layman took no part. That was exclusively the work of the religious intermediary and formulator. Now, while his whole personality as thinker-artist impelled him toward objectivity, certain conditions had to be fulfilled before this urge toward objectivity could be properly made to function. A professional competency and technique had to be acquired, his role as intermediary had to be accepted and respected, and his ministrations had to become sufficiently remunerative to give him both economic security and a measure of independence. Having obtained this he could then turn his attention to perfecting a mechanism for attaining the conscious and unconscious goal he had in view. He possessed as prototypes for translating constraint into independence two activities with which he was well acquainted—the practice of magic and the curing of disease. Magic was both positive and negative, the imposition of spells and the laying of spells; the curing of disease likewise had its positive and negative side, on the one hand the restoration of the soul or of some other entity of which a diseased individual had been robbed, on the other the removal of some foreign object from his body. This gave him a formula which he could use, a tangible mould into which he could pour his experience and his ideas.

Historically one of the first situations which had thus to be resolved was that of spirit-possession; and it had to be resolved by a very particular type of mentality, one which, in a way, could be said to represent the very apotheosis of the relation subsisting in magic between the subject and the object to be coerced, that, namely, where subject and object had for the moment coalesced. The method of attacking this problem was self-imposed. The shaman had practically no other recourse but to defend himself. And this it was that became paramount in the formula which he finally devised for expressing his relation to the supernatural. He must ward it off, exorcize it. Both activities were old and deeply rooted in the magical mentality. But this was only part of his task. We know that the shaman-priest had another side of equal importance for himself and for the function he was to perform, the one, namely, that was connected with the training to which he was compelled to submit during his initiation into the priesthood and which was designed to fit him properly for the reception of the divine. The cardinal practical concept behind this preparation was conciliation and propitiation, the two last historically later activities which the shaman-priest was to combine with the older one, that of exorcizing the spirits. Eventually these became the animating principles activating the transformation of gifts to the deities into offerings and sacrifices and directing the development of spells and incantations into prayers.

Concretely, we may visualize these developments somewhat as follows. Spirit-possession, in its simple form, is invariably connected with mental anguish and physical suffering. This is true where the shaman is admittedly a neurotic-epileptoid, and it is even more patent either where he is compelled, by the demands of the layman, to induce artificially a trance condition or true seizure, or where he is forced to simulate one. Pain is indelibly written across the whole situation as seen from his viewpoint. There is, first, his own personal anguish; secondly, the suffering induced by the spirit's forcibly entering his body, and, lastly, the unwelcome pressure of the layman who has become accustomed to regard a trance state as the only *bona fide* indication that the shaman is functioning properly or effectively.

The concept of evil is the social expression of this mental anguish and physical pain. Manifestly it is not the only source from which the concept arose. But it is an important one; in many respects the fundamental one in religious thinking.

To the shaman then the spirits were evil, were, at least, easily oriented toward evil activities. And so were those members of his group who were directly responsible for his pain. In a sense so was he himself when enmeshed in such a situation. To express this became his most immediate task. Here the magical mentality came to his aid. Was it not an essential constituent in that mentality that the individual should attempt to protect himself against danger by the performance of certain acts and the abstention from others? Both had early become basic ingredients in man's relationship to the supernatural and had been given significant form by the shaman in his function as religious intermediary. This was now to be specifically recognized and to receive its most characteristic social-economic expression in taboo.

Now whatever may be the ultimate origin of the concept of taboo, there can be no question but that it was the shaman and medicine-man and, subsequently, the priest, who elaborated it, fixed the precise form it was to assume, and who were most directly concerned with its functioning. They likewise were those who reaped the most obvious pecuniary benefits—and they were not inconsiderable—arising from the operation of taboos. But what we are interested in here is not taboo as such, but the fact that taboo represented one of the first stages in the breaking up of the constraint relationship between a man and the spirit who possessed him. By this breaking up, evil became associated not with the spirits themselves but with certain activities of the layman. In other words, the shaman transferred the cause of his suffering from the spirit to the individuals who were forcing his hand.

Taboo must consequently be regarded as the first link in the evolution that was to lead to the establishment of an objective relationship between the worshipper and his god. It was in fact an incipient form of conciliation. Its ambivalent nature has frequently been pointed out. This ambivalence is rooted in its strictly human implications, however, and not in the ambivalent nature of the supernatural. Marett's well-known statement that, "negatively, the supernatural is *taboo*, not to be lightly approached, because, positively, it is *mana*, instinct with power above the ordinary," [1] indicates only too clearly what happens when a purely ideological approach dominates the viewpoint of the theorist. Religious phenomena and concepts are then described in terms of generalized men and women who are made to serve as a kind of cement for vague ideas and still vaguer emotions. If, on the contrary, we start with taboo as an incipient form of the conciliation of the supernatural and visualize the environment, personal and economic, out of which it has sprung, then it becomes divorced from its customary and meaningless designation as an inherent attribute of human activity and takes its proper place in an intelligible history of the evolution of human consciousness in general and of religion in particular.

Taboo, however, is only the prelude to a true conciliation of the spirits. It could never, by itself, one may assume, have led to any mature theory of offerings or sacrifice. For that, it was too deeply rooted in magic, and the magical mentality has always constituted both a threat and an obstacle to the progress of religion. But if the concept of taboo has had no perceptible influence upon the more developed theory of offerings, it has been utilized and manipulated by the shaman and religious formulator for other aspects of religion as, for instance, the development of the idea of the sacred and of the notion of sin.

The same conflict that led the shaman to elaborate the idea of taboo in his attempt to alleviate the pressure the spirits were exerting upon him, led him to predicate evil as one of the natural attributes of the spirits. This is well illustrated in the séances so plentiful among all those tribes where the shaman is completely dominant. Let me give one illustration from the Bagobo of the Philippines.[2] Here some of the spirits who enter the medium are connected with diseases and epidemics and they take considerable delight in frightening their victims. "I am the sickness of Malik," one of them exclaims; "I am travelling around the world to make the people sick and it is I that give them chills and coughs." [3] Another one complains about the breaking of a taboo. "Malik does not respect me because he has spoken to some-one during the eight days that he was forbidden, at *manganito*, to speak to anyone. Now I am not angry with him but he must give me eight pieces of betel-leaf, or eight pieces of areca nut." [4] And still another says: "If you do not hasten the celebration of *Ginum* [a ceremony], you will soon be attacked by sickness, be-cause I will send the sickness." [5]

In the interests of the community, as well as for the shaman's own profit, the evil tendencies of all the spirits and the machina-tions of wholly evil spirits must, however, be prevented, nulli-fied, or rendered harmless, and this was done by presenting them with gifts. It is this development to which must be attributed the manifold and complex rites of conciliation so frequently found among primitive peoples, as well as the prevalent theory of offerings encountered there. According to the earliest form of this theory, its main purpose was to ward off harm. The gifts made were essentially as much payments to the shaman and medicine-man as offerings to the spirits. Then, as the relation between the medicine-man and the spirit became more clarified and the spirit took on a more precise physiognomy, it was only natural that the fiction should have arisen according to which the offerings belonged to the spirits themselves, and were accepted by them, if not visibly, at least invisibly. A final stage in this evolution was reached when the offerings no longer represented objects that could be used by man and when the spirit or deity no longer accepted them physically but did so only symbolically. Thus, for instance, in many tribes the belief was current, at least such was the official theory, that a deity did not actually eat the gross food offered him but only the essence of the food. With this purification of the idea of the offering went the purification of the subjective attitude.

Economic factors were manifestly largely responsible for these numerous changes, but associated with them was also the fact that, as we have already repeatedly pointed out, the personnel of the official religious profession had also changed. When, in addition to neurotic-epileptoid individuals, normal people also became medicine-men and priests, the whole picture necessarily changed. Not only did a new sense of proportion and a new, if somewhat cynical, realism develop, but the intellectual level of the profession was raised. Among other things the dependence upon the community at large was rendered less exacting and direct. For the intellectuals in the profession this meant, above all, a certain degree of leisure and the opportunity for the elaboration of the theory of ethical qualifications in the approach to the supernatural, as well as of a more refined and abstract concept of offerings.

Three stages can thus be discerned in the history of the concept of offerings. In the first stage, it represents purely a mechanism for insuring the separation from the undesired and unwilling proximity of a spirit; in the second, it represents a free exchange of gifts and amenities between voluntary parties to a contract; and, in the third, it represents an expression of gratitude and thankfulness on the part of a humble suppliant toward a wise and understanding deity. Examples of all these stages have been given in other connexions, but I would like to add one more example of the last stage, taken from the Zuñi Indians of New Mexico, in order to show the manner in which offerings have been transformed and transfigured and how the whole relation of suppliant and divine donor has been wrapped in a mystical envelope that effectively disguises the fact that we are still in the presence of a matter-of-fact exchange of goods between human beings and deities. I will quote only the prayer accompanying the offering [6]:

This day my children have prepared food for your rite, for you, their fathers and their ancestors, for you who have attained the far-off place of waters [i.e., the dead].

Now our sun father has gone in to sit down at his sacred place (and) taking the food my children have prepared at their fireplaces, (I have come out).

Those who hold our roads [the supernatural beings], the night priests [i.e., the night itself], coming out rising to their sacred place, will pass us on our roads.

This night I add to your hearts. With your supernatural wisdom, you will add to your hearts. Let none of you be missing but all add to your hearts. Thus on all sides you will talk together.

From where you stay quietly, your little wind-blown clouds, your fine wisps of cloud, your massed clouds you will send forth to sit down with us; with your fine rain caressing the earth, with all your waters you will pass us on the roads.

Your waters, your seeds, your road-fulfilling [long life], your old age, you will grant us.

Therefore, have I added to your hearts. To the end, my fathers, my children: you will protect us. All my ladder-descending children will finish their roads; they will grow old. You will bless us with life.

In its highest ideological form an offering, of course, loses its character as an object with a definite exchange-value and becomes a sacrifice, a gift charged with deeply emotional and symbolic significance to the suppliant. But even here it rarely loses completely its older form of being an offering proper and is frequently still to be found in a context that is, strictly speaking, even magical. What marks it off from offerings, no matter how sophisticated they may have become, is, however, this loss of an exchange-value. Only to such an offering should the term sacrifice be properly applied. Such a concept could, of course, originate only in the mind of a truly religious man. And since this is so, it follows that, even where we are formally dealing with an offering proper, this offering may be a true sacrifice from the point of view of a specific suppliant. Because of this fact it also follows that, what are probably the essential traits of sacrifice—the slaying of an animal, the killing of a human being, or self-mutilation—may all exist in societies where there is no formalized animal or human sacrifice. Yet, if it occurs sporadically everywhere and finds some formalized expression very early, the explanation for this is to be sought in the fact that, for the religious thinker, a gift could easily take on this character without in any way affecting the more realistic and practical conception that it retained for the community at large. That this would naturally lead to confusion in form and meaning and to the development of "mixed" types, goes without saying. Indeed these mixed types are far more numerous than "pure" types. The latter, in fact, are encountered only in those civilizations where a highly organized and independent priesthood has developed or in the particular democratic societies where great latitude was allowed individual expression, at least on matters which, for the group at large, were regarded as inconsequential.

We must therefore expect that sacrifice will become associated with elements from all the various layers of man's religious evolution and expect to find unselfish ideological motivations closely intertwined with crass and selfish ones and with crude economic exploitation. Among the southern Becwana of South Africa we find this neatly illustrated in what is called "the sacrifice of reconciliation." [7] Here two differently coloured animals are selected: one black, to be sacrificed for the sin, and one white, to be used in the purification of the sinner. Only the contents of the stomach and the entrails of the animal offered are used for the purification, the flesh remaining the perquisite of the priest. Where the rite is performed for an individual, the animal is slain while the penitent is on bended knee and after he has made a full confession of the fault he has committed. The blood of the slain animal, which had been collected, before it was quite dead, from the heart and the contents of the paunch, is drunk, while it is still fresh, by the person on whose behalf the sacrifice is being made. After he has drunk it, the fatty membranes of the bowels are placed upon his head. Then the priest cries out that this is a sacrifice of reconciliation and calls upon the name of the estranged ancestor or god.

It is with such rites of purification that sacrifice is generally associated. They may be at times connected with magical purposes of the simplest kind, as, for instance, among the tribes of the upper

Volta of West Africa. There, when a hunter has killed a lion, he has to submit to a rigorous ceremonial cleansing accompanied by a simple sacrifice. The sacrificial priest takes a little chick and calls upon his divine protector in the following words: "We are going to give this man the medicine called *kele* in order to free him from all impurities that he may possess and so that he may not become ill. If you consent to it, accept this chicken, if you do not, refuse it." [8] That is simple and direct enough. Then the victim is sacrificed, great care being taken that it expires in the proper position. After that the throat of another chick is cut and its blood allowed to flow over the left shoulder of the man who is to be purified, as well as over his relatives and all others present who have killed lions.

Wherever human sacrifice exists, this intermingling of gross and refined ingredients, of an altruistic and of an egotistic motivation, is very marked. Among the Tahitians, for instance, human sacrifice is supposed to have arisen at a time of drought when all other methods of appeasing the deities had failed. "Let us humble ourselves before God," the king is supposed to have said. "We must tremble with fear. Let us offer a man as a sacrifice to atone for unintentional offences and regain God's favour in this our great distress." [9] Human sacrifice quite obviously plays more definitely into the hands of the religious egotist and the dominant group than any other form of sacrifice. The reason lies in the fact that it can develop easily into a form of appeal practically identical in nature with the tyrannous constraint exercised by a man seeking power and prestige, and it thus becomes only too welcome a weapon, in a caste or class society, for those in control not to resort to its use continually.

As an example of the first, let me refer to the case of a Winnebago medicine-man who sought to coerce the Supreme Deity into appearing before him by offering up his only child, and as an example of the second, Miss Henry's account of the manner in which victims were selected in Tahiti [10]:

The victims for human sacrifice were always taken unaware [she tells us], and were men chosen from among the war-captives, the men of lowest rank, and the men of the middle classes who made themselves obnoxious to those in power. When one of a family was taken, the others were decreed to follow. Consequently, expectant victims fled and hid in terror when an occasion for such sacrifice arrived, and they did not breathe freely until the drum announced that the man was obtained and offered upon the altar and finally buried. From this custom arose the ironic old taunt: "What are you? a remnant of sacrifices!"

This same incongruous intermingling of ingredients is illustrated by the belief among the Marquesans that, although the gods consume only the immaterial counterpart of the sacrifice, the individual on whose ghost-body they are feasting in typical cannibalistic fashion is destined to be actually sacrificed within a short time.[11] This is exactly the reverse of the example previously cited from the Winnebago,* where the buffalo-spirits must appear as real buffaloes to be killed if they inhale the tobacco fumes from the offerings made on earth.

Our last example brings us to another and important aspect of sacrifice, its significance as a rite of consecration. In the historic religions of Europe and Asia the concept of consecration has generally been associated with the more abstract and, ostensibly, the more spiritual aspects of faith. But the original idea of consecration in religion carries no such implication. It simply signifies that the object to be sacrificed and the deity to whom the sacrifice is to be made have both been more accurately defined and delineated and their relationship more specifically circumscribed than is the case in offerings proper. The offering may, in a consecration-sacrifice, as obviously have an exchange-value as in the crudest form of gift, and its motivation may be as cynically egotistic and utilitarian. In fact it most frequently is, particularly where human

* See p. 32.

sacrifice is found. Thus a ruling chief among the Maori is known to have consecrated a new house by sacrificing his favourite child.[12] The killing of a slave would not have sufficed.

Indeed, consecration generally meant simply a more sophisticated type of coercion of the deity. Handy has pointed out [13] that, among the Marquesans, the main purpose of a sacrifice is to attract the tribal deity to his temple and his prophet. The consecration of an object or a person for sacrifice cannot then be regarded as ennobling either the suppliant or the god worshipped. It is simply the reflection of a more firmly organized and frequently a more grasping and unscrupulous priesthood.

The idea of consecration takes on an entirely different aspect where an individual sacrifices himself or some part of his own body. Even if we were to accept the theory that in Polynesian worship, for instance, consecration meant release from taboo and the endowing of a person with supernatural power, it must be remembered that this was always done in the interests of a specific and small group or in the interests of an individual. But consecration through self-sacrifice or its substitute, self-mutilation, does seem largely to have had the welfare of the whole social group in view. This is admittedly not absent in the other forms of sacrifice, but here it forms the essential core of the sacrifice and that is why it is most frequently found associated with elaborate rituals like the Sun Dance of the Plains Indians of the United States. If it is, on the whole, rarely encountered in primitive religions, that is because such self-annihilation was regarded as socially justifiable only where the salvation of the whole community was concerned or in the interests of one's loved ones. This also is the answer that must be given to all those historians of religion who insist that a "eucharistic" conception of sacrifice, one that is free from the desire to secure material benefits in the future, does not exist among aboriginal civilizations. No man, so it can be dogmatically stated, in his relation to other individuals, whether they be human or divine, rises above the theory of the exchange-value of goods prevalent in his society. Among all aboriginal groups a gift always entailed a return gift of some kind greater in value than the one given. Only when the theory of exchange altered, did the theory of sacrifice alter. That holds as true for our own as it did for aboriginal societies. In both cases, those who sinned against it and substituted absolute values for a negotiating value were stigmatized by their contemporaries as antisocial.[14]

Before we turn to the consideration of prayer, it might be well to pause and cast a brief glance at the history of the discussions of sacrifice, for very few aspects of religion have received such rich treatment and played so great a role in the history of the subject. That history begins significantly, at least as far as anthropology is concerned, with W. Robertson Smith.[15] The latter's formulation, particularly his famous theory of the sacramental meal by which the community and the gods are united in a common bond, has influenced all subsequent theoretical inquiries. With certain specific reservations, most theorists in England and France have followed in the wake of his stimulating and daring leadership. The most significant departures from his main thesis have been made by Durkheim [16] and Hubert and Mauss.[17] Their criticisms have been directed against the exclusive role which Robertson Smith assigns to the sacramental meal. Durkheim, the most important of the critics, accepts Hubert and Mauss's definition of sacrifice as the more valid one. According to this definition, the essence of sacrifice lies in the consecration of the victim. "It has been demonstrated," says Durkheim, "how, in sacrifice, a whole series of preliminary operations, lustrations, salvings, prayers, etc., actually transform the animal which is to be offered up into a sanctified object whose sacredness is then communicated to the faithful who partake of it." [18] What our attitude toward these theories is, the previous discussion has amply indicated. We can accept none of them in so far as they claim to be based on the data obtained from aboriginal peoples. Hubert and Mauss's theory, we know, is based on the religions of ancient India, and Durkheim's on a very special and completely unjustified reading of the native Australian civilizations. If the *intichiuma* rites of the Australians represent an initial form of sacrifice, then it can be said with equal show of reason that chaos is an initial form of order or that zero is an initial form of the integer. . . .

If it was somewhat presumptuous to attempt to dispose of so intricate a subject as sacrifice in a few pages, it must seem the height of temerity even to try to broach the problems connected with a subject like prayer. Fortunately, most individuals have had some direct experience with its nature and implications. Prayer in its most general form may be described as consisting of two parts: first, the statement of certain wishful thoughts; and, secondly, the enunciation of the facts of everyday life. Man is not naturally given to monologues unless, indeed, he be a mystic, and, consequently, the statements included in prayer had from the beginning to be addressed to some person or object. Wishful thinking, we know, has always been deeply anchored in the facts of everyday life. But this obviously was not enough to constitute a prayer. An additional anchorage was both desired and required, one more immediately pertinent and congenial to the nature of prayer. This it secured by first attaching itself to the supernatural beings that man had created for validating and reinforcing the values of life and then by addressing them directly. Prayer is thus, in a sense, the overflowing of a full mind rather than the overflowing of a full heart. The deities are called upon as much to continue their benefits and blessings as they are to help a man or the community in distress.

Yet no aspect of religion has remained so recalcitrant to official regimentation as prayer. This is easy to understand. Wishful thinking is personal, economic distress is personal, sorrow and anguish are personal, and all have at one time or another sought expression with compulsive urgency. It is not surprising then that simple and spontaneous prayers persist even in the most sophisticated societies. The prayers of aboriginal people may possibly differ from ours in the form that has been given them but not in their general content or in the attitude of the individual. The same variability in content that characterizes the prayers of civilized peoples is to be found wherever analogous social-economic conditions prevail. A Polynesian nobleman does not offer up the same prayer as does a Polynesian bourgeois or slave, nor does a West African king call upon a deity in the same fashion as does a simple tiller of the soil or a merchant.

The same holds true as regards the variability in the formal expression. The gamut is enormous, stretching, among aboriginal groups, from a simple "Help us!" to a prayer lasting practically half a day, as among the Batak; and from the crude unadorned exclamation of a person in distress to the sophisticated poem-prayers of the West African, Polynesian, and Zuñi priests. If, both in form and content, they are often specifically different from ours, this is because their connexion with magical spells and incantations is still very clear and because their intimate relation to the realities of the world has not yet been broken. Indeed, prayers are frequently lengthy reports to the deities on the mundane state of affairs or extended conversations between a man and his god.

Because of the limited space at our disposal we shall confine ourselves to only two phases of our very complex subject: first, the stages in the evolution from spell to prayer, and, secondly, the development of prayer from a simple, spontaneous, and personal request to an elaborate, sophisticated, and impersonal invocation. For a fairly complete, if somewhat uncritical, account of all phases of prayer—at least as far as aboriginal civilizations are concerned—I must refer the reader to the well-known work of F. Heiler.[19] The other works of importance are the famous essay of R. R. Marett [20] and the useful discussion of J. W. Hauer.[21]

Let us begin with the simplest of all magical rites, an Ainu charm against palpitation of the heart. After rubbing his chest six times the patient says: "As I do not wish to hear any bad news, I now brush myself six times." [22] We are here really in the presence of the break-up of a magical act. As a true magical act it should have read: "By brushing myself six times I prevent bad news from happening." It is not difficult to see how the words "I now brush myself six times" could be omitted, since the act itself is performed under any conditions, and the ease with which the statement could be changed into "May I not hear any bad news" and the name of a deity added. We would then have a *bona fide* prayer. And yet all this has been achieved by the simple and natural device of transforming the compulsive interrelation of the wishful thought and the motor activity of brushing into two separate acts. If anyone objects that this is too intellectualistic an explanation, it must be remembered that the order of evolution is not from spell to wishful thinking but precisely the reverse, from wishful thinking to the spell, and that the spell is simply the matrix into which this wish has been cast. It does not at any time lose its inherent dynamic character. A wish, be it remembered, is practically always on the verge of becoming a prayer. Thus it is the formal magical wrapping that is secondary and unstable and not the prayer-wish. The latter actually antedates religion and is, at least, contemporaneous with magic.

Yet magic is as much the handservant of prayer as it is the handservant of the life-values of man. The extent to which this is true can be easily demonstrated. I cannot, however, enter into a discussion of this here and must refer my readers to the ample evidence for it that they can find in works such as those of Malinowski [23], W. W. Skeat [24], etc.

But we must now turn to prayer proper. We need not dwell on such simple appeals as "Help us!" "Save me!" "Do not annoy us!" "Give us rain!" etc.; we may turn directly to those with more content. Perhaps none is more instructive than the one addressed to the Jesuit priest Allouez when he visited the Algonquin:

It is good, blackcoat, that you have come to visit us. Have pity on us! You are a manitu and we give you something to smoke. The Naudouessies and the Iroquois are swallowing us. Have pity on us! We are often sick and our children are dying; they are hungry. Have pity on us! Hear us, O manitu. May the earth give us corn; may the rivers give us fish; may illness never assail us and may hunger never torment us. Hear us, O manitu, we give you tobacco to smoke.[25]

This contains the complete formula for a prayer—an appeal to a spirit, a statement of the specific condition of affairs, a general statement of the natural ills of life, a request that the usual food supply be continued and that the organic ills and the economic ills of life be kept from the community, and ending finally with a sacramental payment to the spirit. It differs from a Christian prayer in that we are told nothing about the attitude of the suppliant and very little about the nature of the deity to whom the prayer is made.

Now whether the subjective attitude of the suppliant is formally expressed or not will depend entirely upon the specific temperament of the suppliant and the degree to which the formula of the religious thinker has been generally accepted. Its formal absence does not necessarily imply its non-existence. The case is different with regard to the specific characterization of the spirit or deity. Such a characterization is, in fact, very rarely encountered in aboriginal cultures. The reasons for this we shall, however, have to postpone to the next chapter. Suffice it to say here that this is intimately connected with the economic conditions, with the existence of classes and castes, of an organized priesthood and of specialized cults. It is only in a society where a highly organized priesthood exists that you will find a psalm-prayer like the following from the Yoruba of West Africa:

> O Sango, you are the Master.
> It is you who hold in your hand the fiery stones,
> To punish the guilty and to cool your anger.
> All that they strike is destroyed.
> Fire devours the woods,
> Trees break and tumble down,
> All that exists is threatened with destruction.[26]

And where, in the ritual of the higher religions, can we find a prayer-hymn of the simple beauty of this one from the Gold Coast?

The stream crosses the road
And the road crosses the stream;
Tell me, which is the older?
Did we not cut our way through to the road, that we might meet this
    stream?
But the stream itself existed long, long before all this.
It had its birth in the creator,
In him who created all things
Holy, holy Tanno.[27]

For examples of other prayers I refer the reader to those scattered through this volume *, and I shall content myself with giving *in extenso* a kind of prayer-duel between the Polynesian god *Tane* and *Kiho-the-All-Source*. Here we have not only the enunciation of an abstract conception of a deity but also an illustration of how a prayer-hymn of the most sophisticated kind can still be used essentially as a magical incantation [28]:

As for Tane, when he had brought the Sky-sphere to completion, he went upon Ahu-ragi (Sacred-temple-platform-of-the-heavens), the temple where Atea had been sanctified by Kiho-the-all-source, and there Tane prayed to the Creator-of-the-gods to lend him his aid in the task of completing the skies, and also to accord him his favour; this is Tane's prayer:

Prayer of Tane-of-the-Crimson-Cloak to Kiho-the-All-Source
That the God Awake

Awake in the Eternal Night!
Arise in answer to the supplication of Tane who does here address
        Thee,

---

* Cf. pp. 20, 35, 64–65, 95, 120–121, 128–130, 131, 139–140, 177–178, 180, 186–191, 200, 202, 203, 216, 217, 223, 228, 249 ff., 260, 261, 298–299, 305–306.

Thou through whom all plant life has evolved!
Thou the upholding hand of all living trees!
Thou the gleaming Star!
Bestow Thy divine power upon Tane, O my guardian God!
    Awake! O Source-of-propagation of the Earth!
    Awake! O Source-of-propagation of the Skies!
May my difficult task receive Thy aid!
O Kiho! Turn Thy Face toward me!

Now, Kiho-the-all-source awoke. Again Tane prayed to the supreme God; this is his prayer:

Prayer of Tane-of-the-Crimson-Cloak to Kiho-the-All-Source For His Favour

I

Kiho dwelt on the ascending rock-foundation floating free,
The First-Cause of continuous unfoldment.
Bestow upon me Thy great compassion!
    O Kiho, Source-of-All!

II

Kiho is the Source through whose divine power the primordial winds
        first blew,
The First-Cause of evolving growth.
Yield unto me Thy deep affection!
    O mighty Creator-of-the-Gods!

III

Thou art the supreme Sanctifier-of-Kings, O Kiho!
    Thou who dost turn Thy favour toward me,
    Thou who dost now extend Thy grace to Tane,
The Primal-Cause of teeming propagation.
Grant unto me Thy unbounded love!
    O Thou the All-Source!

In soaring flight I mount to the Realm-of-Night,
   Now I, Thy vassal, do acclaim Thee Lord!

Kiho-the-all-source gave ear to Tane's prayer; he arose and sent his wind called Gentle-westerly-breeze-loosed-from-the-divine-hand, as a herald to Tane to blow lightly upon him and thus to inform Tane that his song of supplication had come all the long way to Kiho-the-source-of-all.

This is the chant of Kiho-the-all-source which the Gentle-westerly-breeze-loosed-from-the-divine-hand had wafted all the long way to Tane!

Song of the Exalted-Presence of Kiho-the-All-Source Concerning His Deep Love for Tane

I

I am Kiho-the-all-source, Lord of the Sky-spheres!
Winds, whip the surface of the sea into scurrying ripples;
O gentle Westerly-breeze, loosed from my hand,
Waft unto Tane-of-the-Crimson-Cloak, word of the deep love of the
   life-giving Sanctifier-of-Kings!
Tane shall live on high the vast dome of his Heaven,
That ever he muse upon the supernal Creator-of-the-Gods,
   The Veritable Source-of-All.
      O Holy! Holy!

II

It is I who shall give into his keeping the lightning that shall flash and
   flicker, the rolling thunder that shall crash and rumble in the
   skies.
Multitudes and unnumbered myriads with voices stilled in awe shall
   adore the Lord of the Sky-world!
That the supreme Creator-of-the-Gods, ever abiding in the mysterious
   abyss of the Night, may know

The fullness of the loving thoughts of Tane, there, in his Sky-realm.
  O Holy! Holy!
I lean upon the rushing wings of the winds ruffling the troubled sur-
  face of the sea!

10

From Ghosts to Gods:
Ghosts, Spirits, and Totems

WHETHER or not it is correct to say that man fashions his gods in his own image, it certainly is correct to say that whether he fashions them at all depends largely upon the economic and social structure of his particular society. No correlation is more definite or more constant than that between a given economic level of society and the nature of the supernatural beings postulated by the tribe at large or by the religious individual in particular. Naturally it is not so much the method of food production as such that is correlated with the degree of definiteness given to the notion of a supernatural being as it is the extent to which this method of production leads to the development of a priestly class and the extent to which this class, in turn, finds it necessary or profitable to elaborate the notion of a supernatural being. Throughout Melanesia and in many parts of North and South America, agriculture exists but caste and class distinctions are, at best, only slightly developed and, accordingly, there is no trace of the presence of true deities or gods. Some exceptions occur but they are rare. In the vast majority of cases, unless true class distinctions exist, little attention is paid to the form the spirit assumes. In civilizations with a food-gathering or a fishing-hunting economy we encounter a belief in inconsistently defined spirits only. This does not, however, mean that these spirits are not at times clearly enough outlined either as human beings or as animals, real or imaginary. But the concept of a deity or a god, it can be said, consists, among other things, precisely in the fact that it is fixed and static and that the line of demarcation between gods and real men, on the one hand, and animals, on the other, is sharply drawn and cannot be crossed. If the gods do, at times, possess human or animal forms, this is simply one of their attributes and disguises.

It is not difficult to understand why this should have been so. The shaman or medicine-man in the cultures with simpler economies was too much occupied with his practice to spend much time or thought on formulations that were not necessary for his trade, that brought him no additional remuneration or prestige, and that were of no interest to the laity. We cannot insist too definitely on the well-authenticated fact that the official practice of religion in the simple societies was a practical matter, one of the accredited methods for obtaining wealth and security, often indeed in a somewhat terroristic manner. This is well brought out in one of the accounts in the *Jesuit Relations* concerning the Hurons.[1] The author insisted that "the sorcerers ruin them; for if anyone has succeeded in an enterprise, if his trading or his hunting is successful, immediately these wicked men bewitch him or some member of his family so that they have to spend it all on doctors and medicines." Such men were not likely to be interested in theory.

But the lack of any sharp delineation of the spirits is not to be accounted for exclusively in special economic terms. There was a psychological side too. The only thing, for instance, that interested the matter-of-fact man—and his viewpoint was largely dominant in simple societies—was the proof that some supernatural agency had contributed to the successful conclusion of an enterprise. All that the ordinary shaman and medicine-man were called upon to do was to give such proof. Everything else was of subsidiary importance. These proofs varied from the most meticulous enumeration of the details of the immediacy of a spirit's presence to a broad and almost meaningless predication of his existence. So, for instance, an Indian might falsely claim, as did one of my Winnebago informants, that he had been blessed by a specific spirit to heal a specific ailment only to become puzzled as to whether he had actually been blessed when, through chance, this ailment had actually been healed. For, after all, success was the criterion for the existence of a spirit.

In such an atmosphere we cannot expect spirits to take on the characteristics or attributes of true deities. Whatever ingenuity, whatever urge to religious speculation, the medicine-man or shaman possessed, went therefore into the elaboration of the methods of approach to the spirits: how they were to be propitiated and conciliated, what was the nature of the soul, and what were its vicissitudes. But even more important than these, as an outlet for his creative and organizational activity, were the shaman's description and analysis of the preparation and initiation into his profession. This we have already described in a preceding chapter. To this description and analysis we must now return if we wish to understand the genesis of that characterization of the divine which is to take us from the belief in ghosts to that in gods.

Let me begin with two interesting papers in which J. W. Layard [2] has summarized the essential characteristics of the Malekula shaman and compared them with those of the shaman of aboriginal Siberia. He arrives at the following conclusions: that

the initiation of the *bwili* [the Malekula analogue of the Siberian shaman] consisted of a ritual death and resurrection conferring on the candidate the status and supernatural powers of ghosts—powers themselves attained through the association of these with gods [i.e., spirits in my acceptation of the term—P.R.]; that, to this divine character was added a second series of epileptoid features due to the apparent death and rebirth of epileptics during their attacks and that, finally, the dual supernatural and irresponsible nature of ghosts was itself a result of the fusion of the two lines of reasoning. [3]

While we can hardly accept all of Layard's contentions and certainly not his attempt to connect the Malekula tricksters with the Egyptian Osiris ritual and beliefs, still there are some suggestive correlations to which he calls attention and which are particularly pertinent to the present discussion.

To what an extent, in aboriginal societies, especially in the simpler ones, does the ghost of the shaman or of the medicine-man differ from that of an ordinary man and, if there is a distinction, wherein does it lie? The answer is simple. The ghost of a shaman possesses all the traits ascribed to that of an ordinary man plus certain others, and these latter are closely associated with the shaman's occupation and his powers when alive. We know what they were: his ability to fall into a trance state involuntarily and to put himself into one voluntarily; his capacity to transform himself into an animal; his power to travel through space and time and to journey to the spirit-world; and, finally, the fact that he is possessed by some spirit either unrelated to him or an ancestor. To this we may add his dual character: unconscious at one moment, and not only conscious at the next moment but the most practical of men. The difference between the ghost of an ordinary man and that of a shaman lies then, it would seem, in the ease with which the ghost of the latter becomes a spirit. If we go further and ask why this should be so, we admittedly enter the realm of speculation. Yet here it seems to me speculation is both justifiable and remunerative, and I shall accordingly attempt it.

For the ultimate origin of the concept of ghosts, it is impossible to advance any satisfactory or illuminating theory. But we may legitimately ask why ghosts are almost universally represented as mischievous when they meet living human beings. Jealousy can unquestionably be regarded as one of the reasons, and this jealousy of ghosts and of the gods persists into historical times as has been recently demonstrated in a convincing manner.[4] This jealousy is not simply the resentment of the dead against the living; it is the resentment of those dead who can never return to life against those who can. It is, in other words, the continuation of one of the attitudes assumed by the layman toward the shaman when both were alive. In the tenuous atmosphere of spiritland it takes the form of a generalized mischievousness. But it is also a characteristic of the ghosts of shamans that they are evil. And here we manifestly have a reflection of the unconscious attitude of the layman toward them while alive. We need not be psychoanalysts to understand this. Jealousy and its analogue mischievousness, as well as evil, are not inherent attributes of the supernatural but qualities associated with specific human beings which are subsequently projected into the supernatural. The dual personality of the shaman and the ambivalent attitude of the community toward him, all this sets him definitely apart from the rest of his group. In a sense it may be said that he continually casts the shadow of his future divinity before him.

Manifestly the ghost of the shaman is not the only source from which the notion of the supernatural has been developed. Yet it is clearly his personality, his life, his symbolic death and rebirth, his hallucinatory experiences, that form the concrete mould into which the supernatural has been thrown. It is he who gives the ghost whatever flesh and blood it contains and it is he who endows a spirit with whatever vitality and activizing force it possesses, over and above that of being simply a specific designation for an end-result, for *that-which-succeeds*. And it is his dramatic and neurotic figure that is continually reinforcing and anthropomorphizing the notion of spirit and which, with the aid of certain social and economic forces, transforms spirits into deities as it had previously transformed ghosts into spirits. What fascination he possessed is indicated by the fact that even in a sophisticated civilization such as that of Periclean Athens, a mature mind like Socrates' could justify the acceptance of certain beliefs by saying that they had been arrived at by "priests and priestesses who have been at pains to understand the acts they perform"!

We are now in a much better position to answer the question posed before: How did the ghost of a shaman so easily become a spirit? The answer is: because the shaman was and remained for a long time one of the basic constituents in the necessary formation of the whole concept of the spirit. Without the addition of this ingredient the notion of spirit would have remained permanently inchoate, and religion would never have become differentiated from magic.

Thus it can be claimed that man created spirits and deities

originally in the image of the shaman; that his personality, his powers, his experiences, in short, his *vita* and his *via*, served as the mould for the divine. But this is not equivalent to saying, as some of our modern euhemerists would seem to imply, that spirits and deities are deified shamans or kings or, as those pseudo-euhemerists, the psychoanalysts, insist, that we are dealing with a deified phallus or a deified castration symbol.

The hypothesis I have here advanced prevents us from falling into the amazing psychologizing which scholars like Durkheim, Marett, and particularly Lowie seem so much to enjoy. For them the divine, the supernatural, is "poured" copiously and generously into a man. Lowie [5], in stating his position, begins with Durkheim's famous dichotomy of the universe, the sacred and the profane, but interprets it in Marett's sense as the differential response to normal and abnormal stimuli. The response, he insists, is "that of amazement and awe and its source is the supernatural, extraordinary, weird, sacred, holy, divine." [6] We should not be surprised then if, in describing the religion of the Crow Indians, we are wafted on ethereal wings into the following definition: "Crow religion . . . consists in the memory of an ineffable experience of an extraordinary character . . . the thrill here . . . apotheosizes its concomitants." [7]

Psychology apotheosizes its concomitants. Such is the inevitable catastrophe which overwhelms the ideological approach when applied with logical precision. "In the study of comparative religion," says Dr. Lowie, "it is the psychological point of view that requires emphasis; and however important history may be for an elucidation of psychology, its part is ancillary." [8] In other words, history and economics have no applicability, and religion becomes an entity in itself utterly divorced from the other aspects of individual and corporate life. A dogmatic Catholic theologian like Father Schmidt, a Protestant mystic like Otto, can shake hands with an extreme evolutionist like Marett and a critical ethnologist and anti-evolutionist like Lowie. Now it is one thing to take issue with the excesses of historicism; it is quite another thing to take refuge in an ideological position where there is no room left for any dynamic development. However, it is not the philosophical implications of such an attitude which interest us here but rather the question of whether this helps us to understand the basic problems of religion better than does an historical approach. I do not think so. On the contrary, it has led so sane and critical an anthropologist as Lowie[9] to attempt "to disengage the least common denominator of all religious phenomena," a dangerous procedure.[10]

But it may be asked: Does not what I here contend, conflict with the fact that all aboriginal peoples share the belief in an animated world? Is not animism their basic religion? To this we must reply that animism is not a religion at all; it is a philosophy. The belief in the general animation of nature has nothing to do with the supernatural. An object, animate or inanimate, derives its supernatural quality from its association with a number of distinct elements and from the transference to it of certain ideas, concepts, and activities.

Into the concept of spirit there has entered a large and diversified assortment of ingredients. There is, first, the whole magical relation of actor and thing acted upon, that is, of a constraint and the tension that have to be mitigated; then there are all the ideas and emotions clustering around the bond between the living and the dead, as well as around the antagonism between the living and the dead that have to be resolved; and, finally, there is the figure of the shaman, exemplifying in his person both the formula of coercion-subjection and of life-death, both of which have to be transformed. Thus magic has contributed to the notion of the spirit the element of constraint; the memories connected with the dead and the long-continued existence of his body, or some portion of it, have contributed the concept of the ghost; and, finally, the person of the shaman has contributed the concrete and dynamic image, the individualizing factor which acts as a kind of catalysing agency. If inanimate or animate objects function as spirits, it is, let me repeat, because of their fusion with these elements or, perhaps more correctly, because of their fusion with the synthesis that has resulted from their mutual interactions, positive and negative. Only in this sense can we speak of animism as a religion.

Tylor [11], with his usual acumen, was quite right when he spoke of animism as arising in response to an intellectual need. He did not, of course, realize—and this is pardonable for a person writing in 1871—precisely those whose intellectual need was to be therewith satisfied; that the need of the shaman, the religious formulator, was different from that of the layman; and that their two viewpoints were always pitted against each other. If, therefore, animism, at times, appears to be a "philosophical system," a theory of souls, this impression is quite justified. It was a theory, the theory and formulation of an individual with a specific temperament and a specific experience and one who possessed a definite status—the shaman and medicine-man. If this philosophy seems riddled with inconsistencies and contradictions, it is because, after all, the shaman was a participant in as well as an organizer of his culture, and the viewpoint of the layman, in so far as he had one, was in part different, in part antagonistic, to his. These two factors, among others, militated against the development of a consistent system of thought and to these are due likewise the varied forms which the spirits have assumed in different places as well as the inconsistencies in their delineation and the variability of the attitude adopted toward them.

Bearing all these facts in mind, let us see the extent to which they can be illustrated by concrete instances. I shall begin with the simple food-gathering and hunting-fishing tribes. The Wintun of north-central California [12] may serve as an excellent example of a group having both economies. They are, moreover, famous in the history of American ethnology because of the clearcut conception of a Supreme Being which they were supposed to possess according to the description of a well-known observer.[13] Subsequent investigation has demonstrated clearly that both the clarity of this concept as well as the systematization found in the creation legends of the tribe had been the work of a highly gifted individual with marked religious inclinations. No better demonstration of the role of the religious formulator could possibly be desired. When, however, Miss Du Bois states that the concept of a Supreme Being was immanent in Wintun thought, she misses the whole point.[14] It is only in the thought of the Wintun shaman that this belief was immanent. The people at large, as she herself indicates, have only the vaguest notions of any Supreme Being. For them spirits can be either sharply defined, as in the case of the shamanistic spirit, or indefinite, as in the case of the soul of an ordinary man, which manifests itself in the form of a whirlwind and to which acorn-meal is to be offered. On the other hand, a natural object with a definite shape, like the sun, can, for the everyday man interested in obtaining some outside validation for his life-values, function only in a most tenuous fashion. Take, for instance, the following prayer, which is a declaration of a state of affairs and the expression of a wish that life continue in its regular way. It is essentially immaterial who is addressed and what the addressed person looks like. All this can, presumably, be filled in according to one's liking and one's temperament. The prayer runs thus:

> Behold the sun above the south.
> Look down at me to the north.
> Let me wash my face with water; let me eat; let me eat food.
> I have no pain.
> Let me wash my face with water.
> Today let me kill a deer and bring it home to eat.
> Look down at me to the north, grandfather sun, old man.
> Today I shall be happy.[15]

Among the Wintun, Miss Du Bois assures us, supernatural experiences were obtained by the majority of the tribe, and a shaman was distinguished from the layman only in the strength of his rapport with the spirits.[16] The shaman's function as a formulator was quite secondary to his importance in the social and economic life. There he was second only to the chief.

All this is clearly indicated by the lack of any coherent theory of the spirits. If we compare this with the Eskimo, also a fishing-hunting tribe but where the shaman dominated the whole life of the group, the difference emerges immediately. There we find a most intricate and all-embracing theory of spirits. They are regarded as scattered over land and sea, each spirit localized, however, in a special place, and we find a specialized doctrine of taboos. "No bears have come," answered an Eskimo shaman when he was asked to explain the strange absence of bears at a time when they should have appeared, "because there is no ice, and there is no ice because there is too much wind, and there is too much wind because we mortals have offended the powers." [17] The religious formulator's theory rules supreme: all happenings are referred to the intervention of the spirits.

What diverse forms the organized belief in spirits can assume, and how impossible it is to prophesy what aspects will be emphasized, is illustrated by the Bushman and Hottentot as recently summarized by Schapera.[18] Here the medicine-men are regarded as being endowed with supernatural powers, and they can, in a sense, become spirits after death, for, on occasion, dead rain-makers and dead game-magicians are asked to send rain and give success in hunting. The forms which the organizational activity of the medicine-men took here centred around the heavenly bodies— the sun, the stars, and particularly the moon—and the individualization of the vague spirits associated with the primary need of this community, rain. As in most of the very simple cultures, the beliefs and the viewpoint of the layman always play havoc with all the attempted schematizations and clarifications of the medicine-man and thinker. It is not surpising then to find the figure of the rain-being either not outlined at all or represented as an animal who is sometimes to be identified with a bull or an eland, at other times simply with a nondescript animal-like being living in a waterhole, and, at still others, as a non-existent imaginary animal-like being accompanied by those animals he protects—the frog, the fish, the tortoise, the snake. It is the folkloristic background of the people at large that determines what attributes he is to have. Thus it is believed that when the rain-being is angry he carries people off in a whirlwind and transforms them into various kinds of objects. Young women, in particular, are liable to harm and they must accordingly propitiate the waterhole where he resides by offering different kinds of aromatic herbs.

Miss Bleek [19] gives an invocation-address to the rain-being in which this folkloristic background is clearly expressed. The first part refers to the dead men riding the rain-being, thought of here as a magic animal:

I

O gallopers, O gallopers, do ye not know me?
Ye do not seem to know my hut.

II

Thou shouldst put thy tail between thy legs,
For the women are looking shocked at thee;
Thou shouldst put thy tail between thy legs for the children.

It is the same folkloristic background that has forced the figure of the trickster upon the attention of the religious thinker. He is called Mantis among the Bushmen and he is the buffoon-hero of the people, mischievous, stupid, perverse. When raised to the position of a spirit he had to be given a positive side as best could be done by the thinker. It is the same problem that confronts the formulator everywhere, and he seems generally to have solved it by making the trickster the object of a cult. He becomes the first being who creates all things—the sky, the moon, the stars, and the animals. Among the Basuto Bushmen he is called Cagn, and a simple prayer is addressed to him:

O Cagn! Are we not your children, do you not see our hunger?
Give us food.

To the question where Cagn resided the Bushman informant responded:

> We don't know, but the elands do. Have you not hunted and heard his cry, when the elands suddenly start and run to his call? Where he is, the elands are in droves like cattle.[20]

What more perfect illustration of the extraverted lay mind can one demand? A pragmatist of pragmatists!

The lay mind is written across all their prayers. When invoking the new moon it is magical constraint they are thinking of in such phrases as: "New moon, come out, give water to us; thunder down water, shake down water." [21] And it is constraint, mitigated somewhat by the notion of an interchange of gifts, when in a prayer to the star Canopus, they exclaim:

> O star coming there, let me see a springbok, let me dig out ants' food with this stick! O star coming there, *I give thee my heart; do thou give me thy heart!* Let me eat, filling my body, that I may lie and sleep at night.[22]

The societies we have so far discussed were all non-totemic. The moment we deal with those organized on a totemic basis, a new element enters into the conception of the spirits. The overwhelming majority of totemic organizations have an agricultural economy. There are a few exceptions, however, like the simple food-gathering and hunting Australians and the highly complex fishing-hunting cultures of British Columbia.

We cannot, of course, enter here into a discussion of totemism as such but some points must be cleared up. The various views of the nature and origin of totemism have all been summarized in M. Van Gennep's work *L'Etat actuel du problème totémique.*[23] Their number is legion. Van Gennep has conveniently catalogued and characterized them in a table which he gives in his book. He finds that from the first use of the term *totem* until the present day the explanations have fluctuated between two sets of extremes, between individualist as opposed to collectivist theories and between magico-religious as opposed to non-religious economic theories.[24] Certainly the most satisfactory one would seem to be a combination of that which J. G. Frazer advanced in 1899 based on the Australian *intichiuma* ceremonies and which has been designated as the *magico-économique* by Van Gennep, with the one advanced by Durkheim, designated by Van Gennep as the *emblématique-collectiviste*. However, our concern is naturally enough not with these theories but with the extent to which a given social organization, characterized by a number of very distinctive features, influenced not only the concept of spirits but also the type of spirits to be selected for elaboration and clarification.

In spite of the fact that the totem of a group can be practically any object, organic or inorganic, natural or artificial, in the overwhelming majority of cases the totem is an animal or plant. Far less frequently, though not rarely, we find natural phenomena—the sun, moon, stars, sky, fire, features of the landscape, etc. The general consensus of opinion, however, is that animal totemism is the oldest and the original form.[25]

Inevitably the problem arises: what was the attitude of the individual toward the totem animal? Volumes could be written on this subject. Volumes have been written on it. The answer of most ethnologists and ethnological theorists has always been the same: that this attitude implied the virtual equation and identification of animals with human beings and must be taken as the reflection of the inherent viewpoint of aboriginal man. Thus it has been pointed out that the early observer of native Australian life, Taplin, was informed by the Narrinyeri that, when they first saw white people on horseback, they believed the horses to be their mother because that is the manner in which Australian mothers carry their young. Similarly K. von den Steinen was told by the Xingu Indians of central Brazil that the only difference between men and animals was that the former could make bows and arrows and hammocks, and the latter could not. Strangely enough it never occurred to any of those theorists who have written so voluminously on the subject to ponder upon the source of the answer which they received. Had they done so, they might have found the key to many things, particularly to the reason for the somewhat conflicting explanations given in regard to the specific relationship of an individual to his totem. They would probably have discovered that there was as wide a contrast between the view of the religious formulator and the layman on this subject as there was on most others and that it was both inaccurate and indefensible to speak of the tribe or, for that matter, the clan as such, as believing this or that. Let me illustrate the extent of the variability encountered and the explanation for it by reference to the Winnebago Indians.

Among the Winnebago there were at least four different explanations given for the relationship of a man to his totem animal: he was descended from that animal; he had been changed from an animal into a human being when the clan first originated; his totemic clan name was derived from the animal without descent being claimed at all; or, finally, he derived his totem name from the fact that his ancestors had imitated the actions of certain animals. There were, likewise, two different conceptions of the original clan animal. According to one he was a real animal; according to the other he was a generalized spirit-animal who took on a real and specific animal form when he appeared on earth. According to this latter theory, when a man of the deer or buffalo clan, for instance, killed a deer or buffalo, he was not killing his totem animal at all.

How are we to account for this variability? Shall we dismiss it as an inherent attribute of culture much as extension is an inherent attribute of matter, or shall we seek for some more specific connexion? And if we seek for such a connexion, are we to be content with vague interpretations concerning the historical implications of these variations or are we looking for a specific and realistic type of causation?

The latter approach is the only one that yields satisfactory and intelligible results; this fact emerges as soon as we apply it. Then we discover that—while it is true that a universal belief existed according to which life had much the same content for animals as it did for human beings and that their thinking processes were the same, their struggle with the environment the same, and their emotional reactions the same—the belief in the transformation of human beings into animals and animals into human beings was a specific construction of the shaman. In fact the shaman was believed to possess this power. The ordinary man, as we might have suspected, was fundamentally uninterested in such questions and accepted the interpretations of the shaman in his capacity as formulator just as he accepted the fact that the shaman alone possessed the power of transforming himself into an animal. As this interpretation, in turn, was taken over by the layman, it naturally led to all types of distortions, vaguenesses, and inconsistencies.

The religious aspects of the totemic animal, we may consequently insist, are the result of the activity of the religious formulator and, in large measure, were stimulated by the analysis of his own hallucinatory experience. This we have already described a number of times. But what was it in the social and economic conditions of the group that led to the sudden and fairly universal stressing of animals as either semi-divine or wholly divine? In other words, what was it that led to the appearance, all over the world, of the specific characteristic of religion in totemistic societies?

Here we are again admittedly in the realm of hypothesis, and the one I wish to advance is this. Leaving aside other and important aspects of totemistic societies, totemism can be said to represent a group attack on the power and the influence of the shamans and medicine-men, an attempt of the "lay mind" to overwhelm the "religious mind." This would explain adequately why, with the advance from a simple undifferentiated social-economic structure, like that of the food-gathering and fishing-hunting peoples, to the agricultural structure of the totemic societies, there should have been, at first, no marked elaboration or increase in the complexity of the religious concepts and no sharp formal delineation of the spirits. We find instead an overwhelming stress laid on animals and the development of a new reverence for them. Animals and their adventures now become the primary subject matter for treatment by the medicine-man, and the latter has to include it in all his formulations. Why this overwhelming of the religious by the lay mind occurred just then must be ascribed to the new system of food production that had either developed in a given area or been introduced from without, namely agriculture.

Agriculture entailed, inexorably, the development of larger and firmer social units; it united individuals into co-operative groups by bonds that protected each against the amazing terrorism that so frequently, as we have seen, prevailed in the simpler societies. In those societies it was generally difficult for a layman to resist successfully the exactions of the shaman, particularly when the latter united with the chiefs. Agriculture thus increased the security and the independence of the matter-of-fact man and, of course, improved immeasurably the position of women, since the latter were almost always the individuals who worked the fields. This meant that the average man and woman could impose their point of view on the shaman in a way that had, on the whole, been barred to them before. The shamans had now to come to terms with them and not they any longer with the shamans. A compromise was effected. The shamans thereafter included in their formulae the new folkloristic background which the laymen had forced upon them and then proceeded to reinterpret and reformulate it in the interests of both their own security and their retention of power and influence. In part, likewise, this new evaluation may have sprung from the promptings of the shaman-thinkers' intellectual-artistic temperament.

It was to this new practical adjustment to the laymen and the group at large that the shamans and medicine-men devoted all their energies. Speculation as such was little encouraged except in so far as it was connected with the creation and elaboration of rituals and secret societies. These, however, were definitely and blatantly in the complete possession of the medicine-men and priests.

Thus it can be seen that the totemistic structure of society meant an increase in organization for both laymen and medicine-men. The emergence of such social units as the clan and the phratry, the development of the concept that all those who reckoned their descent from a common ancestor were related, that the same emotional attitudes existing toward the members of your immediate family extended to them—all this also implied the development of what might be termed a "national" consciousness. At times it even meant the consciousness of a bond that leaped tribal barriers as when, for instance, a man belonging to the bear clan regarded himself as related to the members of any bear clan, irrespective of tribal or linguistic affiliations. But with this new form of tribal cohesiveness there also appeared new dangers. Traits like common descent, reverence for a specific totem, special taboos, and innumerable other characteristics differentiated each clan so clearly and decisively from the next, that enmities and jealousies were bound to develop.

The one factor in the totemistic society that tended to counteract this disruptive tendency was, of course, the rule of exogamy which constrained the members of one clan to marry the members of another. Where clans were clustered into a number of phratries, or where they were all grouped in two such phratries or moieties, this meant that the blood bond, or some semblance of it, was extended so as to include, at times, one half of the tribe. In spite, however, of this extension of the blood bond implied by exogamy, the tendency was for these larger units to be pitted against each other, either in friendly or in hostile rivalry, and for the development of two loyalties, one tribal and the other clan or phratry, the latter immeasurably more profound and fundamental. Some interesting results flowed from these contrasting conditions. While the layman was freed from the more obvious attempts at extortion or terrorism at the hands of the shamans and medicine-men of his own clan, he had now to protect himself against those of other clans. The struggle between the two thus continued but on another level and in a much more intricate manner.

In the last analysis, however, the various facts we have just mentioned strengthened principally the power of the medicine-men, a power that was still further consolidated by the crystallization in totemic societies of the position of the chief and by the appearance of a number of new administrative positions necessitated by the totemic type of organization and, finally, as already pointed out above, by the power which the cults and secret societies now acquired. While the chiefs were at times in marked rivalry with the medicine-men, that rivalry as often as not led to co-operation and, in a number of instances, to the fusion of the two positions and of their functions. The divine king, who plays so great a role in the later evolution of civilizations scattered over the whole world—the Mediterranean, Africa, Asia, Oceania, and the two Americas—may be taken to represent the final stage of this fusion.[26]

This, in brief, was the social-economic setting in which the religious formulator had to work throughout that long period in the history of mankind during which the concepts of ghost, totem-ancestor, and supernatural spirit were formed and elaborated.

The task of the religious formulator in totemistic societies was thus definitely circumscribed. Let us see what the nature of this new interpretation of animals and of the popular mythology clustering around them was. As my first example I shall take a non-typical instance, that non-agricultural totemistic culture which has now, for more than two generations, been the centre of anthropological discussion, the aboriginal Australians.

If we begin with the assumption, as I think we must, that the non-shamanistic interpretation of the difference between human beings and animals implied no more than what the Xingu Indians told von den Steinen, namely, that the latter in contradistinction to the former could not make implements, then all the various conceptions of the totem animal as a spirit or semi-spirit may be attributed to shamanistic speculation. Among the Arunta of Central Australia this took the form of a belief that every individual was the reincarnation of a spirit left behind by totemic ancestors in a far past time.[27]

To the influence of the medicine-man's speculation and his desire for systematization must also be ascribed the clarification of the mutual obligations toward each other of a man and his totem. The principal obligation of the individual, it must be remembered, was not to eat his totem. Although his attitude toward it was one of reverence, it was never one of true worship. The whole nature of his conception of the totem and the tie that bound him to it were, in fact, fundamentally magical and not religious. This dominance of the magical mentality is also apparent in the avowed purpose of the numerous magical rites. Their object was to increase the supply of the material object from which the totemic group took its name. Thus we are here after all still in the realm of constraint, the realm where subjectivistic thought is dominant. This also comes out definitely in the type of service the individual expects from his totem. What is the latter to do? To help and protect him, to warn him and his fellow-clansmen when danger threatens them by intervening either visibly or appearing in a dream, and, finally, to act as a messenger to inform him immediately whenever a friend or a relative has met with misfortune.[28]

It is clear then that these Australian totems are in no sense real spirits. In fact we can say that animism as a religious belief is very poorly developed here. The explanation for this peculiar state of affairs lies, for me at least, in the fact that the concept of spirits previously held was completely overwhelmed by that of the totem animal and its accompanying mythology. Such an interpretation is supported by the peculiar development of the so-called high-gods in Australia, for, apart from its philosophical flavour which we shall discuss later on, this concept seems deeply rooted in the figures of Australian mythology. Van Gennep has indicated fairly clearly that these high-gods are either developments out of vague mythical ancestors or transformations of culture-heroes or, possibly, a fusion or confusion of both.[29] The elaborate criticism to which Father Schmidt has subjected this interpretation in no way invalidates Van Gennep's argument.[30]

In other words, the new subject matter which accompanied the appearance of totemic societies temporarily relegated the older religious ideas to the background, and the religious formulator had, for a time at least, to begin his task practically *de novo*. The importance of the Australian case, as I see it, lies in the fact that, in spite of admittedly special developments, it represents a very early form of totemic society, one in which the essential democracy inherent in this type of government has as yet not been qualified too definitely by the growth of complex cult organizations and secret class fraternities.

An entirely new attitude toward the totem developed in all those groups where agriculture existed even in a marginal fashion. Let us take, for instance, the case of the Ojibwa of north-central United States and south-central Canada, the tribe from whose language the word totem actually is derived. Here we know quite definitely that agriculture and the totemic organization were introduced from the south within comparatively recent times, at the very earliest a thousand years ago. This totemic structure was imposed upon a non-agricultural fishing-hunting people whose religious ideas, as moulded by the medicine-men, centred, among other things, around the idea of spirit-possession. When the clan developed and the new insistence on animals was introduced, the concept of the totemic animal ancestor was merged with that of the spirit who possessed the shaman. To the totem was thus transferred whatever magico-religious practices it had been customary to associate with the spirit and, since totemic society was basically democratic, the idea of spirit-possession became universal, naturally undergoing certain changes in the process.

Instead of spirit-possession there then came into prominence the concept of a guardian spirit and protector to whom a regular worship was to be extended and who was to be approached in much the same manner as was a true spirit or deity. Here then, among the Ojibwa, the new world of the totemic civilization did not wholly submerge the old one as had apparently been the case in Australia, but the one, on the contrary, to a certain extent reinforced the other. Since, however, the old anarchical-individualistic world of the fishers-hunters had to give way to the new co-operative democratic world of the agricultural totemic peoples, the intellectual energies of the religious formulators, for a considerable time, were completely absorbed in classifying and re-interpreting the new subject matter that had now been brought in and little attention was accordingly paid to any sharp delineation of the spirits. The task of the medicine-men was primarily the accustomed one, to convert the animal totems into spirits as rapidly as that was possible.

All totemic civilizations remained on this plane as far as concerns religion until, under the impulse of economic conditions whose origin is not clear to us but which we can confidently claim were connected with the struggle of the shamans and medicine-men to retain their power and if possible to extend it, the cult organizations and secret fraternities took on a complex form and began to elaborate highly intricate rituals. This development was then specifically reflected in the remodelling and the reformulation of the concept of the spirits. But when this stage of evolution was reached, the totems, in turn, were relegated to the background except in so far as they had become *bona fide* spirit-deities and had lost their specifically totemic associations.

Strictly speaking, of course, we have then left behind us that phase of religious evolution in which supernatural beings are represented almost exclusively as spirits and entered the stage where they can generally be called true deities, meaning by deities supernatural beings with considerable individuality who are, on the one hand, to be clearly distinguished from ghosts or spirits of the dead and, on the other, from semi-divine mythological beings. As an example of this new setting I shall select the Winne-bago Indians.

In dealing with a group like the Winnebago we are confronted by historical problems that are absent in the simpler cultures, for there is always the possibility, indeed the probability, that, under the impact of the new conditions brought about by their contact with the whites, there has been both a hypertrophy of certain religious beliefs and a deterioration of others. After we have made generous allowance for these types of change, a picture emerges that is of considerable importance for the general history of primitive religion as reflected in what may be called the middle period of totemic civilizations, and I am willing to hazard the statement that this middle period is essentially similar wherever it is found, be it in the two Americas, Africa, Asia, or Oceania.

The main characteristic of Winnebago totemic society was the existence of a clearly developed dual organization and of clans with very distinctive functions and individualities. When first encountered by the whites, the Winnebago lived in definite villages in which members of all the clans were represented. Their method of food production was twofold, agriculture and fishing-hunting. The technique for food preservation and food storage was moderately well developed, sufficiently so, at least, to afford some protection against the somewhat rigorous winters of Wisconsin. That protection was, however, not always adequate, and this, in addition to the pressure of their neighbours, militated against any real permanency for their villages and engendered as its corollary an emphasis on war and military prestige.

The implications of the dual division of the tribe struck in two directions. On the one hand, it made for a solidarity and cohesiveness, enlarging the conception of the unity of interests of all the clans that belonged to the same phratry-division and extending the fiction of the blood bond of the clan to that of the phratry-division; on the other hand, it made for the sharpening of the rivalry between the two divisions and for increased differentiation of their functions, economic-social and religious, and, indirectly, of the functions of their constituent clans. If we bear all this in mind and also remember that only one major ceremony existed which cut completely across all clan affiliations or guardian-spirit implications, then we can approach the examination of the forces that made for the development of the Winnebago pantheon and theogonies.

Since the religious formulator is the prime factor in articulating the religious elaborations, let us begin with that ceremonial among the Winnebago which is most specifically his, the Medicine Dance. It happens to be, in many ways, the oldest, and is also the only one open to members of the tribe at large. What do we find there? A ceremonial of a highly complex kind dealing with a symbolic death-and-rebirth rite that is patently a reinterpretation of a magical and shamanistic performance, a strong emphasis on reincarnation, and a sharply outlined and highly ethical concept of a creator god. These are, with the exception of the last, the basic constituents of non-totemic civilizations. They belong to the archaic stratum of Winnebago culture, and they have been brought together, combined with new elements, and fused into a coherent whole by the very shamans who had profited most materially, we have seen, from the old order of things and who, when the old civilization was overwhelmed by the new totemic society and, later, by Christianity, perfected their organization and their techniques in this extremely dramatic and effective manner. How loose-jointed and individualistic this organization originally was can best be gauged by its analogues among the simpler tribes that lived in the vicinity. This same remodelling, reformulating, and eclecticism is also obvious in the whole structure of the ceremony. It is, in fact, a vast conglomeration of practices and beliefs of various ages and diverse provenience. The impelling force behind this creative activity of the shaman, we may surmise, was the new order ushered in by the totemic society, with its co-operative democracy, its implied threat to the dominance of the shamans, and its stress upon a new attitude toward animals, plants, concrete living objects, and natural phenomena in general.

But totemic society also meant the emergence of totemic cults and cult societies. These worked to the advantage of both the average man and the medicine-man. Both became organized. It may be assumed that here the medicine-man, as far as concerns the subject matter to be treated, was passive and that his freedom of action was essentially limited to evolving some compromise. In the domain of religion proper this compromise meant the merging of his notion of the spirit involved in spirit-possession with that of the clan animal and the generalizing of the concept of the animal totem. The resultant figure, the guardian-spirit, became the dominant influence in the life of the individual. Every individual could and was compelled to obtain one. Contrasted with this democratization of the technique for approaching and conciliating the supernatural was the sectarian and aristocratic attitude which led to the guardian-spirit cult societies where admission was limited to those who had been blessed by the same spirit. Still another essentially separatistic attitude was fostered by the clan cult ceremonials given in honour of the clan ancestor.

While there was thus ample opportunity for the religious formulator to indulge his gifts to the full, the mass participation in the worship of the guardian-spirit and the totem-ancestor must have continually interfered with his efforts at clarification, integration, and abstraction. One can easily visualize the religious thinker-poet echoing the well-known words of the director in the introduction to *Faust*:

> *Was hilft's, wenn ihr ein Ganzes dargebracht!*
> *Das Publikum wird es euch doch zerpflücken.*

Such a situation was by no means peculiar to the Winnebago and those North American Indian tribes who shared many of the specific traits of their culture. It is just as characteristic of many parts of Melanesia and South America. We cannot, in fact, insist too strongly upon the fact that totemic society had a broad, cooperative, and egalitarian base which militated very strongly against the type of individualism favourable to the development of clearcut deities. Only when special economic conditions developed—such as trade and a definite unit of exchange as found, for instance, among the Melanesian Trobriand Islanders and related tribes or on the north-west coast of Canada, with the attendant appearance of classes and castes—did the situation materially alter.

The composite picture that emerged from the fusion of the spirit and the totemic animal was not so very different, on the whole, from that of the gods of the Homeric world, at least the gods as depicted in the Iliad. When, in one of the incidents of the great prose epic of the Winnebago entitled *The Twins*, the great hero deities Trickster, Turtle, Bladder, Hare, Sun, Red Horn, and Earth assemble in heaven to ask the supreme deity, Earthmaker, to help them redress the injuries suffered by their absent colleague Morning Star, the atmosphere is almost that of a meeting of the gods on Olympus. And Earthmaker, like his cynical prototype, the Homeric Zeus, has no illusions as to their purpose in coming. "Certainly, my children," so he addresses them, "you must have come here with some object in view. I have never known you to come without one." Is this not amazingly reminiscent of the Zeus of the Iliad? So likewise is the delightful touch where the supreme deity points out to Trickster the difference between the manner in which he speaks of the purpose for which he has come and the way in which he himself behaved when sent on an analogous mission. And so, too, is the whole theory of sacrifice that has taken shape—the suppliant's offering and the deity's acceptance. Listen to this prayer:

Hearken, father, you who dwell above, all things you have created. We desire to make you an offering which we know is ever welcome to you—a handful of tobacco, some buckskin for moccasins and a white-haired animal cooked to your taste so that you and yours can feast upon it. Give us in return the honours we crave, the opportunity to lead a victorious war-party and the privilege of killing an enemy in the midst of battle and in sight of all.

And what does the departed soul request when it reaches spirit-land?

I was to ask for life. May the flames from our lodge-fires ascend straight upward. Yet the living would be satisfied, so they said at my departure, if the flames only swayed to and fro.

And in typical Homeric fashion, we are told that "our ruler, Earthmaker, will nod assent and express his approval by word of mouth."

But let us return again, for a moment, to the Winnebago pantheon as depicted in the epic. It is a remarkable mixture of old and new. We find Trickster, Turtle, Bladder, the oldest of the figures of the esoteric mythology, the mythology of the people. Hare also is a principal figure in the mythology, but becomingly purified because of the nature of the mission to be entrusted to him. Red Horn is a strange intermingling apparently of a primal mythological figure and one of the stars; the Sun and the Earth are the oldest of the spirits. If the Morning Star and the Moon are not present, that is because they are the principal *dramatis personae* of the epic; the Morning Star being the decapitated deity whose head has to be restored and the Moon, his devoted sister who is to give birth to the great heroes destined to accomplish this task. Manifestly the elevation of the heroes of the popular myth cycles to the rank of spirits and then progressively to that of deities could not be resisted. The actual mechanism for accomplishing this was found in the functioning of the cults. They individualized the spirits and deities, and the latter aided in the differentiation of the cults. Thus the Hare, originally an out-and-out trickster and an inchoate culture-hero, became the patron of the Medicine Dance, and, conversely, the Medicine Dance made his *vita* the cardinal incident in the creation legend. Similarly the Thunderbird spirits became the patrons of the clan war-bundle rituals. This enabled them to receive a triple emphasis: first, as the totem of a clan; secondly, as the clan from which the tribal chief was drawn, as guardian-spirits; and, thirdly, as patron spirits of the war-bundle rituals. They were, in addition, popular figures in the mythology.

But there is no need for giving further details. This brief sketch of what I feel were the salient facts in the evolution of Winnebago religion should make clear to the reader what part the religious thinker plays in the formulation of the concept of totem-ancestor, spirits, and deities, and the extent to which he is reinforced and his activity circumscribed by political and economic conditions.

11

From Ghosts to Gods:
Ancestor-Spirits, Deities, and Gods

AS we pointed out in the previous chapter, intricate and complex forces and counterforces came into play throughout the history of the religion of the totemic civilizations, seizing upon one aspect for emphasis in one instance and another in another. Yet the priest-thinkers always seem to have restricted themselves to a certain fundamental subject matter until a new order of things was brought about. And when this new order developed, it developed directly out of the totemic world and through the operation of the very forces and events engendered by it. Let us, for lack of a better term, call this the polymorph stage of totemic society. It was characterized by the appearance either of well-defined stratified classes or of a highly intricate economic organization. Where classes existed the contrast was generally between a free and a slave group although frequently there were two true classes, nobles and common men, to which must be added, as a floating population, the slaves.

With few exceptions the basic traits of the totemic system still persisted unimpaired although the appearance of true classes and castes naturally subjected it to far-reaching modifications. Agriculture remained the fundamental economy. Instead of villages, however, one frequently encountered fixed settlements with pretensions to the name of towns. The population had, in many cases, increased by leaps and bounds. Overpopulation, friendly contacts with other civilizations, invasions, conquests, all conspired to make for confusion and disturbance. The processes we know so well from documented history were unquestionably operative in these undocumented cultures. All this makes the task of correctly evaluating and describing the religious ideas of these people almost hopeless. Added to the normal difficulties is the utter inadequacy of our record.

Yet I shall make the attempt and illustrate, as best I can, the salient traits of the deities in these civilizations. Because of lack of space I shall confine myself to the Baila of northern Rhodesia, the New Caledonians, the Ewe of West Africa, the Tanala of Madagascar, and the Zuñi of New Mexico. I well realize the risk I run of being severely criticized for making just this selection or for having the temerity to draw general conclusions from so few examples. But this risk must be taken and it seems an infinitely better and wiser procedure than simply to make generalizations and expect the reader to find the proof.

Among the Baila [1], the egalitarian principle immanent in the totemic form of society is still in full operation although the population is divided into two distinct groups, the free people and the slaves. Theoretically the slaves have no status at all; in practice this is not true.

The extensive territory over which the Baila are spread necessitated a clearcut division of the land. There are actually today almost eighty communes varying in size and population, each one strictly delimited. Each one has a number of villages, sometimes of the same size, sometimes very unequal. But far more disruptive to the implications of the totemic organization than these facts is the age-grade grouping. All those born in the same year and all those who have gone through the initiation ceremonies in the same year belong to one such group and regard themselves as bound together in a very special way. This, in a real sense, constitutes a definite threat to the clans, and this threat is perhaps best reflected in the fact that the clans have become, as Smith and Dale correctly state,[2] simply mutual-aid societies. Finally there are certain new factors that have entered into the connotation of clan, indicated by the different names a clan may possess. Thus, for instance, the buffalo clan is known, first, by the common appellation of the animal; secondly, by its so-called praise-name; thirdly, by the name of a man who was once its chief; and, lastly, by some place-name. That all these forces, which are fundamentally inimical to the clan, disrupted it so little was due to the "industrial" organization of the tribe and the existence of slaves whose function as workers effectively prevented the chiefs or the priests from centralizing and solidifying their power over their own people. Baila culture remained definitely a totemic-democratic one, and this is reflected in the conception of the deities.

So great, apparently, was the impact of the totemic society upon the older structure of Baila society that the task of the first formulator seems to have been concerned primarily with developing a theory of ghosts that would transcend all group and clique affiliations. Metempsychosis and reincarnation, instead of being limited to a few individuals, became the privilege of every person. Ghosts were found everywhere and could become transformed into anything. They could live in a tree or rock or ant-hill; could become animals, evil spirits, or deities to be worshipped; and, finally, they could possess a person. Unfortunately our authorities leave us in the dark as regards the relation between the different types of transformation which the ghost enjoys and the status the individuals possessed while alive.

But this theory of the ghosts makes it perfectly clear that, as usual, the medicine-men and thinkers began their task by attempting to co-ordinate into some semblance of a system those features of the older religion which were specifically connected with their own power and their particular personal experiences. The one experience destined to play the greatest role in the future evolution of Baila religion was spirit-possession. Why spirit-possession should loom so important in totemic society, we have already pointed out in our discussion of the Winnebago.* Here among the Baila we have the same fusion of spirit-possession with the animal totem and the same significance attached to the guardian-spirit. Here, however, the resemblance stops, for the

* See pp. 213 ff.

guardian-spirit, instead of being, in the main at least, freely selected, is equated with the ghost of a closely related kinsman. In other words, the worship of the ghost has beome ancestor worship. Among the Baila ancestor worship is manifestly only in its initial stage and still shows quite clearly its genetic affiliation with the spirit who possessed the shaman. Yet in spite of all these secondary developments, the clan tie holds sway over practically everything. A wife's guardian- or clan-spirit may sicken her child, but the husband's may not, for the Baila are matrilineal and the child belongs to the mother's clan.

How it has come about that spirit-possession so easily developed into ancestor worship in Africa, Melanesia, Malaysia, and Polynesia while it did not do so among the Eskimo, the peoples of Arctic Asia, and so many tribes that have both agriculture and the totemic organization, it is hard to say. There is no record of ancestor worship among any peoples who do not have either a totemic organization or a stratified society and, since many of the tribes with a totemic organization are without it, we must think of ancestor worship as more specifically associated with civilizations on the particular political and economic level of the latter. The materials for ancestor worship—spirit-possession, the tendency for the spirit to be inherited, and the not infrequent tendency for this spirit to be some deceased relative—these are present in almost all cultures.

With ancestor worship a new type of divinity entered as the subject matter of religion. As our authorities on the Baila very well put it:

In putting off the flesh the ghosts have by no means divested themselves of human nature. The best of living men are subject to moods; ordinary people are jealous, touchy, fickle; you have to be on your guard not to offend them, for if put out, they are apt to be vindictive. And so it is with the ghosts; you can never be quite sure of them; any omission on your part to do them reverence will be visited on your head or on the head of someone dear to you. Then they must be placated by offerings. It is a good thing they are placable, for if they kept up resentment where would you be? [3]

Only if this is remembered can one understand, for instance, the conception that the ghosts who have gone into the other world embittered by their treatment in this, are never to be trusted. These are always regarded with unmitigated dread.

The divinity of a man is not good [said a native]. It is a person who was not pleased in his death because he was bewitched by a relation, desirous of "eating" his name; so he goes off indignant when he dies saying: "We will see to that one who killed me." [4]

And does this prayer not sound as though it were addressed to a close older relative?

Tsu! If it be thou, O leave me alone, that I may get well. What is it thou requirest? See, here is tobacco, here is water, here is beer. Leave me alone that I may enjoy myself.[5]

These ancestor deities must be cajoled and flattered in the manner of human beings. Their names are given to oxen, dogs, spears, canoes, any possession one has, so that one will be in a position to utter the name of the deity often, for that is pleasing to him.

It is by making the deities so utterly like normal human beings that ancestor worship became so important in the history of religion, and it was undoubtedly this characteristic that eventually led, under special political and economic conditions, to the identification of a living individual with the deity and paved the way for such developments as that of the divine king of the Shilluk.[6] On the other hand this humanizing of the whole supernatural world meant the wiping out of the specific features of some of the older deities and the merging of newer ones with the ancestor-god. Few cults could arise, and under these conditions no real gods with specific theogonies could, in consequence, develop. Much of this levelling was due to events and forces of which we are ignorant; much of it, however, can be ascribed to the fact that the essential co-operative democracy of the totemic organization still persisted unimpaired.

Surely it is not too much to state that this realistic and cynical attitude and this human, all too human, interpretation of the supernatural world represented the viewpoint of the average matter-of-fact man whose mentality is dominant in every phase of Baila life. All that the priest-thinker could do was to direct it along certain channels and dam it up by attempts at ethical and philosophical formulations. But all was of no avail, for even in the most abstract formulation achieved, the concept of a cosmical Supreme Being, Leza, the realism of the matter-of-fact man still obtruded itself. Leza, for instance, has many epithets and many names. Those in common use and apparently the oldest are concerned with his ambivalent character. For instance we find: He-Who-Besets-Anyone, He-Who-Persecutes-Anyone-with-Unremitting-Attentions, He-Who-Stirs-Up-to-Do-Good-or-Bad-by-Repeated-Solicitation, He-Who-Trades-On-a-Person's-Good-Name, He-Who-Asks-Things-Which-He-Has-No-Title-to-Ask-For.

To offset these and to define him clearly and as a positive force, the priest-thinker developed another series, the so-called praise-names. There Leza is called: The Creator, The Moulder, The Constructor, The Everlasting-and-Omnipresent, He-from-Whom-All-Things-Come, The Guardian, The Giver, He-Who-Gives-and-Causes-to-Rot, Deliverer-of-Those-in-Trouble, He-Who-Cuts-Down-and-Destroys. But the answer of the lay realist was devastating and mordant. It is contained in such names as Dissolver-of-Ant-Heaps-but-the-*Maumbuswa*-Ant-Heaps-Are-Too-Much-for-Him, He-Can-Fill-Up-All-the-Great-Pits-of-Various-Kinds-but-the-Little-Footprint-of-the-Oribi-He-Cannot-Fill, and finally The-Giver-Who-Gives-Also-What-Cannot-Be-Eaten.[7]

Much of what we have said for the Baila holds also for the New Caledonians, except that among the latter the totems have played even greater havoc with the older beliefs. Here they have completely moulded ghosts and spirits in their own image. Even ancestor worship, which overlays everything in New Caledonian religion, did not succeed in effectively displacing this new concept of ghost-spirit-totem. The explanation is to be sought in the fact that the New Caledonians never developed any stratified classes, had no slaves, and that, although a chief of the tribe existed, with considerable power and prestige, each clan had a chief with almost equal power and with an infinitely closer hold upon the members of his group. Their civilization was predominantly a bourgeois one; trade and money were their main interests. We are thus in the presence of a commercial co-operative democracy, and the religion reflects it.

Since the medicine-men and priests themselves participated actively in the trading life of the community, they had little opportunity or desire for intellectual speculation and co-ordination. The spirit-deities remained vaguely outlined and only loosely systematized. Léenhardt distinguishes three types:

The totem-deities, that is to say those totems who in the remote past had fused with ancestors and become gods; ancestors whose tradition had been lost and who, in the popular imagination, had retained one single attribute which had been exaggerated and intensified; and, finally, the more recent ancestors, so recent that one can recognize some of their personal characteristics.[8]

But, as he adds, the newer they are, the more frequented are their altars. In fact the transient character of their form and influence is the outstanding trait of the religion of the natives. The deities themselves seem to have been but recently differentiated from the places they inhabit. They were originally the guardians and possessors of these places, and the conception of their nature and attributes had become transformed when they were merged with the totems and ancestors.

How unstable the systematization here is, how loosely superimposed are the various layers of religious belief and practice, and how everywhere the matter-of-fact man and his point of view assert themselves, Léenhardt has well indicated and I shall let him speak:

The ancestors have conserved the attributes of human beings and acquired, in addition, some traits of which human beings are deprived. They are *bao*, gods, with very human tempers and they kill all those who do not pay them proper attention. They are particularly sensitive to any propitiatory offerings made by their relatives. They desire the latter to accord them all that was due them when they were living in this world and that they recognize their authority and their ability. And they, in their turn, now possessing the attributes of a god, give them the power and the magic that can be employed in war, on the hunt and for love.

But though the ancestors are the creators of specific roles and of specific religions, and possess very great magical powers, they still are not the dispensers of life and they do not have an organizational influence comparable to that which we have seen exhibited in the rules of life as embodied in the taboos and the ritual acts of totemism. Since the memory of man rarely extends more than four or five generations, these gods are born and perish far more speedily than do the totems, whose worship is rooted in a past extending back many generations. The gods have thus become so definitely reduced to the role of mere dispensers of magic that the belief in them as well as their influence and power disappear as rapidly as does the recollection men have of them. And the people turn to other magical practices and welcome new gods of whose origin they are in ignorance and whom they call *bao*.[9]

These *dieux fainéants*, like their analogues the later *rois fainéants*, are always threatened with displacement by newer deities. Léenhardt speaks of such a one, *bao mii*, the red god who left the Island of Lifour with his people after it had been Christianized, but who, when they decided to stay on the Island of Pines, continued on to New Caledonia. This travelling of deities, this passing from one place to another, is a marked feature of all religions where ancestor worship is fairly well developed. It is fundamental for an understanding of the religion to which we shall now turn, that of the Ewe of West Africa.

There we find a society of the most complicated structure, with stratified classes, a king, and clans. Although the totemic basis has been fairly definitely submerged, enough of it still persists to prevent the complete centralization of power in the hands of the king. A limit to this centralization was also set by the power of the sub-chiefs, the secret societies, and the necessity of ratification of the king's election by a public assembly of the people. His influence thus depended upon the alliances into which he entered with these sub-chiefs and with the secret organizations. Such alliances, however, were not always effective or of long duration. As a result, the general picture we get is that of a society split up into essentially antagonistic factions and autonomous units with historical traditions often quite distinct, the one from the other. The unifying factor present was not so much that of the king and the symbolism associated with his office as that of the markets, the legal system that had grown up, and the great secret societies, although the latter of course also possessed a definitely disruptive side.

The helter-skelter atmosphere so apparent in the social organization, in spite of the thin veneer of consolidation, was even more marked in the realm of religion. Ancestor worship ruled supreme and coloured all the older beliefs. To the realism which the ordinary man brought to this worship was now added the materialism of the priests of the various sanctuaries. Rivalries existed everywhere, and these led to secessions and the setting up of new deities and gods to the detriment naturally of both their permanency and their prestige. New ones also were added through friendly or hostile contact with other peoples. The test of a god's power became his effectiveness in a concrete situation. What he looked like, where he came from, how he derived his power, that was immaterial. All this is realistically summarized by the cult of Dente.[10]

According to his worshippers, Dente is the supreme chief of all the gods of the Ewe as well as of those of the Tshi, from which country he originally came. He was a cripple, and when the people who were caring for him got tired of their charge, he left and wandered to a town named Late. There he found a cave near the top of a flat mountain. Into this he crept for refuge. The following morning, seeing some children playing near the cave, he called out to one of them. The children, however, ran away and told their parents what had happened, and a man standing by said he would go and look into the matter. He accordingly went but, when he approached the mountain, the cripple shouted at him so ferociously that he fell to the ground in a faint. The cripple then spat upon him and the man arose again. He could not see who had done this to him and he made haste to return. There he told his brothers what had happened, and they inferred that a powerful *tro* had come to this mountain. They immediately prepared to bring him gifts. Taking two chicken's eggs with them, they approached the dread place to pray and they addressed him as follows:

When our brother approached this place a little while ago, something happened to him, we know not what. We do not know whether it was a *tro* or a ghost. But here are some eggs for you and we pray you to withdraw your hand from within.

No sooner had they finished their prayer than they heard a voice from within the cave.

Yes, indeed, I am a *tro,* but I did not come to kill. On the contrary I came to guard your city. Tell your king, therefore, to come and visit me and tell your brother that he should come to get some medicine that I have, so that no harm can come to him

On the following day the king came and the cripple said to him:

You must bring me a dress so that I can come to the entrance of this cave before you approach any nearer. Who doubts and attempts to look upon me, him will I make blind. All those who come here must approach me walking backward.

All this was done and the man who had first seen him became his priest. To him he disclosed the fact that he was a living being and had to eat like any other living being. When subsequently the elders of the community came with presents and asked him how they could serve him, he gave them the following orders:

My worship is to consist of the following: No goats are to be allowed in the city; no one is permitted to whistle and no one must light a light at night. I will drive all evildoers from the community; all the witches, all evil magicians, all adulterers, all sinners. If anything unpleasant happens to you either at midday or at night, come to me, for I am your father. If you obey my rules you will have peace and all the neighbouring towns will become subservient to you. You are to worship me on Sunday and Monday.

After a while the community began to realize, however, that the exactions of this new *tro* were exceedingly heavy, and soon discontent developed into doubt and doubt into suspicion. They suddenly remembered that this cave had never been dangerous before and that their children had played in it, and they decided to enter and see what the *tro* looked like. Although warned by the priest that they might be overcome just as he had been, the first time, they nevertheless persisted. The cripple was dragged out and, after cursing them, he left.

Dente had no less than twenty-five epithets associated with him, such as the following:

I am the king of the cave; I am he who drags the cliff; When you serve Dente, you are serving a real king; Dente is the great *tro* of Kratsi; Dente is the owner of the town; Kwasi died in vain, for it is I, Dente, who killed him and took possession of his things; Bestower of gifts; Dente is bad because the people of Kratsi are bad; I am he who sees the occult; I seize the sinner in his sin; I confuse the people; If you see anything beautiful, give it to your guardian-deity; I break without reason; I break certain things and I destroy others; If your grandfather gives you nothing, do you believe that your guardian-deity will give you something? ; I, who adorn myself with trifles, visit the people at night; I am the great liar of the world; I am the *tro* of the tribes; I am he before whom the great kings kneel; I am the great hunter who gives nourishment to those who wish me to be with them; If you will not give it to me, I will take it from you; I am the great pot; I send the rain; Do not forget him who helps you; If no other *tro* can help you, I, Dente, can do so.

The whole history of religion, primitive and civilized, is epit-omized in these names.

Some interesting results flowed from this pragmatic attitude toward gods. It meant, among other things, that, despite the large number of priests, their power could not easily be centralized and consolidated and that, monarchy and class distinctions to the contrary, individualism and much of the co-operative democracy associated with totemism still held considerable sway. It also implied that the priest-thinkers were free to indulge their talents for elaborating the details of the ceremonials.

Rarely in any religion, historical or aboriginal, can thesis and antithesis be seen so definitely and clearly at work. The priest-thinker formulated the beliefs and the ceremonial details and the layman then unhesitatingly accepted them. But the layman's ac-ceptance was due to his indifference to the actual beliefs and the precise formulation of the nature of the god appealed to. The priest-thinker, accordingly, aided by the political-economic set-up, was not prompted to develop any real personality or individuality for the god and allowed the ancestor-image and the archaic ghost beliefs full scope. This freedom of treatment, however, interfered in turn with the permanence and the prestige attached to the particular god. The only static element here is the ceremony with the priest in charge. On its basis there then developed fixed sanc-tuaries. But fixed sanctuaries gave increased power to the priests and their cults, and this led, on the one hand, to their taking common action with the king and the sub-chiefs. How this could be used for terroristic purposes, the Nupe instance shows.* But, on the other hand, it also led to increased tension between the civil and the religious dignitaries. In other words, as many conditions conspired to consolidate the power of the priests as to disrupt that power after it had temporarily succeeded. The final victory was destined to be with the priest. But that rarely occurred in primitive civilization. Where it did occur the priest had become merged with the king.

In the domain of religious speculation the contrasts were just as great. Toward those who came to them as suppliants the priests could be the most materialistic of bargainers, and toward the god whom they worshipped they could be the humblest and meekest of mortals. They could extol him in special names, preach the highest of ethical creeds, intone psalms to him that have a biblical quality, and speak of him in a universal language.

We can never attain a knowledge such as God's [so runs an Ewe discourse [11]]. You saw me bring back a calabash and you now see me working on it. I have scraped it and in this fashion made a drinking vessel for myself. The seed that lay within it was exceedingly small, but I placed this seed in the ground and, as you now see, it has become a useful utensil. I (man) cannot do that; but the wisdom with which God made it, that, too, I do not understand. The child must not say to its father, "I surpass you."

These contrasts and contradictions should never be underestimated or effaced. Unfortunately the tendency has always been for anthropologists, even for those who, like Lowie [12], stress the existence of individual differences among primitive peoples, to do so or to overemphasize either the utilitarian or the non-utilitarian side of a given religion. Linton, for instance, in an otherwise critical description of the religion of the Tanala of Madagascar [13], states that the outstanding feature of their religion is its extreme

* See pp. 45–48.

practicality. But such a characterization of so complex a cultural phenomenon as religion is perfectly meaningless. It is particularly meaningless for the religion of the Tanala, as we shall see.

Among the Tanala, as among the Ewe, we find a monarchy, stratified classes, and clans. We also find ghosts, spirits, deities, ancestor worship, and the belief in metempsychosis. This should not surprise us, for changes have taken place so frequently and over so long a period of time in this region that the religious beliefs have never been properly integrated or systematized. Yet that the religious thinker has been active here as elsewhere is patent. The very division into the two types of supernatural agencies which Linton describes as the core of their religion is the best evidence for it. Linton designates them as Beings and Fate. They are credited with having equal power for good and evil; the Beings are supposed to interfere capriciously, in contradistinction to Fate, which is supposed to be impersonal and mechanistic. Surely we may hazard the interpretation that the origin of this basic dualism is to be sought in their history. The former concept represented the culture of the conquering Indonesians, who invaded the country at least five hundred years ago—much earlier than that, if we follow Linton—and who brought with them totemism and ancestor worship, probably already merged at that time. The latter, on the other hand, represented the older indigenous African peoples with their much simpler culture, which certainly possessed no social classes. It is no accident that there should be so clearcut a distinction between the priests, who deal with the Beings and with the ancestral spirits, and the medicinemen, who concern themselves with Fate. Fate apparently was but an elaboration of magic. Nor is it strange that the natives should have found it somewhat difficult to describe the interrelation between the Beings and Fate. Theologians of unusual acumen would have been required to disentangle this intricate enmeshment.

Political and economic events actually made the integration and consolidation of the religious beliefs possible over and over again, but these same events also disrupted them. That these kaleido-scopic changes should have been reflected in the conception of the nature of the supernatural powers goes without saying. They led to two somewhat contrasting results: on the one hand, to an identi-fication of the position of the king with the position of high-priest, and, on the other, to the loose superimposition upon one another of all the various stages through which Tanala religion had passed. No apparent unification had taken place, that is, no integration. What we do find is a somewhat uncritical eclecticism. Such a condi-tion presaged the complete breakdown of the totemic order of things. But this lack of definiteness concerning the nature of the deities was coupled with the concentration of civil and religious powers in the hands of a theoretically absolute king. Added to this there was the fixity of the ceremonial details themselves. Both factors paved the way for that development of the conception of a divine king which was to appear so often both in the Old and the New World and which was to end in the complete destruction of that type of co-operative democracy and controlled individualism which was the essence of the normally functioning totemic so-cieties.

Our last three examples have dealt with the varying fate which befell the concepts of the ghosts and spirits when the new economic and political conditions present in totemic societies brought about the formation of true classes and the emergence of ancestor wor-ship, these appearing either singly or combined. As a contrast to these examples I shall now turn to a tribe, the Zuñi of New Mexico [14], which is a classical instance of the degree to which a totemic culture can persist, be fully operative, and yet lead to an attempt at the co-ordination of religious beliefs into a system where the individual and individual initiative would be com-pletely obliterated. Because of this fact and because of the unusual detail and excellence of the data gathered, we shall treat it in considerable detail.

Class distinctions are completely absent among the Zuñi, and at no time did there exist the slightest tendency for political-economic or religious power to be consolidated in the hands of one man. Today one gets the impression that all power is invested in a small group of priests, but actually the co-operative principle on which Zuñi totemic society is based has prevented any real theocratic government from developing. In fact we shall see later on that, in many ways, the present-day Zuñi culture actually represents what was originally a complete victory of that democratic co-operative principle which is inherent in the totemic structure of society. This victory apparently, at different times in Zuñi history, suffered a number of definite setbacks but was never really threatened or even seriously neutralized.

The Zuñi live today and apparently have always lived in one or at best two compact pueblo-villages. They are organized on a totemic basis with kinship reckoned in the female line. Crisscrossing the clan are a number of other important social units—the household, the tribal and special secret societies, and the cult societies. According to Miss Bunzel [15] :

A man must belong to several of these groups and the number to which he may potentially belong is almost unlimited. There is no exclusive membership. He is born into a certain household, and his kinship and clan affiliations are thus fixed, unless altered by adoption. At puberty he is initiated into one of the six dance groups that comprise the male tribal society. He may, through sickness, be conscripted into one of the medicine societies; if he takes a scalp he must join the warriors' society; and if connected with a sacerdotal household he may be called upon to join one of the priesthoods.

Since there were no classes and no slaves, every man could, so to speak—was indeed forced to—have a public career. In view of this situation it is somewhat puzzling to know what scholars like Bunzel and others who have written on the Zuñi mean when they speak of the complete absence of a stress on individual expression.[16] It would be just as correct to state that the Athenian citizen of the time of Pericles found no expression for his individualism.

All that they can legitimately claim is that the official formulations made by the priests took no cognizance of the individual. Most of the writers on the Zuñi, particularly Bunzel, have taken these formulations at their face value. Indeed the latter writer insists, with almost devout fervour, that the Zuñi priest "strips his life of trivial, irrelevant, and distracting matters in order to have his mind free for his great work—the material and spiritual welfare of his people." [17] What is it in this culture that is responsible for such ecstatic eulogies and exclamations of wonder on the part of alien observers? The answer seems to be that, apart from the amazing richness and beauty of its poetry and rituals, we seem to be here in the presence of a civilization that has, like few others, succeeded in becoming welded into a harmonious whole. Actually this is an illusion. It is simply a feeling that we have. What is true, however, is that the scheme of things as articulated by the priests does so represent Zuñi life. These poet-priests and organizers really have achieved an integration that is almost unbelievable, and they deserve all the greater credit for it when one tries to visualize the disparate elements out of which this unity had to be wrought, the environmental obstacles with which they had to cope, and the social and political vicissitudes through which the Zuñi have passed in their history.

The Zuñi religious and ceremonial system as at present constituted consists of a single non-esoteric cult to which everyone may belong—the cult of the ancestors—and six major esoteric cults. The cult of the ancestors is the basis of all their ceremonialism. This fact, the fundamental significance of this cult alone, is the most eloquent testimony to the original democratic basis of their society and illustrates admirably the amazing feat which the religious formulators have accomplished and what they have done to the old archaic beliefs. These ancestors are not the ancestor-spirits with whom we have been dealing in Africa and Melanesia; they are simply the generalized ghosts of the dead. The more distant the dead the more specifically beneficent are they supposed to be. Toward the more recent dead, however, the attitude of the Zuñi is one of fear; at best it is ambivalent. How are we to explain this? Why should what seems the most archaic stratum of beliefs still hold so important a place in a ritualistic organization entirely controlled by a small group of priests belonging to the esoteric societies? It was certainly not in the interests of these priests to allow a ceremony to flourish unhampered where individuals were permitted to establish a direct relationship with the supernatural world without priestly intermediation. It is not reasonable to suppose that even priests who, as Bunzel states, regarded themselves as "too sacred to contaminate themselves with dispute or wrangling" would calmly allow so direct a challenge to their power and prestige. It is in fact quite clear that they did not let it pass unchallenged. For instance, within the memory of people still living, those priests to whom the police powers were delegated, executed individuals under the charge of sorcery. Under this term was included not only sorcery as such but any expression of individualism, particularly any attempt on the part of an individual to act on his own initiative.

The only reasonable inference from these facts is that we are dealing here either with the priest's usual type of compromise when facts and events became too strong for him or that this ideal of conformity—a conformity which, incidentally, holds largely not only for the Zuñi but for all the Pueblo tribes—was due to special economic-environmental causes or to some special and possibly some recent historical event. The same holds true in other Pueblo groups. "The typical sorcerer in Hopi theory," says Mrs. Aitken, "is the man in charge of an orthodox ceremony who has altered it for private ends." [18]

Mrs. Aitken sees it as springing from the necessity of the subordination of the individual to the group because of economic necessity. A civilization, so she contends, that has staked its all on agriculture under the semi-arid conditions existing in the southwest of the United States had to emphasize conformity, had to develop unanimity.[19] But explanations of this general psychological type never carry much conviction. They do not possess sufficient specific content. A far more satisfactory and concrete explanation can be given, namely the influence of the contact with the Spaniards and the far-reaching series of events, political and economic, in Zuñi history since Vásquez de Coronado set out in 1540 on his adventurous journey to the Seven Cities of Cibola. Mrs. Parsons [20], who was the first to emphasize these influences, has also pointed out a number of facts and traditions in the Zuñi sources which indicate that the clan has only recently lost its function and that individualism played a significant role in the Zuñi order of things not so very long ago.

Apart from the cult of the generalized dead, all the societies of the Zuñi are esoteric secret cults, each cult connected with the worship of a different group of spirit-deities and each one in charge of a special priesthood. In addition, each society has its own fetishes, its own place of worship, and its own calendrical cycle of ceremonies. Following Bunzel we can distinguish six such major cult-types: the cult of the sun; the cult of the water-spirits; the cult of the *katchinas,* i.e., certain supernatural beings identified with the dead; the cult of the priests of the *katchinas;* the cult of the gods of war; and the cult of the animal-deities. Of these all except the *katchina* cult are restricted in membership. The latter cult, on the contrary, is unrestricted in the sense that all male members of the tribe must belong to it and participate in its ceremonies. There are thus two large cults that rest on a mass, or better, lay, basis, contrasted with those controlled entirely by the priests. The interweaving and overlapping of the various activities, functions, and personnel of these various societies indicate only too clearly that here the unity attained is of recent origin. In fact Miss Bunzel herself admits that the intricacy of the ceremonies is due in part to the piling up and telescoping of distinct rituals, in part to a coalescence of independent cults.

If we now turn to the organization of the priesthood, in order to determine the degree of integration and unification achieved there, we find a council of six priests: three from the chief priesthood, and the heads of the other three priesthoods. The head of this hierarchy is also the head of the sun cult. Aiding these six, there are two bow-priests, members of the war society, and the heads of the *katchina* societies. The powers and functions of this council are multiple. They choose the impersonators of the deities at the annual festival, insert important ceremonies into the regular calendar, decide what action is to be taken in cases of calamities such as earthquakes and drought, and determine the general tribal policy whenever new contingencies arise. To them alone belongs the power of appointing the civil officers.

What strikes one most definitely in this priestly council is its representative nature. No religious group is absent, yet no particular society has seized absolute control. On the other hand, the clan does not participate as a unit although the clan bond is still very close, for an individual still feels his closest ties to be with members of his clan and it is upon them that he calls for assistance in such undertakings as the harvest, housebuilding, and initiations.

Where we find such a tremendous development of ritual, one would naturally expect the deities worshipped to be clearly outlined. This is precisely what one does find. The delineation, however, is not in terms of idols but in terms of masks and principally in connexion with the *katchinas*. Unfortunately the *katchina* worship is legitimately suspected of having been subjected to strong Catholic influence. If we were to exclude it from consideration, at least in its present form, as being of aboriginal origin, then we would find ourselves in the presence of a ritualistic system of bewildering complexity and intricacy, but one which had no conception or delineation of deities higher than that generally encountered in the normal totemistic cultures. We are consequently forced to the conclusion that what we are accustomed to regard as the distinctive achievement of the Zuñi and of Pueblo religion in general must be a very late aftergrowth, due to the displacement of the clan and of its religious associations by the esoteric societies. This displacement in turn we must attribute to a very special economic-geographical environment, to the struggle with hostile tribes, and to the gradual merging and coalescence of all kinds of social units during the long history of the tribe, facts about which we have some information from the archæological remains.

To the reasons enumerated for the decline of the clan's power we must add the history of the contact with the Spaniards. It is to this same contact that we must also ascribe the exuberant development of the cults. Only in part, and probably only in small part, was this due to the influence of the rich ritual of the Catholic Church. But as the influence of the Church waned, particularly in the eighteenth century, a new crystallization of native culture apparently took place which produced a real hypertrophy of ritualism. That is what we find today. It is the answer that not a few American Indian tribes have given to the threat of cultural annihilation. The Zuñi culture, being so much older and representing a highly complex civilization to begin with, developed this hypertrophy to a more marked degree. The individual was temporarily submerged. We are here consequently not in the presence of a positive integration where the individual has consciously surrendered his rights and his initiative of action for the good of the whole, but in the presence of a negative and adventitious integration which betokens the end of a people.

The history of the Zuñi, as we can reconstruct it from archæology, ritual, and mythology, suggests quite definitely that they must have been subjected to native foreign influences time and again, and long before the coming of the whites, and that crises rivalling in importance that which the contact with the Spaniards produced were not new to them. But each new realignment, each new readjustment, meant a blurring of the older structure of their society and a break in the normal course of evolution. It is only too clear that for the Zuñi, as for all the other Pueblo cultures, there had been a steady loss, coupled with deterioration and confusion, for a number of centuries before the coming of Coronado in 1540. It is on such an assumption that we can best explain why the subject matter of the priest-thinkers remained so exclusively confined to mythological figures and why no greater progress was made toward the development of true deities. Their time and

energy were engaged elsewhere. Not that other causes were not
likewise at work. True deities and gods do not develop where the
totemic structure still functions significantly; they do not, in other
words, develop where there is no social-economic basis for them.
The truth of this generalization is confirmed as soon as we turn to
those aboriginal civilizations which, like the Malayan and the
Polynesian, either have never had a totemic organization or have
developed their cultures under the influences of an agricultural
society which had passed through its totemic period long before
they came into contact with it.

If we have found it difficult to estimate properly the influence
exercised by the great Western European and Eastern Mediterranean peoples on the tribes so far discussed, our difficulties increase
tenfold when we approach such civilizations as the Malayan and
Polynesian. Not only have they been subjected to the direct influence, first of Hindu and later of Mohammedan civilizations,
but they must have already brought with them to their island
homes cultures of a markedly mixed kind.[21] For the Malayan-
speaking groups, wherever they are found, it is impossible to exclude the influence of Hindu religious ideas although this does
not necessarily imply an old contact. For Polynesia the situation
is different. Whether or not many elements in their religion are to
be regarded as ultimately of Hindu or Indian origin, we know
that the Polynesians were not subjected to any major invasions
from that source. It is also quite clear that they have so completely
reorganized and reinterpreted any older ideas and beliefs they
may have borrowed that little is to be gained by putting these
ideas and beliefs into the forefront of our discussion.

Because of lack of space I shall confine my remarks to two
tribes for whose religion we have unusually good records: the
Bagobo of south-eastern Mindanao in the Philippine Islands, and
the Tahitians, each one presenting a definite social and religious
system contrasting markedly with the other.

The Bagobo have no stratified classes. Their economy is based
on agriculture—on the planting of rice, maize, and sweet pota-

toes. They have three domestic animals: the horse, the dog, and the water buffalo. Characteristic of their material culture are the highly specialized forms of overlacing and colouring hemp, the use of iron, and the casting of various bronze and brass objects from a wax mould.

Corresponding to the somewhat heterogeneous character of their economic life is the political and religious structure of the tribe. Whatever it may have been at one time, today there is no effective centralization of power in the hands of any one person, in spite of the fact that the chief is actually both the civil and the religious head of the community. This means that he is in charge of the central liturgies of the main ceremony, that he offers up the sacrifice, and that all problems connected with religious behaviour or with secular activities are referred to him for decision. In this decision, however, he is aided by the prominent old men and a few of the old women of the village. It was this direct participation of the layman in all the affairs of the group that prevented the development of any close organization of the priesthood or the assumption of autocratic shamanistic control on the part of any particular functionary belonging to the four official religious classes into which the priesthood was divided. And to this direct participation of the layman must also be attributed the composite make-up of the rites, rites in which we encounter not only the offerings of the blood of slain victims and of agricultural products, but also public and private sacrifices.

Next to the chief stand a group of warriors, each of whom has distinguished himself by having killed one or more persons in the proper and orthodox fashion and who have, as a body, specific duties to perform in the ceremonies. Then come the medicine-men proper. Their functions are not connected with the treatment of disease but with the rites performed during the harvest, with marriage, and with the conducting of séances. The mediums form their own group, in part related to the medicine-men, although their primary function is to transmit messages from the supernatural beings.

From a superficial view we should not expect to find in a society such as we have just described any marked development of true deities or gods. And yet not only do we find them, but we find them delineated in far more positive fashion than among civilizations so immeasurably more complex and sophisticated as those of West and East Africa. How are we to explain this? Part of it manifestly is to be ascribed to foreign influence. Part of it is the result of the type of speculation and interpretation which resulted indirectly from the various modes of food and commodity production that had developed. Yet equally important were the facts that no totemic period had intervened to bring a new religious content and emphasis and that this highly diversified economic system had been introduced from without. The first factor prevented the development of any true social-political cohesiveness and left the religious beliefs unintegrated, while the second, on the contrary, permitted just such a systematization. A compromise thus arose which is neatly expressed in Bagobo religion, where, on the one hand, we find well-defined gods and deities and, on the other, malignant supernatural spirits.

The gods proper are regarded as being far removed from human affairs and neither harm nor good is to be expected from them. The deities, i.e., individualized spirits, in contrast, are closely associated with man's interests and are the constant objects of his worship. They all represent reinterpreted older nature-spirits to whom specific and specialized functions have been assigned. Thus we find a deity Tigyama, protector of the household and healer of the sick; Tarabume, who takes care of the growing rice and the hemp plants; Paneyangan, who protects the industry of casting brass and secondarily or, more probably, primarily, protects the swarms of wild bees that hive in the flowering trees; the hunting-deity Abog; the water-gods Gamo-Gamo; the ground- and air-gods, Linug; the sky-gods Sebandal and Salangayd; and the war-gods Mandarangan.

Intermediate between gods and deities are the unseen divine

beings called *tolus*. Their names are never mentioned. They are regarded as omniscient and infallible, and their relation to the people is a very direct and intimate one. They seem to be specifically connected with the guardianship of the industrial arts of the Bagobo.

In a group by themselves are two semi-divine figures: the divine man Malaki t'Olu k'Waig and the half benevolent, half malevolent Tagamaling. Both belong to the archaic stratum. The first stems from the popular mythology, the second from the magical background. It is perfectly clear that Malaki t'Olu k'Waig is an old culture-hero of the people who has been purified and remodelled and then elevated to the rank of a deity. Dr. Benedict describes him as follows [22]:

[He] represents the highest ideal of goodness and of purity, as the native visualizes that ideal. He figures as a hero in mythical romance, where, indeed, one finds many Malaki t'Olu k'Waig, who go through remarkable adventures and achieve distinction. On the devotional side, however, all of these fabulous characters are fused into the impersonation of one beloved individual, whose home is associated with a legendary spring far up in the mountains which is called "the source of the waters." Here two rivers are said to take their rise, and it is just at the point where the two streams separate that the Malaki t'Olu k'Waig lives. He is the great healer, and to his home are carried all the diseases which the Bagobo, by magic rites, have coaxed into leaf-dishes or into little manikins. Here, at the mythical spring, the Malaki destroys all sickness that is sent to him. He winds one end of a string, or fibre, around the neck of each disease, ties the other end to some post or tree, and quickly strangles the disease. The Malaki t'Olu k'Waig is believed to know the whole world; he never sleeps, he answers prayers wherever offered.

Tagamaling likewise represents an attempt at purification and reinterpretation. He is an old mountain-spirit who, I take it, was at one time identified with the malignant spirits *buso* and then secondarily "reclassified" with the benevolent nature-deities. His dual nature is well described in a myth collected by Dr. Benedict [23]:

Before the world was made, there was Tagamaling. The Tagamaling is the best buso, because he does not want to hurt man all of the time. Tagamaling is actually buso only a part of the time; that is, the month when he eats people. One month he eats human flesh, and then he is buso; the next month he eats no human flesh, and then he is a god. So he alternates, month by month. The month he is buso, he wants to eat man during the dark of the moon; that is, between the phases that the moon is full in the east and new in the west. . . .

Tagamaling makes his house in trees that have hard wood, and low, broad-spreading branches. His house is almost like gold, and is called "Palimbing," but it is made so that you cannot see it; and, when you pass by, you think: "Oh! what a fine tree with big branches," not dreaming that it is the house of a Tagamaling. Sometimes, when you walk in the forest, you think you see one of their houses; but when you come near to the place, there is nothing. Yet you can smell the good things to eat in the house.

The figure of Tagamaling brings us to those supernatural beings whom the Bagobo fear above all others, the so-called *buso*. To understand their origin we have but to remember that they are, on the one hand, associated with natural objects and physical phenomena and, on the other, with the ghosts of the dead. It is the *buso*, likewise, who cause disease. It can be safely assumed then that we are here dealing with the oldest of shamanistic systematizations, one which has been revitalized by the medicine-men in order to cope more effectively with the other individuals who participate in the various religious activities—the chief, the warriors, and the mediums. In this revitalization, however, none of the terror traits always associated with the supernatural beings of the shaman have disappeared. They have in fact, if anything, been accentuated and generalized. Thus a *buso* is defined as a being that preys upon human flesh and that sends sickness to the living in order to kill them and feed upon their dead bodies.

One subdivision, the *tigbanua,* are supposed to live in a state of perpetual cannibalism. They are unbelievably repulsive in aspect, possessing only one eye and that one situated in the middle of the forehead, and a hooked chin two spans long and upturned so as to catch the drops of blood that may chance to drip from the mouth. Their bodies are covered with coarse black hair. From mountains and forests they come flying to every fresh-dug grave to drink the blood from the corpse and gnaw the flesh from the bones. They are the impersonations of evil in its most unmitigated form. As Dr. Benedict says [24]:

> There is, for the most part, no idea of an interaction between stimuli from bad spirits and the religious or ethical transgressions of man. Buso does not incite a Bagobo to break taboo or to steal rice.

Assuredly this is the phantasmagoria of the disordered mind of our neurotic-epileptoid shaman that has acquired a special concreteness and an added virulence through its association with a complicated economic structure.

But to sum up. The characteristic of Bagobo civilization is the marked contrast between its well-integrated economic organization and the lack of such an integration either for its political institutions or for its religious beliefs. This contrast is all the more marked in the realm of religion because we do find there a considerable degree of systematization. Each group apparently—that of the chief, the warriors, the medicine-men, and the mediums—elaborated its own system. But each of these systems was more or less in competition with the others and was prevented from taking on any final form by the vicissitudes of Bagobo political history, which subjected them to far-reaching influences from the outside.[25]

Yet those very influences must be regarded as fundamental in encouraging the development of true gods and deities. Particularly is this true of those outside influences that were responsible for the introduction, first, of agriculture and irrigation and domestic animals, and, much later, of bronze and brass casting. The necessity for caring for their fields and their water supply, for instance, added definiteness and rigour to a legal development based on currency and on an exchange system which probably arose in connexion with other aspects of Bagobo culture but which would otherwise have never attained the clearcut character it actually possessed. Finally, the specialized professions, like bronze and brass casting, brought into existence an artisan class that was prompted to convert vague supernatural protectors into well-defined deities jealously guarding its rights and privileges. Superimposed upon all these influences were two other facts: one positive, the direct borrowing of Hindu religious concepts; and the other negative, the absence of what, at all times, seems to have acted as an inhibiting factor in the development of true gods or deities, namely the totemic structure of society with its emphasis on democracy and its stress on animal-deities.

None of the peoples so far mentioned, no matter how clearly the concept of their supernatural beings or deities was defined—the Pueblo Indians possibly excepted—ever made images of them, and only the great African civilizations had true temples. And yet it is clear that only where supernatural spirits are fashioned into idols, are housed in special and sacred structures, and have true theogonic myths associated with them, can it be claimed that they are true gods in the ordinarily accepted meaning of the word. To the type of society that has led to such a development we shall accordingly turn, taking as an example the Tahitians so well described by Miss Henry.[26]

The Tahitians shared most of the characteristics of the other Polynesian groups. Their economy was based on an intensive agriculture; they were divided into distinct classes that partook somewhat of the nature of castes; they practised human sacrifice on a large scale; and they developed a highly elaborate literature, sacred and profane, and a complex religion which included a most amazing assortment of elements, some crude and belonging to the most archaic stratum of society, some, on the other hand, sublime and of the most refined nature and worthy of finding a place at the side of the highest expression of religious thought. Wherever such variability and complexity in the religious beliefs of a people exist, we can be certain that they are definitely an outgrowth of an elaborate economic and social structure and the result of a long history full of political vicissitudes. The Tahitians, indeed all the Polynesians, form no exceptions to this generalization. Indeed, for no other primitive group, not even for the great civilizations of native Africa, is it more important to bear in mind all these factors. The complexity which they have introduced into Polynesian religion makes it practically impossible to describe these in brief compass and it is only with considerable trepidation that I attempt it.

The nature of the Tahitian religion, as well as its history, is best epitomized in their temples and their theogonic myths. Let us begin with the temples, the *marae*. Against one thing the reader must be cautioned immediately, namely, that practically all our material has been gathered from individuals belonging to the royal entourage or to the higher nobility.

There were formerly eight classes of temples, three connected with the welfare of the community at large—the international, the national, and the local—and five of a more private nature—the family or ancestral, the social or so-called "clan," the doctors', the canoe-builders', and the fishermen's. To understand these divisions we must correlate them with the social units and the social classes with which they were connected.

Be it remembered that there were four social classes among the Tahitians—the members of the royal family proper; the chiefs, that is, the nobility of the land, who were intermarried with the royal family; the landed gentry; and the common people. The international and the national temples were completely and directly controlled by the royal family, the local temples by the chiefs, the family or ancestral temples apparently by the landed gentry, the social temples by the landed gentry and the common people, the canoe-builders', the doctors', and the fishermen's controlled by the members of these special professions. The temples, in turn, were the visible emblems of land-ownership—the international and the national symbolizing the power of the royal family over the whole land; the local, the power of the chiefs over their smaller domains; and the family or ancestral, the power of the landed gentry over the smaller strips. This intimate connexion of the temple with land-ownership is best illustrated by the fact that to the family temples, which were erected upon every portion of the land a man owned, were attached the hereditary names of the family. Without these they could give no proof of their ownership, and even up to her day, according to Miss Henry, "the memory of this class of *marae* does not cease to be of importance to the heirs of these families, for it is necessary when dealing with land, to state that their title-name is from the *marae* named so-and-so." [27]

Naturally, since the members of the royal family were regarded as descended from the gods, in fact, from the highest class of gods, and were recognized as gods incarnate by all the other people, it followed, first, that the land would be considered sacrosanct and, secondly, that the gods connected so concretely with the symbols of economic domination would be clearly outlined and their characteristics catalogued with meticulous and jealously guarded detail. The prestige attached to genealogies would still further reinforce these tendencies by establishing a presumptive historical evidence to divine descent and by developing genealogies for the gods themselves. These divine genealogies, in the hands of priest-thinkers belonging to the royal or noble families, often assumed the most abstract forms. Finally, attention must be called to the spread of a particular god from one island to another either peacefully or by conquest, and the frequent absorption, by a particular god, of the characteristics of the god he had displaced. All these are well-known processes in the religion of the so-called higher civilizations. Nowhere, among primitive peoples, can they be seen at work better than among the Polynesians.

Let me illustrate these processes in connexion with one god, Oro, who was specifically worshipped at the most important of the international temples and was the patron god, *par excellence*, of the royal family. I am following Handy's excellent summary.[28]

According to the traditional history, Oro was a war-god first worshipped at Opoa Raiatea in the Leeward Islands. In connexion with his cult, there was associated, from the very beginning, a particular tuft of red feathers called *ura*. It was believed that the particular chief who owned it became thereby invincible in war. This talisman, which was to become so integral a part of the king's regalia and for which many battles were in later times ostensibly to be fought, was identified with Oro, the ferocious war-lord of the most famous of all the international temples. Subsequently Oro, because of his renown as a war-lord, was introduced in Tahiti. There he apparently superseded the original patron gods of the chiefly families, the gods Ta'aroa and Tane, and we finally find him simultaneously the ferocious war-lord, the recipient of the peacetime harvest offerings, and the patron of the dancers and singers whose activities were intended as fertility rites.

How specific the gods may become in appearance and in power under the influence of a genealogical authentication, the chant sung by the high-priest of Tane, one of the most important gods of the Tahitians, clearly demonstrates. It begins in approved Polynesian fashion with nothingness [29]:

O shapeless, O shapeless! No face, no head, no ears, no mouth, no ribs, no abdomen, no umbilicus, no neck, no back, no chest, no thighs, no buttocks, no knees, no legs, no sole of the foot! O, what growth is this little child! Who could have borne such a child? He is born of Atea and Paputu-oi, the handsome offspring of Ta'aroa.

Then messengers are sent to summon the artisans who fashion the bodies of gods. They fashion the face and back of the new god but are afraid to apply their hands to him, fearing the dreaded majesty of his mother, Atea. Finally Atea herself comes and provides the new child with a skin for every kind of weather and hardship. Then he was given, in specific detail, all the parts of the body that man and the gods need. The traits he is to have are often symbolically foreshadowed. For instance, his ears are "deaf ears to become open ears, ears that could hear far off, ears that could hear close by, deep ears, nice and erect and thin." [30] Similarly his eyes are "frowning eye-brows that join, and . . . bright eyes, glancing eyes, fixed eyes, winking eyes, observing eyes, eyes that have tears." [31] The cheeks are "smooth cheeks, cheeks full of rage, flushed cheeks," [32] and the lips are "set lips, pliant lips, pouting lips, laughing lips, sneering lips, thick lips," [33] and when they made the vitals, care was taken that they contained a conscience.

At last all was ready and Atea covered the child with a sleek, brown skin and then taking some gimlet-shells she bored into the round skull of the child. But let me continue with the chant [34]:

She bored into the ears to listen by, and placed wax in them. She bored into the nose and the talkative mouth and the throat of the child. The child then moved, he wept, and cried: "O Atea, I am in great pain!"

Thus the development of the child was perfected, accomplished it all was. The child became a living being, it was the spirit of Ta'aroa that directed the work, and caused Tane-mata-morari (Tane-of-Shapeless-Face) to become a good-looking boy. None of the artisans touched Tane, they were all afraid of the majesty, the power of Atea.

Tane matured; Tane who stood outside. Tane who stood inside. Tane breathed heavily, Tane the heavy breather. Tane whistled, Tane the whistler. Tane of many friends. Tane the friend of armies. Tane the heavenly friend. When the hosts of gods saw Tane's hair, which was not like their feathers, they named it moss.

Now Tane stood up and said: "And so this is I, great Tane, god of all things beautiful! With eyes to measure the skies! I whose eyes will unite with those of Ro'o (Fame), the famous."

These are Tane's attributes: Tane friend of armies, Tane of long breath, Tane of distant lands, Tane the extirpator, Tane the resounder, Tane whose touch subjected, Tane who drew away the sky of Atea, Tane of the tenth sky, Tane of the open sky, Tane of extended arms.

Tane had two great spears, Vero-nu'u (Dart-upon-Armies) of coconut wood, and Vero-ra'ai (Attacking-Dart) of 'aito. These are the two dark streaks that still remain along the Vai-ora (Milky Way), in the sky. When Tane vented his rage above, there was death! When he vented his rage below, there was death! When he vented his rage at sea, there was death! When he vented his rage inland, there was death! When Tane's wrath was poured forth in the house the shadows vanished from within, and people got ill. When Tane struck a man, he became a pulp. Tane was the god of all artisans in this world. Tane was a bailer of the sea. He was Tane who caused a restless, anxious mind.

The characterizations of the gods so far discussed were the work of members of the royal and noble class, of their warrior-statesmen and their priest-thinkers. Parallel with these were the characterizations emanating, we have a right to assume, from the landed gentry and the common people. In these the gods were represented by post-like figures or small sennit-covered stakes. Among the Tahitians there were well-carved wooden figures of their creator-god Ta'aroa although in most parts of Polynesia only distinguished ancestors and heroes were so depicted. Among the Marquesans, for example, there exists a representation in stone of a famous chief, Takaii by name. The figure is about eight feet tall, square and massive, with a cylindrical head, and the mouth, nose, and eyes in low relief. The body itself is short and broad; the hands are clasped across the stomach. The base is formed by the legs which are short and heavy and represented in a semi-squatting position.

It has been contended ever since the Polynesians were first described that the information as obtained from the natives seemed to indicate that we are not here dealing with true idols and that these images are not true emblems of divinity.[35] There is some validity to this objection. But we are justified, I think, in regarding this attitude as probably the interpretation of the priest-thinker. The very fact that the vast majority of these figures were those of heroes and chiefs is the best proof that they represented the viewpoint of the two lower classes. The higher priests apparently had to take cognizance of this viewpoint and, in characteristic priestly fashion, elaborated a theory that they were not the gods themselves but that, at certain seasons or in answer to the prayers of the priest, the gods entered them. They had even to compromise further and admit that, during this indwelling of the gods, the images themselves were powerful.

So once again we have two streams of thought meeting, two contrasting attitudes contending with one another; on the one hand, the thinker, and, on the other, the man of action and pragmatist. Here in Polynesia these are further contrasted because only those thinkers who belonged to the two higher social classes were permittted to express themselves significantly. This does not mean that the attitudes of the ordinary man did not find expression in Polynesian religion. The great role played by charms, incantations, and magical rites in general is the best evidence that the priest-thinker, even when he was selected from a special ruling caste, was powerless in their presence. And this is but natural enough since the common people represented the overwhelming majority of the population.

In the last two chapters we have attempted to characterize briefly the fundamental traits of a number of primitive religions in regard to one feature, the nature of their beliefs in supernatural beings, deities, and gods. Even if the reader cannot accept the historical implications and interpretations which I have introduced, this much surely will have become clear: that throughout the primitive world, whether we are dealing with tribes possessing a simple food-gathering economy like the central Californians or with those having complex and intricate economies like the Polynesians and the major cultures of native Africa, the economic factors have always been the determining ones. Everywhere we find two classes or groups in conflict: that of the priest-thinker and that of the matter-of-fact pragmatist and essentially non-religious individual. Everywhere the priest-thinker has functioned in three ways: first, as a person with a special temperament and psychic make-up whose experiences have impressed themselves indelibly upon the form of religion and its constituent formulae; secondly, as an individual seeking for power and privileges who has invariably associated himself with those individuals or groups in his community striving for the same; and, thirdly, as a thinker attempting to bring order into the folkloristic background surrounding him on all sides. At no time was he permitted to be simply a thinker. But he did occasionally find some opportunity to indulge in purely intellectual speculations. To some of these, such as speculations on the concept of a Supreme Deity and its ethical implications, on the nature of the soul and its destination, on the concept of immortality, and on the synthesis of all these ideas and concepts in great ritual dramas, we shall now turn.

12

Monolatry and Monotheism

NO aspect of primitive religion has been more frequently discussed during the last decade than the question as to whether in primitive religions there already existed a belief in a Supreme Being. Ever since the well-known Scotch essayist and polyhistorian Andrew Lang propounded the theory that such a concept is actually to be encountered among the very simplest tribes,[1] this discussion has never ceased. For the last twenty-five years it has formed the main interest of one of the foremost Catholic apologists of our time, Pater W. Schmidt.[2] His completed work is now before us in five stout volumes. It is at one and the same time a pungently uncritical thesaurus of our subject and a contribution to Catholic dogmatics. Yet in spite of its obvious purpose, which is essentially theological, Schmidt and those trained under him, all of them priests, deserve great praise for their attempt to gather together whatever information is still available on this subject among primitive cultures. Independently of Schmidt the Jesuit priest H. Pinard de la Boullaye has discussed the whole question in a far more critical and acceptable fashion in connexion with his comparative study of religion.[3] During this same period a number of other scholars have also dealt with it in a less theologically biased connexion.[4]

In the small space at my disposal only a few aspects of this problem can be broached. Let me begin with the well-known statement of Tylor which sums up admirably the older evolutionary viewpoint as it was understood both by ethnologists and historians of religion. "Among [primitive] races," says Tylor, "animism has its distinct and consistent outcome and polytheism its distinct and consistent completion, in the doctrine of a Supreme Deity." [5] It is to this assumption that Lang, Schmidt, and many ethnologists proper have taken exception, and rightly so. Had Lang and Schmidt rested there, all would have been well. But, as we know, they did not. Instead they attempted to show that the belief in a Supreme Deity was primary and that it had been secondarily contaminated, distorted, and blurred by animistic ideas and magic. To demonstrate this Pater Schmidt, with a very correct historical instinct, devoted himself, and stimulated others so to devote themselves, to the study of this conception among those tribes who today possess the simplest cultures, to those, that is to say, whose economy is either that of food-gathering or simple fishing-hunting. Possibly the most thorough of such studies is that of Schmidt's pupil and colleague M. Gusinde [6] on the Selknam of Tierra del Fuego. By examining his data and the method he pursued in obtaining his facts we shall not only discover what is valid about Schmidt's position but find an added demonstration of the role played by the priest-thinker in primitive societies throughout all stages of their history.

According to Gusinde the Selknam believe in a Supreme Being who lives in the heavens and the meaning of whose name is unknown. His name is seldom uttered and never used frivolously. Because of the awe with which they regard him, whenever he is to be mentioned, circumlocutions are employed. He is a spirit and no one can see him. Since he is regarded as a spirit and since no specific name is applied to him, it follows, insists Gusinde, that he can be regarded as possessing an independent personality. The full force of the strong Christian dogmatic bias of this school emerges when we are informed that, on the basis of the above characteristics, the Supreme Deity of the Selknam can justifiably be described as a "sharply circumscribed and clearly individualized personality." On such evidence it would be possible to call practically every spirit in primitive religions a sharply circumscribed and individualized personality. The legitimate distrust which such a method of proof engenders increases when we examine the method Gusinde has used to obtain his evidence. He worked primarily with one man, a priest, and most of the information was obtained by direct questioning. Yet in spite of this highly reprehensible method of approach and in spite of the fact that much of what Gusinde adduces cannot be accepted as an unbiased and correct report, the fact does remain that here, in one of the simplest of primitive cultures, we do find the belief in a being who has many of the traits of the Supreme Deity of the great religions of Western Europe. How are we to explain it?

As I have repeatedly pointed out in previous pages, beliefs and ideas can be understood only when we know who the people are who share them. Who, in the simplest cultures, are the individuals who do? The moment we put this query we realize that they are a selected group of shamans, medicine-men, and priests, and we discover, in addition, that there is a definite cleavage of belief between these comparatively few individuals and both the other shamans and medicine-men and the community at large. Gusinde himself has unwittingly indicated how definitely the belief in a Supreme Being is limited to a certain group of individuals by admitting that, as soon as the Selknam culture deteriorated, this belief was quite forgotten while all the other religious beliefs remained more or less intact.[7] Why should this have taken place unless the figure of the Supreme Deity was a very special concept confined to those individuals whose power and prestige disappeared as soon as the full Selknam culture became attenuated? This, and other reasons which space forbids us to dwell on here, make it fairly clear that the belief in a Supreme Being among those non-agricultural tribes who possess it—for many do not—was a construct of the medicine-man and thinker and one which rarely, and then only partially, found its way into the ranks of the community at large.

As we proceed from the food-gathering to the fishing-hunting and then to the agricultural tribes, the figure of the Supreme Deity assumes more and more the characteristics of a priestly construct, bears more and more the earmark of a special and privileged group and class. The extent to which it does so depends largely upon how strong the economic-social domination of this priestly group happens to be. Where this is marked, as, for instance, among the Dakota and Winnebago Indians, among the Polynesians, and in West Africa, there its recognition as the private and specific belief of the priest-thinkers as a class is definitely stated by the priests themselves.

With this fact then we must begin: that wherever a Supreme Deity or a High God, as he is frequently called, exists it is the belief either of a few individuals or of a special group. Bearing this in mind we can now turn to an examination of the belief itself, in order to see what light it can throw on the speculative enterprise of the religious thinker in primitive communities. Let us first, however, determine where this belief is encountered. I must again warn the reader against placing any great faith either in its distribution or in the actual nature of its character as given by Pater Schmidt.[8] His bias and the uncritical nature of his knowledge have often unfortunately led him to state as positive facts what are often simply his own idealized conjectures.

As far as our present actual knowledge goes, it can be said that the most typical instances of an aboriginal belief in a Supreme Deity are to be found among the simplest and among the most complex of primitive civilizations. The simple cultures may be taken to be represented by the south-eastern Australians, the Andaman Islanders, the Negritos of the Philippine Islands, and the Selknam of Tierra del Fuego; the complex cultures by the Polynesians, the major civilizations of West, East, and South Africa, and the Caddoan, the Dakota, and the Winnebago Indians of the United States. There are of course others, but most of them are suspect for one reason or another, the main reason being that they represent either secondary borrowings from other tribes or indirect influences from Christianity or Mohammedanism. In fact this may well be the case for the Winnebago. This does not make them any the less interesting or the less valid as examples of speculative thinking, but it does not give them the same importance for the history of the evolution of this concept.

The contrast in the nature of the belief as found in the two groups of tribes mentioned is perhaps not very great, but there are a number of suggestive differences. There are, for instance, no creation myths to be found among the first and, in spite of Pater Schmidt's statements to the contrary, the Supreme Being is there not credited with the creation of the world and its inhabitants, divine and human, nor are prayers addressed to him. Since, in addition, among these simpler tribes no ritual is connected with his worship and he has no direct relation to the world, the conclusion is forced upon us that we are here not dealing essentially with a religious belief at all, but with a philosophical concept. And this interpretation is further reinforced by his ethical traits, by the fact that he is always credited with being good and righteous.

Indeed it was the possession of these two ethical attributes that first struck Lang and which quite naturally Pater Schmidt has avidly seized upon. Yet these are precisely of the type of attributes which we might expect to find that the primitive thinker, groping about for some unity and coherency in an ever-changing external world, would give to a philosophically conceived supernatural being. It represents the conversion of the dynamic spirits, in whom the vast majority of the community believe, into an artificial and static synthesis, into an abstraction, always the earmark of the thinker. It is never a complete synthesis nor a pure abstraction, for, as might have been expected, in those cultures where the belief in a Supreme Being had no economic and social-political significance, in other words, in all but a very few, no real consistency could long be maintained for a conception of such a nature. We find accordingly that even Pater Schmidt finds himself in difficulties in regard to just these two attributes.

It must be remembered that such other of the attributes of a Supreme Being as omnipotence, omnipresence, immortality, and omniscience are by no means confined to him alone. They are the traits of all supernatural beings, the last three, in fact, of a selected number of human beings. One trait alone is ascribed only to the Supreme Being in these simpler cultures, namely that of being unalterably good and righteous. Yet, as I have indicated, even here consistency was impossible. So, for instance, among the Yamana of Tierra del Fuego and the Semang of the Malay Peninsula, he is called hard and cruel because he has instituted death. Pater Schmidt adds rather tamely: "This petulant reproach is at once set right for both these deities [that of the Yamana and the Semang] by the admission that they punish none but the wicked." [9] Similarly with regard to his being unalterably righteous, the same author feels it incumbent upon himself to add:

For the very reason that all evil is kept far from the Supreme Being, those people who lay especially great emphasis on his moral character oppose to him another being who is the representative of evil, who meets all his endeavours for good with protests and hindrances. We cannot properly call this dualism, for the Good Supreme Being is represented as far the stronger and more important; but the origin and continuance of the evil being is often shrouded in a dim twilight which our present knowledge does not allow us to brighten.[10]

Actually a really consistent and completely purified conception of a Supreme Deity, i.e., true monotheism, we encounter only in those few tribes where it has, as among the Polynesians and Ewe, become the special belief of a priestly group in a society based on classes, or among the Dakota, where it represents the speculation of a fraternity of priests who have been consciously selected to be the custodians of certain esoteric knowledge and esoteric rites. Monotheism, strictly speaking, is, in other words, extremely rare. What we have is monolatry, and this is essentially merely a form of polytheism. Even the monotheism we find is not the expression of a religious faith but of a philosophical drive. It would be just as legitimate to call Socrates or Seneca a monotheist. Monotheism in its strictly religious connotation implies that it is the official faith of the whole community. That is never found among primitive people.

This being clear, let us now turn to a brief consideration of both monolatry and philosophic monotheism as an expression of the speculative ability of the priest-thinker. I am selecting such instances as will bring out most clearly how the prevailing beliefs of the people at large have been reinterpreted in the interests of a larger unity.

In the religion of the Shilluk we find three well-defined elements [11]: the limited worship of a god, Juok; the cult of Nyakang and the dead kings of the Shilluk; and the cult of ancestor worship proper. Out of these distinct elements the priest-thinker has tried to develop the concept of a Supreme Being. But at best it is incomplete. On the one hand, he is spoken of as formless and invisible, both one and many, as far away and not concerned with the daily life of the people; on the other hand, he gives rain, directs the spear-thrusts, is the cause of disease, and is functionless without Nyakang. At times, indeed, we find a prayer that sounds almost like the beginning of a Hebrew psalm, for instance: "I pray to Juok, God the Giver, God the Protector; I have taken Juok to me and have become fearful to my enemies so that they scarcely dare attack me." [12] But this alternates with such a medley as the following:

We praise you, you who are God. Protect us, we are in your hands, and protect us, save me. You and Nikawng you are the ones who created, people are in your hands, and it is you, Nikawng, who are accustomed to assist God to save and it is you who give the rain. The sun is yours, and the river is yours, you who are Nikawng. You came from under the sun, you and your father, you two saved the earth, and your son Dok, you subdued all the peoples. The cow, for sacrifice, is here for you, and the blood will go to God and you. [13]

The Seligmans, quoting from unpublished information, describe his traits as even more contradictory and confusing than the above prayer indicates.

He appears to be one, and yet he seems to be a plurality as well and the native himself is puzzled. . . . He will say there is but one *Juok*, and then he will say of one who has been extremely fortunate that his juok is very good, while he speaks of another who is less fortunate as having a bad or angry juok. The foreigner is spoken of as juok, because of the marvellous things he does. He flies through the air or makes a machine that talks, so he is a juok. A badly wounded animal that is lost in the grass is juok, because it walked off dead and could not be found. . . . Juok is the creator of mankind, and the universe . . . but anything that the Shilluk cannot understand is juok.[14]

A far more consistent concept is found among the Azande, where, according to two well-qualified observers, the belief in a dominant all-pervading God exists. One of the observers, Mgr. Lagae [15], obtained the following prayer made when a native is menaced by ill-fortune:

The way in which the Azande pray is to blow water. The Zande takes water in his mouth and blows it near him and addresses it and says: "Father, as I am here, I have not stolen the goods of another; I have not taken the goods of another without recompense, I have not set my heart after the goods of another, all men are good in my eyes." And he blows water near him and says: "Mboli, it is indeed you who settles the difference between us who are men"; or such a prayer as "If Mboli does not desire it let me not die today."[16]

Contrasted with this conception of Mboli is that presented by Evans-Pritchard, according to which the Supreme Being is not the immediate judge of misdeeds, nor the one who deals out appropriate vengeance, but simply the agency that permits magic to function.

Men frightened by thunder [says Seligman, quoting Evans-Pritchard [17]] will say, "I have stolen no man's goods" and "I have not taken another man's wife," because they know that the thief or the adulterer will suffer from the effects of the blowing of a magic whistle and an accompanying utterance of spell. . . . Mboli gave magic to man, and he permits it to attain its end or he is able to frustrate it.

When Evans-Pritchard adds that the idea of the Supreme Being as presented by Mgr. Lagae has been unduly simplified, he is quite right. But he errs in ascribing this simplification to the Monsignor. It is manifestly the work of the priest-thinker.

A similar type of simplification and unification is encountered among the Winnebago Indians. In the oldest myths of this tribe, those concerned with the culture-heroes, there are two superior deities: the good spirit, Earthmaker, and the evil spirit, Hereshgunina, whose name defies analysis. Neither of them is depicted as creator or even transformer. They are simply the respective chiefs of the good and bad spirits. In the origin myth of their principal ceremony, the Medicine Dance, however, and in one of the versions of the clan origin myth of the most important clan, namely the one from which the semi-sacred chief of the tribe is selected, Earthmaker is a full-fledged creator and Supreme Being. In both instances we are dealing with esoteric accounts and in both instances we are fortunately in possession of the non-esoteric versions of the same happenings, so that we are in the enviable position of being able to trace the exact nature of the simplification, purification, and unification that have taken place. We can thus see all the stages in the transformation of the figure of Earthmaker from a mythological and religious supernatural spirit in no way concerned with the creation of the world and with powers no greater than his pendant, Hereshgunina, to a true creator and Supreme Being, who, in one myth, even creates Hereshgunina and thus solves the vexatious problem of having evil associated directly with him by removing it, at least, one step. The main characteristic of Earthmaker as a Supreme Being is his all-embracing creative activity. After a fashion, he even creates himself. Thus the account of creation begins as follows:

What it was our father sat on when he came to consciousness is uncertain. Then his tears flowed and he began to cry. Not long did he think. He saw nothing and nothing was there anywhere. He took something from the seat on which he was sitting and made a portion of our earth.

Then he sent the earth below him. From where he sat, he looked at his own creation and it became similar to our earth. However nothing grew upon it and it was entirely without a covering. It had not become quiet but was spinning around.[18]

His first problem becomes that of stopping this "spinning around" of the world, the old and hoary problem of all thinkers and philosophers, that of transforming a dynamic, ever-changing, external world into a static, immovable and eternal, internal world. Earthmaker succeeds in stopping it without becoming a mystic like his successor M. Bergson. His method is admittedly somewhat crude, but it may have implications and even a deep significance for the psychoanalysts: he scatters a female spirit over the earth, a kind of eternal feminine if you will, which in the form of rocks serves as an anchor to the universe, and it becomes quiet.

He had sent the rocks [a female spirit] clear through the earth, throughout its extent, and only the heads remained uncovered. He looked at his creation and saw that it had become quiet. No clouds appeared anywhere, the light of day seemed motionless, and the vibrations of heat looked like spider-webs going past, floating.[19]

It is only then that he begins to create the animal inhabitants of the earth. As in the biblical account man is created last. But in the Winnebago account a far truer realism and a much better perspective prevail. Precisely because man has been created last, at the end of Earthmaker's thinking, as they put it, he is the weakest, possessing no more strength than a fly, and the problem of his rescue from the beings whom Earthmaker has not created, and who are thus by implication evil, begins. It is at this point that the priest-artist who has developed this myth cleverly utilizes the old tricksters, transformers and culture-heroes, as agents sent by Earthmaker to the rescue. To one of them he says:

You are to go to the earth. As my last thought, I created the two-legged walkers and they were pitiful in every way. They are about to be exterminated and you are to rescue them.[20]

Only the last of these heroes, Hare, whom Earthmaker, in contrast to those he had sent before, created *entirely by the force of his thoughts,* succeeds. He becomes the founder of the Medicine Dance and the intermediary who is to lead its members to the presence of Earthmaker.

Of the characteristics of a true Supreme Being—creativeness, omnipotence, omniscience, omnipresence, immortality, unalterable goodness, and righteousness—the Earthmaker of the Winnebago possesses only the first five. But omniscience, omnipresence, and immortality he shares with other supernatural beings, and omnipotence he can hardly be said to possess. As far as unalterable goodness and righteousness are concerned, there is no trace of them. Both attributes play a great role in Winnebago ethical theory but they have nothing to do with a Supreme Being. In the Medicine Dance, which is Earthmaker's ceremony *par excellence,* goodness and righteousness are acquired by adherence to the precepts of the ceremony.*

The one specific attribute associated with Earthmaker is creativeness, and this is a theme which, it can legitimately be contended, is much older than any clearcut belief in a Supreme Being. It is part and parcel of the priest-thinker's attempt to solve problems that interested and fascinated him. Some of the Winnebago thinkers pushed this theme of creation still further back and represented Earthmaker as lying in space unborn, first moving one limb and then another, then his head, and finally opening his eyes. Only then is he born, a fact signified by his weeping just as does a new-born child.

For a really complete, in fact an almost redundant, example of such a hypothetical history of the earth, the cosmos, consciousness, and even unconsciousness, we must, however, turn to other tribes.

---

* Cf. pp. 166 ff.

Let me select two: the Uitoto of Colombia, South America, and the Maori of New Zealand.

Among the Uitoto the creation legend runs thus:

In the beginning there was nothing but mere appearance, nothing really existed. It was but a phantasm, an illusion that our father touched; something mysterious it was that he grasped. Nothing existed. Through the agency of a dream, our father, He-Who-Is-Appearance-Only, Nainema, pressed the phantasm to his breast and then was sunk in thought. Not even a tree existed that might have supported this phantasm, and only through his breath did Nainema hold this illusion attached to the thread of a dream. He tried to discover what was at the bottom of it, but he found nothing. "I have attached that which was non-existent," he said. . . . Then our father . . . tied the emptiness to the dream-thread and pressed the magical glue-substance upon it. Thus by means of his dream did he hold it like the fluff of raw cotton. He seized the bottom of the phantasm and stamped upon it repeatedly, allowing himself to rest upon the earth of which he had dreamt.[21]

Assuredly this is a creation *ex nihilo.*

Among the Maori this evolutionary process is pushed one step still farther back. If it was a creation *ex nihilo* in the case of the Uitoto, here we should have to call it a creation *ex nihilissimo.* Four stages can be distinguished; first, the development of physical and psychical differentiation and of personal consciousness; second, the development of the external world; third, what might be called the genealogical history of matter; and, lastly, the appearance of the heavenly bodies and of light. Into this creation legend the figure of the Supreme Being, Io, was then fitted. According to one poem-legend:

Io dwelt within the breathing-space of immensity.
The universe was in darkness, with water everywhere.
There was no glimmer of dawn, no clearness, no light.
And he began by saying these words,

That he might cease remaining inactive.
"Darkness, become a light-possessing darkness."
"Light, become a darkness-possessing light." [22]

The concept of Io, we know, became further elaborated at the hands of the priests selected from the highest class of Maori nobles. He became the cosmic deity who gave unity to the universe of unrelated monads, the creator of the world who has retained to himself the three abiding entities—the spirit, the life, and the form. Everything proceeds from him and everything is gathered in his presence. All things are subservient to him. Nothing is outside of him and nothing beyond him, neither life, death, nor divinity. Obedience to his commands is life, disobedience death; and death means only one thing, the preordained termination which Io has given to all things that exist. The great and all-embracing ethical principle that flows from this concept and which is expressed by one of Io's epithets, He-in-Whose-Presence-All-Things-Are-Combined, is that everything must have a function by which it fulfils itself. [23]

This is the highest form that abstract thinking assumed among any aboriginal peoples. To some scholars it seems inconceivable that any aboriginal thinkers could have attained to it unaided and they seek for Hindu and Greek connexions. But there is really no necessity for making this search. The social and economic structure of Polynesian society can explain it adequately.

In the examples given above we are not dealing with religion at all but with philosophical speculation. These Supreme Beings are not meant to be worshipped. When they are, then we see them transformed almost immediately into the highest gods of a polytheistic pantheon and they lose much of their abstract character as well as those traits that set them off as Supreme Beings. The reasons for this phenomenon are simple enough. There was no need for such a concept. Nothing in the social, economic, and political structure of even the most complicated of primitive civilizations demanded it. It remained consequently the possession of a few priest-thinkers and could not be utilized. The moment it left the protecting atmosphere of its creators it became something else, something utterly different. The priest-thinkers, with that intellectual arrogance which their later colleagues have inherited, seem to have sensed this and to have looked with commiserating contempt upon their less intellectual fellowmen who vitalized their idealistic and static construct but who destroyed its abstract qualities in the process.

13

The Soul: Its Nature and Destination

IN the preceding chapters, it may have been remarked, we have attempted to describe the different religions of primitive peoples and their evolution without reference to the conceptions of the soul found among them. Yet it is a well-known fact that for most historians of religion the soul is the basic ingredient of religion. To the founder of modern anthropology, E. B. Tylor, the conception of the soul was, as he expressly states, "the very *fons et origo* of the conceptions of spirit and deity in general." [1] Practically everyone has followed in Tylor's footsteps. A. E. Crawley, who has written a suggestive work on the subject, insists that we owe to it the idea of "an order of spiritual beings and of a spiritual world existing now and hereafter" [2] and quotes the Dutch Sinologist, de Groot, to the effect that the human soul is the original form of all beings of a higher order.

Yet it seems to me extremely doubtful whether supernatural beings in their original form had much to do with the conception of the soul. Many aspects of religion can definitely not be explained in terms of it. Indeed, by reason of its very universality and permanence, by reason of the creative power and morphological influence which it possessed and which Crawley so very rightly stresses, it clearly belongs not to the religious sphere proper but to the evolution of the human mind in general. This too Crawley seems to have recognized. But when he proceeds and states that "Both in the race and in the individual we shall find it to be the first purely intellectual result of human reaction to environment . . . our first effort toward an explanation of things," [3] we enter the realm of those somewhat futile evolutionary-sociological generalizations that have vitiated so many treatments of primitive religion.

Our purpose here is not primarily to inquire into the origin of the idea of the soul or to discuss the many forms this conception has assumed, but to indicate what the priest-thinker has done with certain of its constituent elements. We shall accordingly have to omit much of what customarily fills the pages of the voluminous works on the subject. To these I must refer the reader who wishes more detailed information.[4] Many of these data have been conveniently summarized in Crawley's book and above all in Frazer's well-known work, *The Golden Bough*.[5]

In so vast a subject I can naturally touch on only a few problems. I propose to begin with the one invariable attribute in all conceptions of the soul both among ourselves and among primitive peoples, the belief in its immortality. It seems to be one of the few beliefs which are the common possession of all individuals, of the ordinary man as well as of the medicine-man. It is not surprising therefore that, in the search for the origin of such unanimity, psychological explanations should have been preferred.[6] For Crawley the germ of the belief in the immortality of the soul lies in the fact that it exists in the brains of others.

A man dies, but his image remains. The fact of death does not necessarily alter the character of the memory-image. . . . The permanence of the soul depends on the length of the memory of the survivors, or the affection the man inspired, or the strength of his personality.[7]

For Lévy-Bruhl an individual is himself only because his ancestors inhabit his body, that is, he is simply an episode in an indefinite series of events.

By the effect of this symbiosis of the living and the dead, that is both mystical and concrete at the same time, an individual is his specific self thanks only to those ancestors who have survived in his person.[8]

The psychoanalysts make the same assumption. Róheim, with his hypothesis that all supernatural ideas are simply symbolic representations of biological facts, feels that mankind could have derived the idea of the immortality of the individual or, at least, the duration of the species, only from the power of the propagation which ensures it.[9] Lévy-Bruhl's interpretation represents, in a way, the socialization of the biological fact and he is thus almost at one with the psychoanalysts.

There is, however, no need for having recourse to any such explanations. They arise, it seems to me, from the failure to recognize certain differentiations, economic-social and temperamental, that have existed in societies from the very beginning of time. It is all very well for Lévy-Bruhl to insist that we must not introduce into primitive cultures problems which they have never posed.[10] But why, it may be asked, does he not recognize the distinctions that they have made? Had he and all the other theorists who speak so glibly about the conception of the soul among primitive peoples stopped for one moment to consider the nature of these differentiations, a more correct understanding of their cultures would have been obtained and fewer books written on the subject.

Now what did the idea of immortality mean to the ordinary matter-of-fact individual in a simple primitive community? It signified simply imperishability, the recognition of an endless change, with no necessary implication that this persistence be progressive; it meant the sense of a dynamic indeterminism in a world of objects possessing an infinite capacity for transformation. In this notion there was no beginning and no end, not, however, because, as Lévy-Bruhl contends, "The fate of the individual in the world beyond gave him no inquietude and he had little to say about it," [11] but precisely for the contrary reason, because his type of thinking did not permit of the admission that there was a stoppage or that there was either a beginning or an end. The belief in some form of reincarnation, universally present in all the simple food-gathering and fishing-hunting civilizations, can in part be taken as the socialized stabilization of this attitude.

This is not as strange as it may seem at first glance, for it is implied in the very nature of all thinking which is prevailingly subjectivistic. That of the matter-of-fact man in simple societies was obsessively so. No better demonstration of this tyranny of thought can well be found than is contained in the various descriptions of the nature of the soul, its appearance, its vicissitudes, and its destination. Here Lévy-Bruhl's criticism of Tylor and his school is quite pertinent and his caution is to the point: "We must not try to rediscover in the 'representations' of the primitives our distinction between the soul and the body." [12] But when he continues and insists that the soul is "neither purely material nor purely spiritual" but that it is both, "at the same time, one and the other," and that it is so because "its presence acts as a mystical property," [13] he is falling into an error of interpretation equally reprehensible. Fundamentally, it would seem, Lévy-Bruhl has always remained a closet philosopher and a positivist and this perhaps explains his dogmatic imperviousness to criticism. Had he been more amenable to such criticism he could have transformed his strikingly suggestive book *Les Fonctions mentales dans les sociétés inférieures* into one of the landmarks of anthropology.

Thus we have come again to one of the fundamental problems posed in our book: how was the subjectivistic obsession of early thought to be transformed into a realistic understanding of man and the universe around him and to whom shall we ascribe this transformation? In the light of what I have said in previous chapters the reader can answer this question for himself.

The thinker-priest was, as usual, faced with the task of co-ordinating and unifying the disparate and often contradictory beliefs and practices of his folkloristic background. How difficult such an endeavour was in the case of the concept or concepts of the soul need not be told. As far as the idea of imperishability of the soul is concerned, this was perhaps easiest. The steps were given. Imperishability had to be made more concrete and it had to become the realization that a given specific and individualized consciousness was eternal. This was, for instance, expressed first in the doctrine of reincarnation and secondly in ancestor worship. But this still is not immortality in the religious sense; it is simply persistence. Immortality of necessity implies a division into those who do not die and those who do, a belief that to some things there is a termination, whereas to others there is not. Who introduced this notion? Manifestly the priest-thinker. The concept of a beginning and of an end is after all the necessary condition for all objective thinking.

It is only when this consciousness of an indeterminate series of successive events which is so characteristic of the thinking of the matter-of-fact man has been broken up, that a true concept of immortality can emerge. No such concept can mean anything unless it is contrasted with its opposite, extinction. The primary function of the priest-thinker at this period in the evolution of the mind was consequently to devise a formula for separating what was mortal from what was immortal. He did not have to call attention to the fact that apparent stoppages and cessations existed. This was self-evident. What he did have to do, however, was to emphasize and magnify these stoppages and cessations so that the moment of death could constitute, for human beings as for animals and plants, the visible and concrete criterion by which one set of beings, the organic, was opposed to another set where organic processes were not so much unknown as that they were not applicable. But here the thinker's analysis conflicted sharply with the folkloristic concept of indeterminateness and imperishability, a concept which was rooted in the subjectivistic obsession of early thought and which, to a certain extent, the thinker too must have shared. The final synthesis that resulted was a "compromise." The thinker and medicine-man as thinker predicated beginnings and endings; as a participant in a specific environment, however, he continued to postulate the eternal persistence of one part of the personality, that which corresponds roughly to our concept of the soul.

We are not, however, so much concerned here with the actual

nature of the concept of the soul held, as with the theory of its persistence. Yet we cannot understand this unless we inquire into the theories advanced concerning where, originally, the soul was supposed to have come from, the extent to which it was independent of the body, and its fate after it had left the body.

There is no question but that in those primitive societies of which we have any record, all individuals understood quite definitely the difference between a living person and his corpse, just as it is also clear that they did not believe that all of a man's personality, i.e., everything which characterized him as a living being, disappeared upon death. His body, after all, still remained and, though it decayed, some parts persisted, apparently for ever. Here there was thus visible testimony of its imperishability and, with it, of man's. Yet there was also the undoubted fact that as a living being he was non-existent except in so far as either his memory remained fresh in the minds of his contemporaries or in so far as he appeared to them in dreams and visions or, finally, in so far, of course, as he was considered present in the persons of his children and his descendants.

Two interpretations for this continued "presence" seemed possible. According to the one, two constituents were involved, a body and something which gave life to the body; according to the other, there was really only a single such constituent, although this one could assume multiple forms, of which the two basic were the body proper and that which animated it. The first was roughly speaking a form of dualism, the second a kind of undifferentiated monism. Both interpretations posited imperishability; but the one posited it only for the animating principle, the other for both. I am of the opinion that the second was the earlier "theory" and that it represented the thought of the everyday man, while the first represented that of the shaman-thinker, although I do not wish to press this distinction too far.

Superficially we seem here to be close to Lévy-Bruhl's well-known concept of *participation mystique*. Yet let me say at once that, although both the interpretations given above are often held by one and the same person, he does not confuse any more than he fuses them. I should say that Lévy-Bruhl does both.

Now although it is true that we must not insist too definitely upon the idea that this "dualism" is exclusively the attitude of the thinker while the initial "monism" is that of the matter-of-fact everyday man, yet it was the former who clearly made this contrast of body and life-principle increasingly sharper. We may confidently assert that it was the thinker-priest who developed the theory that the body perished but that the animating principle persisted. As we have stated above, however, the complete disappearance of the body ran counter to the clear testimony of the senses, and apparently the group as such consequently never completely accepted it. This refusal to accept it may be seen in the almost universal presence of the belief in reincarnation, especially among the non-agricultural civilizations, and the development in the agricultural societies of ancestor worship. Yet the victory was eventually to rest with the priest-thinker, for he so interpreted this reincarnation that it became the reward for a certain type of behaviour while alive, a type of behaviour, however, that was definitely linked with his own activities. What it really signified then was that, in the main, only the priest-thinker, or those individuals who participated in ceremonies over which he had fairly complete control, could become reincarnated. And this was closely bound up with the belief that only a few individuals possessed the power to transform themselves at will into animals, a trait ordinarily associated with supernatural beings only.

The shaman-priest's viewpoint is beautifully illustrated among the Winnebago. There a theory prevailed according to which all Winnebago were originally neutral beings, able at any time to assume either human or animal-plant shape. At an early period in their history, however, they all decided to use up the power they possessed in order to transform themselves permanently either into one or the other, into human beings or into animals; all but a few, who retained this ability. They are the shamans and medicine-men. In the same tribe we also find that all those who adhered strictly to the teaching of the Medicine Dance Lodge could become reincarnated. A successful adherence to this teaching, however, depended upon certain definite factors and upon conditions which only the shamans and the medicine-men could fulfil.

The priest-thinker's dualistic theory thus meant that, although the body perished, a distinction was to be drawn between the body of the priest and that of the ordinary man, in the sense, at least, that, for the priest-thinker, the two constituents, the body and the life-giving agency, were always more or less interchangeable. In the case of the ordinary man, however, the two were to be definitely contrasted. In the one instance we are dealing with a *tertium quid* which has assumed two forms, in the other with two distinct and separable elements. The insistence upon this double nature of man, as in part perishable, in part not, brought to the front the whole question of where the imperishable part had come from, what it represented, and what happened to it when the body died. The particular origin of the perishable part, the body, man understood clearly. This was re-enacted before his eyes whenever a human being or animal was born. The origin of the imperishable part and its precise nature were, however, questions the ordinary man did not understand and in which he manifested little interest. They were, on the contrary, of prime interest to the priest-thinker, not only because, as a thinker, he was impelled to deal with them but because the answer to them involved the whole nature of his authority. We are here on the very brink of all the problems connected with the concept of the *mana* or magical power. Space again forbids an adequate discussion and I must therefore refer the reader to what has been said about this concept in the preceding pages * and to the relevant literature.

The manner in which the shaman-thinker answered the first question is definitely connected with what we have already learned about him in the accounts of his initiation.† A reference to these

---

* Cf. pp. 12–13.
† Cf. Chapter 6, especially pp. 111–131.

accounts will show that the spirits who possessed him had no organic substantiality and yet they had existence. Since the same characteristics as held for the life-giving agency also held for the spirits, they could be equated. This left two lines of speculation open. Either this life-giving agency or soul, as we may provisionally call it, had coexisted with the spirits from the very beginning of time or, on the other hand, the spirit itself or some emanation from it had taken residence in man. The first line of reasoning can be regarded as the thinker's formulation of the oldest and most fundamental of the folkloristic beliefs with regard to the nature of the soul. Many ethnological theorists, we know, regard the belief in the soul not as coextensive in time with that in supernatural beings but as antecedent to it, indeed, as antecedent to the source of all concepts of the spirits. Yet both these interpretations, it seems to me, represent a complete misunderstanding of the facts. The concept of the soul takes on its specific "spiritual" physiognomy from that of the supernatural beings, and not the contrary, just as it takes on its specific form from human beings and the organic world around man and just as the supernatural beings, in turn, are given definite outline by their resemblances to or their difference from man.

The second line of reasoning represents the priest-thinker's contribution *par excellence*. It lies at the base of all metaphysical inquiries into the nature of man, civilized and primitive. To imagine, however, that the tremendous interest which certain minds have manifested in it is to be ascribed exclusively, or even largely, to intellectual curiosity or to early attempts at solving the riddle of the universe and of man, more specifically, this, it seems to me, is to disregard the basic fact that it forms part of the shaman's and priest's certificate of authority, an authority to be understood here in a specific economic-social sense. It is this which lies at the root of his persistent interest even if we must be willing to admit that a thinker would naturally be attracted to such problems. Wherever the shamans, medicine-men, and priests play a determining role, we find this second type of speculation prominently developed. A few examples will illustrate it.

Among the Dakota Indians we are told that, according to the esoteric doctrine of the priests, Wakan tanka, the Supreme Being, gives man at birth a *sicun*. *Sicun* is defined as the divine essence of a deity. Let me quote what J. Walker, our principal authority, has to say about it:

The *sicun* is an immaterial God whose substance is never visible. It is the potency of mankind and the emitted potency of the Gods. Considered relative to mankind it is many, but apart from mankind it is one. Skan [the supreme deity] imparts a *sicun* to each of mankind at birth. It remains with the person until death when it returns whence it came. Its functions are to enable the possessor to do those things which the beasts cannot do and to give courage and fortitude. It may be pleased or displeased with its possessor and may be operative or inoperative according to its pleasure. It may be invoked by ceremony or prayer, but it cannot be imparted to any other person or thing. Most of the Gods can emit their potencies and when so emitted their potencies become *sicunpi*. Such a *sicun* can be imparted to material things by a proper ceremony correctly performed by a shaman.[14]

We find the same theory among the Maori and the Batak. In the first tribe every sentient being is believed to possess what they call *toiora*, i.e., the soul of God, that is, of Io, and among the Batak the *tondi* is supposed to be an individualized piece of the soul-substance existing in the universe and of which everything partakes. The concept of the *tondi* is exceedingly interesting. It is supposed to reside in all the parts of the human body and to manifest itself, in addition, in numerous other ways. It first of all becomes materialized in the human shadow; second, in a man's name; third, in the splendour that shines in the face of a happy man; and, fourth, in the personal power he exercises over others.[15]

At times a true pantheism is achieved. Thus among the Winnebago an Indian developed the following theory:

I prayed to Earthmaker [God]. And as I prayed I was aware of something above me and there He was! That which is called the soul, that it is, that is what one calls Earthmaker. Now this is what I felt and saw. All of us sitting together there, we had all together one spirit and I was their spirit or soul. I did not have to speak to them and get an answer to know what had been their thoughts. Then I thought of a certain place far away and immediately I was there; I was my thought. I would not need any more food, for was I not my spirit? Nor would I have any more use for my body. My corporeal affairs are over.[16]

Although the above occurs in connexion with a ceremony that is a mixture of Indian and Christian beliefs its validity as an example of native-religious philosophical speculation is not thereby seriously affected.

The thinker's viewpoint is likewise reflected in many of the myths concerning the origin of man, especially those where man is depicted as having sprung from a divine and a human ancestor. In a well-known Maori account, the god Tane is represented as asking his elder brother how they were to raise up descendants for themselves. It was at first suggested that Tane mate with the divine messengers called Apas. But, as one of the gods pointed out, this would make the descendants gods like themselves. Finally it was agreed that only a female newly created from virgin earth would serve the purpose. In other words matter could not be derived from spirit. "Try the earth at Kurawaka," Tane was told, "and commence your operations [of creation] there for in that place is the female in a state of virginity and potentiality; she is sacred for she contains the likeness of man." [17] When the figure was complete Tane mated with her and from this union man originated. It is this divine spark that is thought to be embodied in the soul.

Such examples, and many more could be cited, definitely reinforce the supposition advanced before that those theorists who think of the idea of gods as having developed out of that of the soul are in error. Either the concept of the soul must be regarded as flowing from that of a deity or at best both concepts are to be regarded as having been coexistent and independent from the beginning. The whole subject has, however, been obscured by so many untoward factors that an intelligible discussion is wellnigh impossible today. Part of the lamentable condition of our data is due to the fact that primitive civilizations were first intelligently described only after the cultures had already begun to decay. In part it can be ascribed, however, to the uncritical manner in which ethnologists have thrown together the theories and beliefs of the thinker with the beliefs and concepts of the ordinary man. Much of the confusion in customary discussions on the nature of the soul, for instance, can be attributed to the lack of realization on the part of the theorists that the folkloristic conception of the soul is one thing, the priest-thinker's another; that both viewpoints are hopelessly intertwined at times; and that, finally, the descriptions which we can, with any degree of assurance, ascribe to the priest-thinkers are often specifically conditioned by economic-social considerations, such as, for instance, the validation and the justification of their authority, the maintenance of their rights and their privileges, and the justification of their desire for prestige. The failure to consider the economic-social side of the problem and its treatment as exclusively an intellectual phenomenon have deprived much of the voluminous literature on the subject of most of its validity. This may seem a harsh judgment, yet it is not made in any spirit of hypercriticism. It is unfortunately true. It remains a tragic reality that a large part of the data so conscientiously gathered together by investigators can be used only with the greatest of caution and that the opportunity for improving the record is irrevocably gone.

I cannot better express the nature of all the confusion that exists on the concept and meaning of the soul than by quoting Crawley's statement of what he thinks it is not and the strictly intellectualistic solution he suggests in order to integrate the various traits and qualities which it is supposed to have. Says Crawley [18] :

Thus the soul is neither a phantom or skeleton outline, nor a second self or double. The origin of these two extremes of which the soul is the mean will concern us later on. The soul, again, is not an illusion—it is not mistaken for the reality; it is not the shadow—it has three-dimensional volume, form, features, colour; it is not a ghost or wraith. When inanimate objects are in question their souls are not animated. It is not a part of or secretion from the organism, such as breath or blood. Lastly, it is not an abstract "force" or "principle," such as "life" or "breath of life"; nor a concept, such as "reason" or "conscience." It is the ideal totality including more or less of the attributes of the reality. Spiritual existence is mental existence; the world of spirits is the mental world. Everything that can through perception lay the foundation of a memory-image can claim the possession of a soul, an existence in the spiritual world here and hereafter. And this world is, in the incomplete and long-suffering term, the supernatural.

We have now come to that part of the doctrine of the soul which seems to have occupied the attention of primitive man most consistently. Where did the soul go when it left the body and how did it reach its new abode? For no aspect of our subject are the answers of the priest-thinker and the everyday man more clearly contrasted than here. In general it can be said that, while the priest-thinker necessarily included in his answer much of the folkloristic background clustering around the beliefs as to the destination of the soul after death, the answers of the everyday man never included much that was specifically his own.

In the necessarily brief summary which we shall now attempt, only the theory of the priest-thinker will be dealt with, not only because his is coherent and clearly articulated but because, by and large, the ordinary man tried to accept it and restate it. I will illustrate my remarks mainly from examples taken from Oceania and North America, the areas from which most of our best information comes.

It is impossible to discuss this journey of the soul apart from the rites and activities connected with death, for the soul is not regarded as becoming a truly independent entity immediately after death. Only after it has become, so to speak, formally dismissed from the living does it become one. Miss Moss has given a convenient summary of the subject for Oceania and, since her discussion holds in large measure for all primitive peoples, particularly her division of this journey into three stages, I shall employ it.[19] According to her the three stages are: first, the temporary sojourn on earth, near the body, before the final departure rites; second, the final departure rites and the formal dismissal; and, third, the journey itself. Much of the detail in all three belongs to the folkloristic background as such and cannot be discussed here. What can be rightly regarded as the contribution of the priest-thinkers, however, is the use to which these details are put, their arrangement and their interpretation. We shall confine our remarks only to that portion of the journey of the soul which begins after its formal and ritual dismissal.

Every reader knows the accounts that have been given of this type of journey. It is generally depicted as of the most arduous kind imaginable. Impenetrable forests have to be traversed, difficult mountains climbed, swinging and dangerous bridges crossed, monsters and unfriendly inhabitants placated or defeated. In short, it is represented as an ordeal of the most trying type.

There is a magnificent description of this inhospitable realm, where there is neither light nor windows, from Aztec sources. This dreadful experience was not imposed on all the Aztecs, but reserved for the souls of those who had died of disease, and for the poorer classes. The first obstacles encountered were two mountains that clashed together and threatened to crush the unwary ghost. Hardly escaped from this peril, the ghost found himself confronted by a huge snake with an enormous and hideous maw and then by a colossal and terror-inspiring crocodile. Eight deserts and eight hills had then to be crossed, and still there was no relief. Here a new affliction assailed the soul, in the shape of a wind consisting of sharp flint knives. Finally the soul arrived at the shores of the river called the Nine-Waters, which had to be crossed on the back of a red-coloured dog who must subsequently be killed in a prescribed manner, by thrusting an arrow down its throat.

The ultimate significance of so representing what might be called the "corporeal" activity of man as contrasted with his "non-corporeal" life, need not be touched on here. It has always been the welcome and happy hunting ground for mystics of all ages and all races, from primitive times to the psychoanalysts. It has not infrequently enabled tired intellectuals to spend the evening of their life in tragic solace and in romantic expiation for the sin of having attempted to think logically and realistically in their more robust years.

The journey of the soul has almost universally been regarded as a test of admission to the afterworld. Irrespective of whether a belief in reincarnation existed, an absence from this world of some duration was always postulated, and this temporary abode had to be properly visualized. The elaborate descriptions which the afterworld has received need not be attributed to any desire on the part of mankind to ease the sorrow an individual felt at leaving the world or as a method he had devised for placating the anger of the dead but, paradoxically enough, it may be most fruitfully explained as due to the prevalence of the belief that the dead man was not leaving the world permanently. Under such circumstances it was only natural for the survivors to manifest an intense interest in the furnishings of the new home, especially since the living realized that they too would, some day, be asked to dwell therein. And because the difficulties besetting the path were so numerous and so exhausting it was only natural that this home should frequently have been thought of as a haven of rest.

We all know, of course, that the horrors, the pain, and the ordeals of the spiritual road have in many of the historic religions been interpreted as a punishment for earthly transgressions and that the beatific character of the new home has been regarded as a reward for those who have led an upright life on earth. Of such conceptions we must completely divest ourselves if we wish to understand both the meaning of the home of the dead and the journey thereto, among primitive peoples. It would be far more reasonable to interpret the difficulties encountered on the road not in reference to the admission to the afterworld but in reference to the readmission into this one. On such a view punishment and reward in the afterworld are really of no consequence. The only thing of consequence is whether a man is expected to find some respite from the ills and uncertainties of life there and what his status is to be. It is at this point that we discover the clearest evidence that most of the accounts of the spirit-home and of the journey to it are the work of the priest-thinker, for in them no attempt is made to depict either the status of the ordinary man or his prestige as being improved in the land of the dead. It is only reasonable to assume that, where we are dealing so largely with an articulated wish-fulfilment dream as in these myths, had they represented the viewpoint of the ordinary man, they would have vouchsafed him more than simply rest in a perfect climate, and economic security. One might have expected an improvement in status as well. As it is, the struggles and the uncertainties of the spirit-road are depicted as the continuation of those of his mundane existence because the goal sought is clearly the earthly one—security and rest for those who have had little of either in this world and the maintenance of their privileges and power for those who had possessed both in life. But let us now turn to some of these ordeals and qualifications.

The ordeals described most frequently include, among other things, the crossing of a bridge, the presence of guardians stationed at some place or other along the path, and, lastly, the meeting with the ghosts who are the inhabitants proper of this realm. The bridge symbolizes generally that the break between life and death is irrevocable. The ability to cross it depends upon a number of circumstances. In Indonesia, for instance, an ethical qualification is essential. But this ethical qualification, this "goodness," as Moss points out, "may mean anything from the manner of death or the possession of high rank, to liberality on the part of the dead man or his friends." [20] Among the Winnebago, on the other hand, it depends upon the "ethical" behaviour of the warriors who are participating at the death-wake. If in recounting their war exploits, they exaggerate or tell an untruth, the soul of the man in whose honour the death-wake is being given falls off the bridge. Small infants, on the other hand, are unable to cross safely because they cannot hold on to the very slippery boards. This sounds almost like some faint adumbration of the later doctrine of infant damnation. In both instances, this failure to cross apparently entails, as a consequence, the inability of this particular individual ever to become reincarnated.

The figure of a guardian or guardians appears in practically every part of the world. In Indonesia there seem to be four varieties: the monster who frightens; the judge who decides the lot of ghosts in the spiritland; the doorkeeper who can be propitiated or deceived; and, lastly, the questioner who requires certain qualifications to be fulfilled before he permits souls to enter. Moss is probably quite right when she says that two different sources are involved in this fourfold differentiation: the monster-doorkeeper and the headman of the spiritland, one simply a folkloristic belief, the other the reflection of a human situation. Both became secondarily reinterpreted. From the bogy there evolved gradually the conception of a porter or guardian, who has to be propitiated or to ask questions of those who wish to pass; and from the second there emerged the concept of a true ruler of the dead, who allots to each individual his appropriate place and who becomes a guide pointing out the path, a judge who examines and passes on the credentials of each new arrival. In no case is he supposed to be a real supernatural being and never a deity. Among those peoples who have developed the concept that the supernatural spirits or deities inhabit the world to which the souls of the dead go, the examination is made long before the soul reaches them and it is rarely at their instigation. In other words it is not a deity who judges but, expressed very generally, a series of experiences and happenings that have mundane references exclusively.

It seems to be one of the delightful ironies in the history of primitive religion that where, in the simple cultures, moral qualifications are demanded for the successful passage of the soul and this in turn is linked with a deity or deities, these deities are largely, if not exclusively, philosophical constructs with little influence on the world, and that where, on the contrary, the deities acquire real significance and true rituals are developed around them, no theory of rewards and punishments seems to prevail. The explanation for this apparent paradox is clear enough. Ethical evaluations belong properly to a philosophical interpretation and are lost or twisted beyond recognition when the attempt is made to introduce them into functioning religions. We know what their fate has been in the complex historical religions even when they were dogmas imposed from above, and we should not be surprised therefore at their almost complete absence in the simpler religions except as secondary interpretations of the priest-thinker.

The soul's qualifications for admission to the spiritland are, we have seen, rarely, if ever, moral. They are based entirely on social-economic evaluations, on the manner of death and on such considerations as the performance of the proper rites. A man must have a specific status to enter these spiritual homes. Strangers, for instance, are not admitted. The soul must be recognized, literally so, for frequently the tribal marks or clan paintings must be presented to the examining judge. Where a rigid caste distinction exists, as in Polynesia, only men of high rank and a few specially favoured commoners can enter. Commoners are in fact not regarded as possessing souls. Where wealth is synonymous with rank, a lavish display of gifts at the death-feasts is required. In New Britain, for example, the reception of the soul in the afterworld depends upon the display of what is termed the "*tambu-money*" of the deceased, which is subsequently distributed among the relatives. Drums are beaten to denote the arrival of a rich man; the souls of the poor men remain in the bush.

When "goodness" is defined as a qualification, it always refers either to liberality in the distribution of wealth, to proper funeral rites, to status, or to the manner of death. The failure of Pater Schmidt and his followers to examine the meaning of what constitutes goodness has vitiated all their discussion of primitive ethics. "Goodness," says Turner [21] in his work on Samoa, "meant one whose friends had given a grand funeral feast and badness a person whose stingy friends provided nothing at all."

However, we could go on indefinitely. What we have said will give the reader an idea of the stuff the soul is made of and the two essentially contrasting interpretations to which its nature and fate are subjected. To emphasize this contrast even better let me quote the pendant to the Winnebago myth on pages 166–168. Whereas, in the former, the ethical-mystical evaluation predominates and illuminates the whole with an almost Early Christian intensity, in the latter we have a picture of a disembodied ego going forth to seek adventures. And as adventures in the spirit of a culture-hero they seem to be visualized, even if they are set ones and even if the outcome is known beforehand. The myth in question is contained in the official speech addressed to the spirit of the departed as he is about to start on his journey [22]:

I suppose you are not far away, that indeed you are right behind me. Here is the tobacco and here is the pipe which you must keep in front of you as you go along. Here also are the fire and the food which your relatives have prepared for your journey.

In the morning when the sun rises you are to start. You will not have gone very far before you come to a wide road. That is the road you must take. As you go along you will notice something on your road. Take your war club and strike it and throw it behind you. Then go on without looking back. As you go farther you will again come across some obstacle. Strike it and throw it behind you and do not look back. Farther on you will come across some animals, and these also you must strike and throw behind you. Then go on and do not look back. The objects you throw behind you will come to those relatives whom you have left behind you on earth. They will represent victory in war, riches, and animals for food.

When you have gone but a short distance from the last place where you threw the objects behind, you will come to a round lodge and there you will find an old woman. She is the one who is to give you further information. She will ask you, "Grandson, what is your name?" This you must tell her. Then you must say, "Grandmother, when I was about to start from the earth I was given the following objects with which I was to act as mediator between you and the human beings [i.e., the pipe, tobacco, and food]." Then you must put the stem of the pipe in the old woman's mouth and say, "Grandmother, I have made all my relatives lonesome, my parents, my brothers, and all the others. I would therefore like to have them obtain victory in war, and honours. That was my desire as I left them downhearted upon the earth. I would that they could have all that life which I left behind me on earth. This is what they asked. This, likewise, they asked me, that they should not have to travel on this road for some time to come. They also asked to be blessed with those things that people are accustomed to have on earth. All this they wanted me to ask of you when I started from the earth. They told me to follow the four steps that would be imprinted with blue marks, grandmother." "Well, grandson, you are young but you are wise. It is good. I will now boil some food for you."

Thus she will speak to you and then put a kettle on the fire and boil some rice for you. If you eat it you will have a headache. Then she will say, "Grandson, you have a headache, let me cup it for you." Then she will break open your skull and take out your brains and you will forget all about your people on earth and where you came from. You will not worry about your relatives. You will become like a holy spirit. Your thoughts will not go as far as the earth, as there will be nothing carnal about you.

Now the rice that the old woman will boil will really be lice. For that reason you will be finished with everything evil. Then you will go on stepping in the four footsteps mentioned before and that were imprinted with blue earth. You are to take the four steps because the road will fork there. All your relatives who died before you will be there. As you journey on you will come to a fire running across the earth from one end to the other. There will be a bridge across it but it will be difficult to cross because it is continually swinging. However, you will be able to cross it safely, for you have all the guides about whom the warriors spoke to you. They will take you over and take care of you.

Well, we have told you a good road to take. If anyone tells a falsehood in speaking of the spirit-road, you will fall off the bridge and be burned. However you need not worry for you will pass over safely. As you proceed from that place the spirits will come to meet you and take you to the village where the chief lives. There you will give him the tobacco and ask for those objects of which we spoke to you, the same you asked of the old woman. There you will meet all the relatives that died before you. They will be living in a large lodge. This you must enter.

14

The Ritual Drama

OF all the elaborations and syntheses of the priest-thinker those in which his creative energy is most apparent are the ritual dramas of the more advanced primitive civilizations. These must be specifically distinguished from certain tribal performances such as initiation rites or the often intricate ceremonies connected with birth and death as well as those connected with some of the major social-economic activities. In the broadest sense of the term, of course, these too are dramas, for they contain elements that are, at least in part, re-enactments of deeds ascribed to some mythical character or characters. Where to draw the line between such rituals and what I am calling the ritual drama is not simple nor always satisfactory. In the main, however, it would seem best to restrict the term drama, first, to the performance of a ritual belonging to a clearly defined non-public organization, in other words, to some society or club whose membership is restricted; and, secondly, to such rituals as are theoretically supposed to be re-enactments of a particular series of events generally embodied in a myth or myth-poem and in which specific individuals or groups definitely impersonate the original actors.

It has frequently been contended, quite justifiably, that a given ceremony bears no genetic relation to the origin myth ostensibly meant to explain it and that, in related tribes, the same ceremony may have a different myth to account for its origin. But this fact, which militates so strongly against the utilization of such myths for purposes of historical reconstruction, constitutes the very best evidence we possess for contending that they are true dramas, in the sense that they represent the subordination of a ritual to a secondary purpose, that being its periodic performance as a play with a specific plot and definite *dramatis personae*. A fairly large number of such dramas exist, but since the rituals with which they are so intimately intertwined are, after all, vital and functioning social ceremonial units, a disturbing element is introduced which shows itself in certain developments. Either such dramas become broken up and, in consequence, fluctuate between real ritual plays and what may be called ritual pageants and processions or the whole ceremonial becomes secondarily utilized for specific and essentially lay purposes. Both types are encountered wherever ritual dramas exist in any form whatsoever. The second type is, however, more specifically confined to West Africa although it is found to a certain extent both in Melanesia and in North America.[1]

This second process, of evolution, represents a definite laicization of the drama. Only rarely, however, did this go to the extent of freeing it completely or even largely from its religious and ritualistic connexions as happened in the case of the ancient Greek theatre or in that of the morality plays of the Middle Ages. Such instances do, nevertheless, exist, particularly in the complex civilizations of ancient Mexico, Peru, Malaysia, and among some of the Pueblo peoples of the south-west United States, particularly the Hopi. With these lay dramas I cannot here concern myself irrespective of whether their subject matter is religious or not. The same applies to the religious pageants and processions. I hope to treat both of them later in a special volume. Here I shall deal exclusively with only a few aspects of the ritual drama proper in order to illustrate the nature of the transformation which the priest-thinker has introduced into the older subject matter of religion and the new syntheses he has substituted.

All primitive ritual dramas can be conveniently grouped into two types: those that seem to bear a transparent relationship to tribal initiation rites and those that do not. According to a well-known theory elaborated by Webster [2], all secret societies, we know, are to be regarded fundamentally as developments from, or outgrowths of, tribal initiation rites. Such a hypothesis seems quite inadequate to me and merely illustrates the manner in which theorists who are still largely under the influence of older evolutionary conceptions unduly simplify their problems. For instance, in the first type of ritual drama, which is mainly found in Melanesia, we have not so much a later development of initiation ceremonies as a reworking of much of the same material in the interests of groups of people belonging to closed societies possessing specific functions connected particularly with such life crises as birth and death. In the main, however, the ritual drama there never succeeded in holding its own against the overwhelming social-ceremonial demands of the community and took on more the character of episodic performances and ritual pageants than of true dramas. We shall accordingly leave them aside and instead turn for significant examples of the ritual drama to North America, where we find both our best examples and our most detailed information. We shall select only three tribes: the Zuñi of New Mexico [3], the Pawnee of Nebraska [4], and the Winnebago of Wisconsin.[5]

The particular Zuñi ritual drama which illustrates most conspicuously both the skill of the priest-thinker at its highest level and the nature of the difficulties with which he had to contend is undoubtedly the ceremony called *The Coming of the Gods*. Bunzel, on whose description we are relying, seems, in a sense, to be aware of this fact. Yet, in consonance with the curious antihistorical principles of interpretation which she has taken over from Dr. Benedict [6], she insists upon describing this synthesis of the priests in terms of what she calls æsthetics.

The problem [so she states] is, perhaps, not a historic one at all but rather one of æsthetics. There is a style of religious behaviour common to all the pueblo peoples. . . . The varied adjustments of the material in conformity to the ritual style are analogous to similar problems in decorative art—the individual reworking and recombining decorative motives within the narrow limits of a tribal style.[7]

Why, having thus recognized the last fact, she still persists in refusing to deal with the individual—this must be ascribed to the influence of her unfortunate adherence to a semi-ideological approach to culture which is a characteristic of so many recent American ethnologists and has often effectively neutralized the value that would otherwise inhere in their data.

The Coming of the Gods or *Calako*, as it is generally called, is not a single drama but a series of dramatic episodes combined with a number of ritualistic pageants and processions with which they have only inconsistently been fused. We have nevertheless a right to speak of the whole ceremonial unit as a drama proper, first, because it is supposed to be the re-enactment of episodes in a myth and, secondly, because the participants specifically impersonate the characters in this myth-plot.[8]

The argument of the plot itself is comparatively simple. The Zuñi in their original wanderings before they came to this world were, at one place, compelled to ford a stream. In midstream the women saw their children transformed into frogs and water snakes. Becoming frightened they dropped them and the children escaped into the water. The Twin Heroes were thereupon sent to the bereaved mothers to console them and to see what had become of their children. They found the children in a house beneath the surface of a place called Whispering Waters. They had been transformed into beautiful *katcinas*. This the Twin Heroes reported and further decreed that thereafter the dead should come to this place and join their lost children. The children, however, pitied the loneliness of their people and decided to visit them. After each visit they took someone with them, i.e., someone died. They consequently decided that they would no longer come in person but that they would, instead, instruct their people to copy their costume and headdresses and imitate their dances.

It requires no great insight to realize the historical development that must have taken place here. In spite of her antihistorical bias, Miss Bunzel seems to be aware of it. At an earlier phase of Zuñi religion the *katcinas* apparently were definitely identified with the dead. Nor were they friendly, as the dire punishment meted out to the sceptical young boy [9] mentioned in the myth clearly indicates.

The task of the thinker-priest is thus his old one. He has either to reinterpret the nature of the spirits of the dead or to break up the identification of the dead with the *katcinas*. He attempted both things although it is clear that the specific conditions, particularly the continuous influx of the folkloristic background, made the attainment of any complete consistency impossible. It seems best to attribute all the confusion that patently exists here, and to which Miss Bunzel calls attention [10], to this clash between the constructive and unifying effects of the thinker-priest and the disruptive influence of the laymen. As the priest-thinker's formulation became more rigidly defined and his theory more clearly enunciated, there was a corresponding disregard of the layman's viewpoint. But this did not do away with it or stop its threat.

Let us, however, turn to a brief characterization of *The Coming of the Gods* as a ritual drama and pageant.

As I have already indicated, the dramatic episodes and the ritual pageants are here hopelessly intermingled and interwoven. The esoteric ceremonies last throughout the calendar year, starting with the winter solstice and culminating in a public festival of fourteen days' duration, in the early part of December of the following year. There are four groups of *katcinas*: the *Koyemci*, or the sacred clowns; the *Culawitsi*; the *Saiyataca*, consisting of four distinct and important subdivisions; and the *Calako*, or giants. The individuals who are to impersonate these various *katcinas* are notified by the impersonator of the chief of all the masked gods, Pautiwa.

Of all the *katcinas* the Koyemci are perhaps the most interesting. There are ten of them, supposed to be the fruit of an incestuous union between brother and sister. They are of grotesque appearance and behave in the most uncouth fashion. They are privileged to mock at anything and to indulge in any obscenity. The attitude of the Zuñi toward them is ambivalent, for they are both the most feared and the most beloved of supernaturals. In the ceremony itself they are particularly adept at black magic. In their drum, for instance, they are supposed to have the wings of butterflies that can make girls sexually crazy, and in the knobs of their masks there is the soil from the footprints of the townspeople to be used as a love charm.

One who begrudges them anything [says Miss Bunzel] will meet swift and terrible retribution. But everyone goes in hushed reverence and near to tears to watch them on their last night, when they are under strict taboo. At this time, from sundown until midnight the following day, they touch neither food nor drink. They neither sleep nor speak, and in all that time they do not remove their masks. This truly heroic self-denial earns them the sympathetic affection of the people, an affection manifested in the generous gifts that are given them on their last day in office.[11]

The esoteric ceremonies begin with the distribution of the appointment-crooks to the impersonators of the gods. This is done, as we have stated, by the impersonator of the chief of the gods, Pautiwa. The duties of the impersonators commence at once. On the evening of their appointment, after having first sacrificed to their ancestors, they meet in the ceremonial houses to learn the prayers and the other details of their office. There then follow innumerable pageants and processions extending over a period of months. Characteristic of these are the innumerable prayers offered up, the sacrifices of food to the deities, and, above all, the ritualistic plantings. For these plantings they gather early in the morning to make their prayer sticks. Then, after prayers have been chanted and the meal consumed, they leave for those shrines lying to the south. Here prayer sticks are deposited. The impersonator of Saiyataca recites the prayer, the others joining in. Finally, toward sunset, the party approaches the village, marching across the plains in regular order and singing the songs of the masked dancers.

The public ceremonies begin with the arrival of the Koyemci. But I shall let Miss Bunzel describe them.

The Koyemci come masked, visiting each of the four plazas to announce the coming of the gods in eight days. They then go into retreat in the house of their father where they remain in seclusion, with the exception of brief appearances in the plaza, until the festival is concluded fifteen days later.

Four days after the appearance of the Koyemci, the Saiyataca party comes in in the evening and goes into retreat in the house of the impersonator of Saiyataca. On the same night the Calako impersonators go into retreat in their respective houses.

On the eighth day there is another planting of prayer sticks with elaborate ceremonies at which the gods are summoned from the village of the masked gods.

After they are clothed and masked they approach the village. The giant Calako gods wait on the south bank of the river, but the katcina priests . . . enter the village in mid afternoon. After planting prayer sticks in six excavations in the streets of the village, they repair to the house where they are to be entertained for the night. This is always a new or at least a renovated house, and the visit of the katcinas is a blessing—a dedication. Prayer sticks are planted inside the threshold . . . and in a decorated box suspended from the centre of the ceiling. The walls of the house are marked with corn meal. In an excavation in the centre of the floor seeds of all kinds are deposited. Similar rites are performed later in the evening by the six Calako and the Koyemci in the houses where they are to be entertained.

After the blessing of the house, the gods are seated by the pekwin, their masks raised. Reed cigarettes are brought and each katcina smokes with the person seated opposite him, exchanging with him the customary terms of relationship. Then the host . . . questions the gods concerning the circumstance of their coming. In the long recital that follows he reviews all the events leading up to the present moment, and invokes upon the house all the blessings of the gods, especially the blessing of fecundity. . . .

All [the chants] are finished at about 11 o'clock at night, when an elaborate feast is served in all the houses. After this all the masked personages dance until day in the houses of their hosts.

At the first sign of approaching dawn Saiyataca ascends to the roof of the house where he has spent the night and, facing the east, unties the last knot in his counting string while he intones another prayer. Returning to the house, he repeats the prayer. He then thanks the members of the society choir who furnished the music during the night. The dancing continues until sunrise when the heads of all impersonators are washed by the women of the houses where they were entertained, as a symbol of their permanent association with these houses. They receive gifts of food, and sometimes of clothing, from their hosts, but these gifts are in no measure a compensation for their services.

At about noon, after planting prayer sticks and performing magical ceremonies in a field on the south of the river, the Calako gods and the Saiyataca group depart for their home in the west. This closes their year, and the impersonators of the Saiyataca group and the Calako are now free after the exacting period of service.

The Koyemci, however, are not yet free. . . .

For five nights following the departure of the Calako gods, dancers from each of the six kivas are supposed to visit all the houses which have entertained the gods. Some of them dance in the plaza during the day. Throughout this period the Koyemci remain in strict retreat in the house where they were entertained. At night they dance in their house; during the day they "play" in the plaza and attend any dancers who appear there. . . .

On the fifth evening they eat early and sparingly, and from this time on food and drink are taboo until the following night. Speech also is forbidden them, nor may they appear unmasked. After they enter upon this period the character of their dancing changes, becoming more solemn. They do not indulge in their usual obscenity. On the following morning they come out early and are taken to be "washed" in the house of the village chief. Here the women give them gifts of food. On coming out, they are taken by men of their fathers' clans to the houses of their fathers' sisters. Here they receive valuable gifts from all members of the fathers' clan. Each personator will receive as many as thirty slaughtered sheep, as many baskets of corn or wheat flour, bread, melons, and miscellaneous gifts of clothing, frequently of great value. The gifts are brought to the plaza where they remain until night. Meanwhile, the Koyemci attend upon the various dancers until later at night.

At nightfall the last of the dancers . . . have departed. Then the Koyemci in pairs visit every house in the village to invoke upon it the blessings of the gods. At each house they receive gifts of food from the female inhabitants. Returning to the plaza, they take their prayer sticks out to plant. They return to the house of their father late at night, and removing their masks for the first time all day give them to their father to return to the house where they are kept. When he comes back, he thanks his children for their year of work and sets them free. Then for the first time since the preceding evening they drink, and after eating and bathing, return to their homes. . . .[12]

In contrast to the voluminous and episodic nature of *The Coming of the Gods,* the Zuñi and other Pueblo tribes have a large number of far more compact and unified ritual dramas. I have selected the above example, however, to illustrate what develops when a ceremonial pattern worked out by a special group of highly specialized priest-thinkers comes into conflict with the multifarious and non-unified folkloristic background.

But we must now turn to another tribe, the Pawnee, and see what happens when the ravages to the unity of a ritual drama, due to the encroachment of the folkloristic background, are checked and strictly delimited. Among the Pawnee, while the purely ritualistic aspect of the ceremonies was never lost sight of, the dramatic side was unusually clearcut and explicitly recognized. Every ceremony was a repetition or dramatization of acts performed by supernatural beings in the mythological age. These ritual dramas were arranged in a definite order covering the whole ceremonial year. The underlying scheme was as follows. The deities were regarded as having withdrawn from the earth during the winter, to return again in spring as soon as the first thunder was heard. To honour this return a ceremony was performed, the Thunder Ceremony. This was followed by one called *Paruxti,* in which the deity of this name was supposed to be called to earth.

Then came the ceremony called *The Planting of the Corn*, to be followed by a whole series of agricultural rites. These ceremonies were, on the whole, more or less public in the sense that the whole village could participate in them. Correlated with them were the rituals of a large number of secret societies, owned and controlled by different coteries of medicine-men. Of these the most important and dramatic was the annual Ceremony of the Medicine-Men. Let us, however, turn to the Thunder Ceremony first.

The first thunder in the spring was regarded as the voice of Paruxti. The latter was the messenger of the supreme god, Tirawa, and the mystical incarnation of the four servants of the deity called the Evening Star, i.e., of the Wind, the Cloud, the Lightning, and the Thunder. As Paruxti passed over the land in a storm, life was kindled anew. He is represented as returning to his lodge in the west, kindling a new fire, and offering smoke to the deities in the heavens. This is supposed to signify that he had visited the earth and that all was well. Thereupon the deities turn their attention to the people on earth and prepare to receive the prayers and offerings from them.

The Thunder Ceremony which ushers in the ceremonial year is essentially simply the series of prayers and offerings to the specific deities made in rotation by the priest-medicine-men present. Each one is supposed to be in charge of the "offering-materials" for a certain deity. The gods appealed to are Tirawa, the chief of the gods, Morning Star, Evening Star, Big-Black-Meteoric Star, North Star, North Wind, the Sun, the Moon, and Paruxti.

The ceremony is divided into two parts, the second practically identical with the first. Toward the end of it, the chief priest, making a circuit of the village, intones the following hymn-prayer to the gods, in gratitude to the young boy for whose initiation offerings have been brought to the ceremonial lodge:

I come! Now we raise our voices for Mother-Corn.
Mother-Born-Again.

Mother-Corn-who-carries-them-through-obstacles.
It is our father who sits in the pathway to receive prayers.
Yonder their fathers dwell in the heavens.
Yonder the Wonderful Being dwells in the heavens.
Yonder their father dwells in the heavens, where the thunders are to
    be heard.
Yonder their fathers dwell in the heavens.
Yonder in the heavens stands Ready-to-Give.
Mother-Corn's kettles are filled with corn brought by a child.
Listen! Boy whose name is Little Son.
Listen! Boy whose name is Little Son.
It is through him that I walk around the circle of the village and call
    upon the gods to look down upon this boy.
I come! [13]

The ritual finally concludes with a speech that is at one and the
same time a statement of its symbolism as a drama and its social-
religious function.

Priests [says the chief medicine-man], we have now gone through
the ceremony that was given us by Paruxti. A young boy wished to see
this ceremony. It is for that reason that you, priests, entered this lodge,
and sit upright in a circle in the lodge, sitting in the places of the gods;
that you sit upright, as they do, sitting close together. You sit in their
places, and we offer stories and rituals that they recited in the ancient
times of the former priests, who long ago sat in the places where you
now sit. Now, priests, the time is approaching, as we sit in this lodge,
for us to move; but before we move, I rise to say that by all the offerings we have made while sitting in this lodge the gods have been made
glad, the gods who stand in the heavens. The offerings were made
to them, and they received those offerings. Well then, we shall see
which one of these gods will send good gifts to the people, and because
of this ceremony will take pity on us. It is time for us to hasten and
rise. Priests, we must now hasten to rise. . . . Now, priests, we are
going to rise. We are going to walk toward the entrance belonging to
Mother-Corn, Mother-of-the-Dawn, Mother-Sunset-Yellow. Now,

priests, we rise! We walk toward the entrance, belonging to Mother-Corn. Rise! Priests! [14]

In the annual Ceremony of the Medicine-Men the ritualistic details do not play as much havoc with the argument of the drama as in the case of the Thunder Ceremony although the social-religious function is even more fundamental, for the objectives here are the renewal of the powers possessed by the medicine-men and the driving of disease from the village. The plot of the drama itself is clearly enunciated in the origin myth. Each performance is supposed to be a repetition of the initiation into the society of its original founder, and the participants represent the various super-natural spirits who conducted the first rites. To the ritual as de-scribed in this origin myth have been added a number of rites, most of them connected with the proper preparations for the ceremony and the paraphernalia and "scenery" necessary for it. Thus the bulls and the cows whose hide is to serve in the building up of the most important pieces of the stage scenery—the images of the Water Spirit, the Witch Woman, the Morning Star, and the nine other tutelary spirits—have to be killed with a single arrow. Similarly when the cedar tree to be used inside the entrance of the ceremonial lodge is cut down and carried to the village, a sham battle takes place between its bearers and a group of medi-cine-men who come out to meet them. The latter naturally are always defeated.

According to the origin myth the ceremony was revealed to the founder by the water-spirit. The dreamer was directed to a stream and told to leap into it. There he found himself in a lodge of animals. In the middle of it was an altar. Two animals, an owl and a beaver, reclined near the altar while other animals sat around in a circle. There were two ponds near the entrance, each of them guarded by a large goose. In the west sat a woman. The water-spirit who had conducted him to the lodge lay to the south of the entrance. It is he who acted as spokesman. He informed the dreamer that he had been sent by Tirawa, the supreme deity, to instruct him personally into the mysteries of initiation with the aid of the other animals present:

My son, when you go home, tell your people to make an image of me and lay it in the lodge as I am now lying. The fireplace you see is not a fireplace but a wonderful turtle. The woman sitting in the west is not a woman but a thing of clay. She is a witch woman. The geese that stand by the ponds, when they flap their wings, make a noise that can be heard in the heavens. The noise wakens the gods to a remembrance of their promise to pity mankind and give them power.[15]

The two most important pieces of stage scenery were the images of the water-spirit and the witch woman. The former was nearly sixty feet in length and encircled the lodge, with its head and tail reposing on either side of the entrance. The framework was made of pieces of ashwood lashed together with sinew. A layer of grass was laid over this and then the whole was covered with mud and painted in different colours. The mouth was large enough for a person to crawl into. The head was covered with a black-dyed buffalo robe and painted and decorated with downy feathers. The figure of the witch woman consisted of a willow frame covered with grass and surfaced with clay. Her features were modelled and her eyes consisted of pumpkin seeds blackened in the centre. On her head was placed a buffalo scalp to which long braids of human hair were attached. Finally the figure was draped in a buffalo robe.

The culminating point in the drama is the "shooting" ceremony. This is described in the myth as follows:

Before they commenced the leader stood in front of the altar of loon skins given him by the animals, and called the men to him one by one. He embraced each and breathed into his mouth. Then he went and sat by the altar. He had taught them a song, and now each man put on the skin of his guardian animal and began to sing this song and dance. At a certain place in the song every one of them fell to the ground as if shot. When the song was ended one of the men got up.

He saw something lying beside him that looked like a small oval frag-
ment of clear ice. Each of the other men found a thing of the same
sort beside him, and all of them laid these things in a line on the west
of the fireplace. The leader told them that these things had been given
to them by the animals. They must swallow them, and then they
would have the power to hypnotize and influence the people. They
did this and returned to their small lodges.

They stayed in the big lodge for several days more, trying their
powers and doing all sorts of sleight of hand. When the last day of
the ceremony came, they all dressed up according to the animal that
was their guardian. They went out and marched around the lodge
once, with two men carrying loon skins from the altar in the lead.
Then they entered the lodge again and crowded around the fireplace,
stamping to awaken the turtle. Then they passed out of the lodge,
dancing, and each man imitating his guardian animal. As they went,
they did all sorts of sleight of hand so that the people could see they
had magic powers. When they had shown their powers to the people,
they entered the lodge once more and sang songs and imitated the
cries of their guardians. They made a great commotion so that the
people outside could see ashes flying up through the smoke-hole. That
night they did more sleight of hand tricks in the lodge, and sang and
worked magic until about two o'clock in the morning. Then they tore
down the little lodges and carried them and the images of the water
monster and witch woman down to the river. As they went along,
they shouted and sang and hypnotized one another. They threw the
mysterious things that gave them hypnotizing power into one another, and the men who were struck fell down as if shot. The rest of
the village looked on, and were mystified by the wonderful things they
did. When they came to the river, they put the little lodges and the
images in the water in the position they had had in the big lodge.[16]

Thus the nature of the objective which the priest-thinker had
in view is clearly transparent in this fascinating ritual drama. It
consisted, first, in the unification of certain aspects of the religious-
folkloristic background; secondly, in the neutralization of the

personal-individualistic implications of his shamanistic profession; and, thirdly, in the dramatic representation of this compromise and synthesis, in a form that would be understood by a selected group of men and one which they and the community would be likely to accept. This, quite naturally, led, on the one hand, to a stressing of common social-economic values at the expense of the artistic side of the drama and, on the other, to just the opposite, namely the undue elaboration of strictly personal and antisocial ambitions. It is not strange, consequently, that after the altar of loon skins has been built up the prayers offered to the deities are: "Give us plenty of rain; let our crops grow so that we may be fed," and that, at the same time, the ceremony should be associated in the minds of non-members and of not a few members with the exhibition of sleight-of-hand tricks. This latter must not be taken to represent a form of degeneration. These two contradictory processes have always been present: the integrating activities of the priest-thinker and the disruptive activities of the individualistic medicine-man and the populace at large. Only rarely can a moderately complete fusion of these contrasting forces be achieved. To such an example I would like now, in conclusion, to turn—the Medicine Dance of the Winnebago Indians.[17]

Even a cursory glance at the Winnebago Medicine Dance indicates clearly that it represents a mosaic of superimposed rites and the fusion of many purposes. According to the official priestly interpretation as embodied in the origin myth, its object is simple enough: to compensate mankind for the introduction of death because of the disobedience of the culture-hero, Hare. On the face of it this sounds almost like Christian influence. Some kind of Christian influence may in fact be postulated, not so much in the specific content of the ceremony, however, as in the need felt to combat its disintegrating influence upon the native culture. The extreme unification of the disparate elements that have gone into its make-up may very well represent the native priest-thinker's answer to the threat that lay in the contact with the white man's civilization. But there were other and older threats to Winnebago culture, such as, for instance, the complete isolation from the southern Siouan tribes and the constant absorption of Central Algonquian elements which must have been just as potent and dangerous. To all these forces must be ascribed the highly integrated simplicity of the whole ceremony. There are no loose ends with regard to either the purposes of the component rites or the argument of the plot.

The plot itself constitutes one episode in the larger history of the creation of the world. It is the last episode, but its proper position in the scheme of things is never lost sight of. What takes place takes place on the island-earth as finally shaped and duly anchored by Earthmaker. The lodge in which the ceremony is held represents that island, and the four basic persons in the ritual impersonate the four primal spirits by whose means the earth is prevented from moving, the four cardinal points or earth-weights. The journey of Hare to these four spirits after he has, through his disobedience, brought death to mankind, is repeated every time a member of the society makes the ceremonial circuit of the lodge. And just as, between the refusal of the last of the four spirits to intervene in the affairs of man and the institution of the Medicine Dance, there lies the whole episode of Hare's visit to Earthmaker, so here in the medicine lodge there stands the personage called Xokera, He-Who-Is-at-the-Root-of-Things, as the word implies, and through whose home one must pass from the south (the place of the disappearance of the sun) to the east (the place of its reappearance), i.e., from death to birth. The whole ceremony is the reiteration of one basic theme, the proper method of passing through life in order to be reborn again. Not for one moment is this forgotten. Whatever it may have been originally, today this journey through life is pictured as surcharged with ethical and mystical interpretations of the most sophisticated kind. And this sophistication runs through the whole ceremony, transforming crude folkloristic beliefs and practices into refined and highly altruistic attitudes and activities. We are transported to a perfect world from which evil, in every form, has been scrupulously excluded. There is not the slightest breath of suspicion in this ritual drama that the dominant passion and ideal of the Winnebago was war or that in real life the people were terrified by the evil machinations of shamans.

In other words the Medicine Dance, from the viewpoint of its leaders at least, was a drama depicting the ideal life and depicting it in terms of a myth from which all the coarser implications of its episodes had been completely obliterated. Such a highly artificial drama can manifestly represent the achievement only of men who have thought deeply on the meaning of life, who possessed the artistic skill to articulate their vision and the leisure in which to do it, not to mention an audience that was willing to accept it.

Our task is now finished. In the preceding pages I have tried to show the nature of religion among primitive peoples, the type of temperament mainly instrumental in building it up specifically, and the type instrumental in disrupting these syntheses of the priest-thinker. Very rarely indeed was it vouchsafed primitive man to attain to a real integration of the various contradictory elements that formed part and parcel of his religion. However, quite apart from the social desirability of such an achievement, an integration of this type has occurred as rarely among so-called civilized groups.

Coexistent with this conflict of the two temperaments that have shaped the form and content of religion there is another, that between the individuals to whom religion is a refuge and a haven of rest from the grim realities of life and those for whom religion is an instrument to be utilized for economic exploitation. It is not strange then that even in so ostensibly devout a community as that of the Sikhs of the Punjab the prayer of the weaver saint Kabir still reflects this conflict:

> A hungry man cannot perform Thy service,
> Take back this rosary of Thine.

I only ask for the dust of the Saint's feet.
Let me not be in debt.

I beg for two *seers* of flour,
A quarter of a *seer* of butter and salt.

I beg for half a *seer* of *pulse*
Which will feed me twice a day.

I beg for a bed with four legs to it,
A pillow and a mattress.

I beg for a quilt over me,
And then Thy slave will devotedly worship Thee.

I have never been covetous,
I only love Thy name.

Notes

CHAPTER ONE

1. Rudolf Otto, *Das Heilige*, Gotha, 1926.
2. R. H. Codrington, *The Melanesians*, Oxford, 1891, pp. 118–119.
3. Beattie in *Journal of the Polynesian Society*, New Plymouth, N. Z., vol. 30, 1921.
4. J. Walker, *The Sun Dance of the Oglala Division of the Dakota*, Anthropological Papers of the American Museum of Natural History, XVI, Part II, New York, pp. 152 ff.

CHAPTER TWO

1. P. Radin, *Crashing Thunder, The Autobiography of an American Indian*, New York, 1926, pp. 56 ff.
2. P. Amaury Talbot, *The Peoples of Southern Nigeria*, London, 1926, vol. II, p. 64.
3. Frances Densmore, *Teton Sioux Music*, Bulletin 61, Bureau of American Ethnology, Washington, D. C., pp. 172 ff.
4. Gunnar Landtman, *The Kiwai Papuans of British New Guinea*, London, 1927, pp. 281–282.
5. Ibid.
6. P. Radin, *The Winnebago Tribe*, 37th Annual Report of the Bureau of American Ethnology, Washington, 1923, pp. 478–479 and 493.
7. Dietrich Westermann, *The Shilluk People*, Philadelphia, 1912, p. 171.
8. H. Labouret, *Les Tribus du Rameau Lobi*, Travaux et Mémoires de l'Institut d'Ethnologie, Paris, 1931, vol. XV, p. 477.
9. J. Spieth, *Die Ewestämme*, Berlin, 1906, pp. 834–836.
10. B. Malinowski, *Argonauts of the Western Pacific*, London, 1922.

CHAPTER THREE

1. A. H. Gayton, *Yokuts-Mono Chief and Shamans*, University of California Publications in American Archeology and Ethnology, vol. 24, 1930.
2. Ibid., p. 399.
3. R. Firth, *Primitive Economics of the New Zealand Maori*, London, 1929, p. 265.
4. E. E. Evans-Pritchard, "Witchcraft," and S. F. Nadel, "Witchcraft and Anti-Witchcraft in Nupe Society," *Africa*, 1935, vol. VIII, pp. 417–448.
5. Nadel, op. cit., pp. 440–442.
6. Gayton, op. cit., p. 397.
7. Knud Rasmussen, *The Intellectual Culture of the Iglulik Eskimos*, Copenhagen, 1929, pp. 55 ff.

CHAPTER FOUR

1. Cf. G. Róheim, *Animism, Magic, and the Divine King*, New York, 1930.
2. B. Malinowski, *Argonauts of the Western Pacific*, pp. 427, 439–440.
3. F. E. Clements, *Primitive Concepts of Disease*, University of California Publications in American Archeology and Ethnology, vol. 32, 1932.
4. P. Radin, *The Story of the American Indian*, New York, 1934.

CHAPTER FIVE

1. A. E. Crawley, *The Mystic Rose*, revised by T. Besterman, London, 1927.
2. C. Strehlow, *Das soziale Leben der Aranda- und Loritja-Stämme*, Frankfurt, 1913.
   B. Spencer and F. J. Gillen, *The Arunta*, London, 1927.
   M. Gusinde, *Die Feuerland Indianer*, vol. I, "Die Selknam," Anthropos Bibliothek, Moedling, Vienna, 1931.
   M. Léenhardt, *Notes d'Ethnologie Néo-Calédonienne*, Travaux et Mémoires de l'Institut d'Ethnologie, vol. VIII, Paris, 1931.
   R. S. Rattray, *Religion and Art in Ashanti*, Oxford, 1927, pp. 69–76.
   H. A. Junod, *The Life of a South African Tribe*, Neuchâtel, 1913, vol. I, pp. 71–92.
3. A. Van Gennep, *Les Rites de Passage*, Paris, 1909, pp. 1–18; 93–125.
4. Strehlow, op. cit., pp. 25–26.
5. Ibid., pp. 11–12.
6. G. Róheim, *Animism, Magic, and the Divine King*, pp. 20–25. Cf. also the same author's elaborate treatise, *Australian Totemism*, London, 1925.
7. Léenhardt, op. cit., pp. 138–139.
8. Ibid., p. 140.
9. Rattray, op. cit., pp. 69–77.
10. Ibid., p. 70.
11. Junod, op. cit., pp. 71–92.
12. Ibid., pp. 85–86.
13. Rattray, op. cit., p. 49.

CHAPTER SIX

1. K. Rasmussen, *Intellectual Culture of the Caribou Eskimo*, Report of the Fifth Thule Expedition, 1921–1924, vol. VII, No. 2, pp. 54–55. The italics are mine.
2. Ibid., pp. 52 ff.
3. C. Strehlow, *Das soziale Leben der Aranda- und Loritja-Stämme*, vol. IV, Part II, pp. 38 ff.
4. P. Radin, *The Winnebago Tribe*, pp. 270–275.
5. J. W. Layard, "Flying Tricksters, Ghosts, Gods and Epileptics," *Journal of the Royal Anthropological Institute of Great Britain and Ireland*, vol. LX, London, July–December 1930, pp. 507–509.
6. E. M. Loeb, "Shaman and Seer," *American Anthropologist*, vol. XXXI, Menasha, Wis., pp. 66–71.
7. Canon Callaway, *The Religious System of the Amazulu*, Natal, 1870, pp. 259–266.

8. R. S. Rattray, *Religion and Art in Ashanti*, pp. 40–47.
9. Teuira Henry, *Ancient Tahiti*, Bernice P. Bishop Museum, Bulletin 48, Honolulu, 1928, pp. 153 ff.

CHAPTER SEVEN

1. K. Rasmussen, *Intellectual Culture of the Caribou Eskimo*, p. 113.
2. Ibid., pp. 133 ff.
3. E. M. Loeb, "Shaman and Seer," p. 74.
4. P. Radin, *The Winnebago Tribe*, pp. 270 ff.
5. F. C. Cole, *The Tinguian*, Field Museum of Natural History, Anthropological Series, vol. XIV, No. 2, Chicago, 1922, pp. 318–319.
6. O. Walker, "Tiurai, le Guérisseur," *Bulletin de la Société des Etudes Océaniennes*, No. 10, July 1925, pp. 7–10.
7. Canon Callaway, *The Religious System of the Amazulu*, pp. 311–313.
8. E. E. Evans-Pritchard, "The Zande Corporation of Witchdoctors," *Journal of the Royal Anthropological Institute of Great Britain and Ireland*, vol. LXIII, 1933, pp. 83–84.

CHAPTER EIGHT

1. Cf. T. K. Oesterreich, *Possession*, New York, 1930.
2. S. H. Hooke, *Myth and Ritual*, Oxford, 1933.
3. Quoted from M. A. Czaplicka, *Aboriginal Siberia*, Oxford, 1914, p. 182; p. 183.
4. P. Radin, *Crashing Thunder*, pp. 17–20.
5. K. Rasmussen, *The Intellectual Culture of the Caribou Eskimo*, pp. 124–127.
6. P. Radin, *Crashing Thunder*, pp. 105–110.

CHAPTER NINE

1. R. R. Marett, *The Threshold of Religion*, London, 1914, p. 99.
2. Laura Benedict, *A Study of Bagobo Ceremonial, Magic and Myth*, Annals of the New York Academy of Sciences, vol. XXV, 1916, pp. 1–308.
3. Ibid., p. 196.
4. Ibid., p. 198.
5. Ibid., p. 199.
6. Ruth L. Bunzel, *Zuñi Ritual Poetry*, Forty-Seventh Annual Report of the Bureau of American Ethnology, pp. 621–623.
7. J. Tom Brown, *Among the Bantu Nomads*, London, 1926. Quoted from W. C. Willoughby, *The Soul of the Bantu*, New York, 1928, pp. 357–358.
8. H. Labouret, *Les Tribus du Rameau Lobi*, p. 440.
9. T. Henry, *Ancient Tahiti*, pp. 196-197.
10. Ibid., pp. 186–187.
11. E. S. C. Handy, *Polynesian Religion*, Bernice P. Bishop Museum, Bulletin 34, Honolulu, 1927, p. 184.
12. E. Tregear, *The Maori*, Wanganui, New Zealand, 1904, p. 280.
13. Handy, op. cit., p. 185.
14. M. Mauss, *Essai sur le don*, L'Année Sociologique, N.S., Paris, 1925, pp. 30–186.

15. W. Robertson Smith, *Lectures on the Early Religion of the Semites,* Third Edition, London, 1917.

16. E. Durkheim, *Les Formes élémentaires de la vie religieuse,* Paris, 1912.

17. H. Hubert and M. Mauss, *Essai sur la nature et la fonction du sacrifice, Mélanges d'histoire des religions,* Paris, 1909.

18. Durkheim, op. cit., pp. 481–482.

19. F. Heiler, *Das Gebet,* Munich, 1923.

20. R. R. Marett, "From Spell to Prayer," *Folklore,* vol. XV, 1904, pp. 132–165.

21. J. W. Hauer, *Die Religionen, Erstes Buch; Das religiöse Erlebnis auf den unteren Stufen,* Berlin, 1923.

22. John Batchelor, *The Ainu and Their Folklore,* London, 1901, p. 305.

23. B. Malinowski, op. cit., and *Coral Gardens and Their Magic,* New York, 1935.

24. W. W. Skeat, *Malay Magic,* London, 1900.

25. Quoted from F. Heiler, op. cit., p. 52.

26. D. Westermann, *Africa,* vol. I, 1928, p. 195.

27. Ibid., p. 200.

28. J. F. Stimson, *The Cult of Kiho-Tumu,* Bernice P. Bishop Museum, Bulletin 3, Honolulu, 1933, pp. 26–29.

CHAPTER TEN

1. *The Jesuit Relations and Allied Documents,* edited by R. G. Thwaites, Cleveland, 1896–1901, VIII, p. 123.

2. J. W. Layard, "Flying Tricksters, Ghosts, Gods and Epileptics," *Journal of the Royal Anthropological Institute of Great Britain and Ireland,* vol. LX, 1930, pp. 501–524; and "Shamanism: An Analysis Based on Comparison with the Flying Tricksters of Malekula," ibid., pp. 525–550.

3. J. W. Layard, "Shamanism: An Analysis Based on Comparison with the Flying Tricksters of Malekula," p. 526.

4. S. Ranulf, *The Jealousy of the Gods,* London, 1933–1934.

5. R. H. Lowie, *Primitive Religion,* New York, 1924.

6. Ibid., p. 322.

7. Ibid.

8. Ibid., p. v.

9. Ibid., p. 321.

10. Ibid., pp. 329–330.

11. E. B. Tylor, *Primitive Culture,* first published in 1871; cf. the famous chapter XI on Animism.

12. Cora Du Bois, *Wintun Ethnology,* University of California Publications in American Archeology and Ethnology, Berkeley, Cal., vol. XXXVI, pp. 1–148.

13. J. Curtin, *Creation Myths of Primitive America,* Boston, 1898.

14. Du Bois, op. cit., p. 73.

15. Ibid., p. 73.

16. Ibid., p. 118.

17. Quoted from E. M. Weyer, *The Eskimos,* New Haven, 1932, p. 241.

18. I. Schapera, *The Khoisan Peoples of South Africa,* London, 1930, pp. 178 ff.

19. D. F. Bleek, "Bushman Folklore," *Africa*, vol. II, 1929, p. 308.
20. Schapera, op. cit., p. 181.
21. Bleek, quoted in Schapera, op. cit., p. 176.
22. Bleek, op. cit., p. 307.
23. A. Van Gennep, *L'Etat actuel du problème totémique*, Paris, 1920.
24. Van Gennep, op. cit., p. 341.
25. Cf. E. Vatter, *Der australische Totemismus*, Mittheilungen aus dem Museum für Völkerkunde in Hamburg, 1929, vol. X, and the famous work of J. G. Frazer, *Totemism and Exogamy*, London, 1910.
26. Cf. the well-known works of J. G. Frazer: *Lectures on the Early History of Kingship*, London, 1905; and *The Golden Bough*, Part I, The Magic Art and the Evolution of Kings, Third Edition, 1910; and pp. 1–175 in the one-volume edition of *The Golden Bough*, London, 1928.
27. B. Spencer and F. J. Gillen, *The Native Tribes of Central Australia*, 1899, London, p. 174.
28. Vatter, op. cit., pp. 82–85.
29. A. Van Gennep, *Mythes et légendes d'Australie*, Paris, 1905.
30. Pater W. Schmidt, *Der Ursprung der Gottesidee*, Münster, 1926, vol. I, pp. 319–334.

CHAPTER ELEVEN

1. E. W. Smith and A. M. Dale, *The Ila-Speaking Peoples of Northern Rhodesia*, vol. I, pp. 283–315. London, 1920.
2. Ibid., p. 296.
3. Ibid., vol. II, pp. 167–168.
4. Ibid., vol. II, p. 168.
5. Ibid., p. 176.
6. Cf. C. G. Seligman, "The Religion of the Pagan Tribes of the White Nile," *Africa*, vol. IV, pp. 1–21, 1931; and W. Hofmayr, *Die Schilluk*, Anthropos Bibliothek, vol. II, 1925, pp. 185–242.
7. Smith and Dale, op. cit., vol. II, pp. 197 ff.
8. M. Léenhardt, *Notes d'Ethnologie Néo-Calédonienne*, p. 232.
9. Ibid., p. 233.
10. J. Spieth, *Die Religion der Eweer in Süd-Togo*, Leipzig, 1911, pp. 149 ff.
11. J. Spieth, *Die Ewestämme*, pp. 327–328.
12. Lowie, *Primitive Religion*.
13. R. Linton, *The Tanala*, Field Museum of Natural History, Anthropological Series, vol. XXII, 1933, pp. 159–240. Cf. also A. Van Gennep, *Tabou et totémisme à Madagascar*, Paris, 1903–1904.
14. R. Bunzel, *Introduction to Zuñi Ceremonialism, Zuñi Origin Myths, Zuñi Ritual Poetry, and Zuñi Katcinas*, 47th Annual Report of the Bureau of American Ethnology, Washington, 1932, pp. 467–1086.
15. Ibid., p. 476.
16. B. Aitken, "Temperament in Native American Religion," *Journal of the Royal Anthropological Institute of Great Britain and Ireland*, vol. LX, 1930, pp. 363–388; and R. Benedict, "Configurations of Culture in North America," *American Anthropologist*, vol. XVII, 1932, pp. 1–27.
17. Bunzel, *Introduction to Zuñi Ceremonialism*, etc., pp. 505–506.
18. Aitken, op. cit., p. 382.

19. Ibid., p. 381.
20. E. C. Parsons, *Hopi and Zuñi Ceremonialism*, Memoirs of the American Anthropological Association, Number 39, 1933, pp. 74–78.
21. R. Heine-Geldern, "Urheimat und früheste Wanderungen der Austronesier," *Anthropos*, 1932, pp. 543–619.
22. L. Benedict, *A Study of Bagobo Ceremonial, Magic and Myth*, pp. 20–21.
23. Ibid., pp. 35–36.
24. Ibid., pp. 29–30.
25. Cf. A. L. Kroeber, *The History of Philippine Civilization as Reflected in Religious Nomenclature*, Anthropological Papers of the American Museum of Natural History, vol. XIX, pp. 37–67.
26. T. Henry, *Ancient Tahiti*.
27. Ibid., p. 141.
28. E. S. C. Handy, *Polynesian Religion*, p. 109.
29. Ibid., p. 364.
30. Ibid., p. 366.
31. Ibid., p. 366.
32. Ibid., p. 367.
33. Ibid., p. 367.
34. Ibid., pp. 367 ff.
35. Ibid., pp. 121 ff.

CHAPTER TWELVE

1. Andrew Lang, *The Making of Religion*, London, 1898.
2. First in French under the title "Origine de l'idée de dieu," *Anthropos*, vol. III, pp. 125–162, 336–368, 559–611, 801–836, 1081–1120; vol. IV, 207–250, 505–524, 1075–1091; vol. V, 231–246: final edition in five volumes under the title *Der Ursprung der Gottesidee*, Münster, 1926–1935.
3. H. Pinard de la Boullaye, *L'Etude comparée des religions*, Paris, 1922, vol. I, pp. 356–385.
4. K. T. Preuss, *Die höchste Gottheit bei den kulturarmen Völkern*, Psychologische Forschungen, vol. II, pp. 161–208, Berlin, 1922.
   N. Söderblom, *Das Werden des Gottesglaubens*, Leipzig, 1916.
   R. Pettazone, *L'essere celeste nelle credenze dei popoli primitivi*, Rome, 1922.
   P. Radin, *Primitive Man as Philosopher*, Chapter XVIII, New York, 1927.
5. E. B. Tylor, *Primitive Culture*, vol. II, p. 336.
6. M. Gusinde, *Die Feuerland Indianer*, pp. 492–522.
7. Ibid., pp. 513 ff.
8. Cf. especially Pater Schmidt's *The Origin and Growth of Religion*, New York, 1931, pp. 257–290.
9. Ibid., p. 271.
10. Ibid., pp. 271–272.
11. C. G. and B. Z. Seligman, *Pagan Tribes of the Nilotic Sudan*, London, 1932.
12. Quoted from Hofmayr in Seligman, op. cit., p. 75.
13. Seligman, op. cit., p. 75.

14. Ibid., p. 76.
15. Mgr. Lagae, *Les Azande ou Niam-Niam,* Brussels, 1926, p. 70. Quoted from Seligman.
16. Seligman, op. cit., p. 519, quoting J. E. T. Phillips.
17. Seligman, op. cit., p. 520.
18. P. Radin, *The Winnebago Tribe,* p. 350.
19. Ibid., pp. 350–351.
20. Ibid., p. 351.
21. K. T. Preuss, op. cit., p. 182.
22. *Journal of the Polynesian Society,* XVI, p. 113.
23. S. Percy Smith, *The Lore of the Whare-Wananga,* Memoirs of the Polynesian Society, III, pp. 105–107; and P. Radin, *Primitive Man as Philosopher,* pp. 324–325.

CHAPTER THIRTEEN

1. E. B. Tylor, *Primitive Culture,* vol. II, p. 247.
2. A. E. Crawley, *The Idea of the Soul,* London, 1909, p. 1.
3. Ibid., p. 3.
4. Cf. also H. Pinard de la Boullaye, *L'Etude comparée des religions;* and L. Lévy-Bruhl, *L'Ame primitive,* Paris, 1927, and *Le Surnaturel,* Paris, 1934 (?).
5. J. G. Frazer, *The Golden Bough,* Part II, "Taboo and the Perils of the Soul," Third Edition, 1935.
6. Crawley, op. cit., pp. 211–224; L. Lévy-Bruhl, *L'Ame primitive,* pp. 291–408.
7. Crawley, op. cit., pp. 211–212.
8. L. Lévy-Bruhl, *L'Ame primitive,* p. 436.
9. G. Róheim, *Animism, Magic, and the Divine King,* p. 25.
10. Lévy-Bruhl, op. cit., p. 292.
11. Ibid., p. 292.
12. Ibid., p. 292.
13. Ibid., p. 293.
14. J. Walker, *The Sun Dance of the Oglala Division of the Dakota,* XVI, Part II, p. 87.
15. J. Warneck, *Die Religion der Batak,* pp. 8–24; and also A. C. Kruijt, *Het Animisme in den Indischen Archipel,* The Hague, 1906.
16. P. Radin, *Crashing Thunder: the Autobiography of an American Indian,* pp. 190–192.
17. P. Radin, *Primitive Man as Philosopher,* pp. 303–305.
18. A. E. Crawley, op. cit., pp. 77–78. Cf. also E. Arbman, "Untersuchungen zur primitiven Seelenvorstellung mit besonderer Rücksicht auf Indien," *Le Monde Oriental,* vol. XX, 1926, pp. 85–184.
19. R. Moss, *The Life after Death in Oceania and the Malay Archipelago,* Oxford, 1925, pp. 88–132.
20. Ibid., p. 110.
21. G. Turner, *Samoa,* London, 1884, pp. 292–293.
22. P. Radin, *The Winnebago Tribe,* pp. 143–144.

CHAPTER FOURTEEN

1. Hutton Webster, *Primitive Secret Societies*, New York, 1932; F. E. Williams, *Orokaiva Society*, Oxford, 1930, pp. 230–260; and J. G. Frazer, *The Golden Bough*.
2. Webster, op. cit., pp. 74–134.
3. R. Bunzel, *Introduction to Zuñi Ceremonialism, etc.*, pp. 467–544 and 837–1086.
4. R. Linton, summarizing G. A. Dorsey's unpublished notes, *The Thunder Ceremony of the Pawnee* and *The Annual Ceremony of the Pawnee Medicine Men*, Field Museum of Natural History, Leaflets numbers 6 and 8, Chicago, 1922 and 1923.
5. P. Radin, MS notes.
6. R. Benedict, "Configurations of Culture in North America."
7. R. Bunzel, op. cit., p. 901.
8. Ibid., pp. 879 ff.
9. Ibid., pp. 606 ff.
10. Ibid., pp. 516 ff.
11. Ibid., p. 521.
12. Ibid., pp. 943–945. Cf. also E. C. Parsons, *Notes on Zuñi*, Memoirs of of the American Anthropological Association, Lancaster, vol. IV, no. 3–4, 1917.
13. Linton-Dorsey, *The Thunder Ceremony of the Pawnee*, Chicago, p. 18.
14. Ibid., pp. 18–19.
15. Linton-Dorsey, *The Annual Ceremony of the Pawnee Medicine Men*, pp. 7–8.
16. Ibid., pp. 12–13.
17. P. Radin, *The Winnebago Tribe*, pp. 350–378.

Index

A CATALOGUE OF SELECTED DOVER BOOKS
IN ALL FIELDS OF INTEREST

A CATALOGUE OF SELECTED DOVER BOOKS IN ALL FIELDS OF INTEREST

CELESTIAL OBJECTS FOR COMMON TELESCOPES, T. W. Webb. The most used book in amateur astronomy: inestimable aid for locating and identifying nearly 4,000 celestial objects. Edited, updated by Margaret W. Mayall. 77 illustrations. Total of 645pp. 5⅜ x 8½.
20917-2, 20918-0 Pa., Two-vol. set $9.00

HISTORICAL STUDIES IN THE LANGUAGE OF CHEMISTRY, M. P. Crosland. The important part language has played in the development of chemistry from the symbolism of alchemy to the adoption of systematic nomenclature in 1892. ". . . wholeheartedly recommended,"—Science. 15 illustrations. 416pp. of text. 5⅝ x 8¼. 63702-6 Pa. $6.00

BURNHAM'S CELESTIAL HANDBOOK, Robert Burnham, Jr. Thorough, readable guide to the stars beyond our solar system. Exhaustive treatment, fully illustrated. Breakdown is alphabetical by constellation: Andromeda to Cetus in Vol. 1; Chamaeleon to Orion in Vol. 2; and Pavo to Vulpecula in Vol. 3. Hundreds of illustrations. Total of about 2000pp. 6⅛ x 9¼.
23567-X, 23568-8, 23673-0 Pa., Three-vol. set $26.85

THEORY OF WING SECTIONS: INCLUDING A SUMMARY OF AIRFOIL DATA, Ira H. Abbott and A. E. von Doenhoff. Concise compilation of subatomic aerodynamic characteristics of modern NASA wing sections, plus description of theory. 350pp. of tables. 693pp. 5⅜ x 8½.
60586-8 Pa. $7.00

DE RE METALLICA, Georgius Agricola. Translated by Herbert C. Hoover and Lou H. Hoover. The famous Hoover translation of greatest treatise on technological chemistry, engineering, geology, mining of early modern times (1556). All 289 original woodcuts. 638pp. 6¾ x 11.
60006-8 Clothbd. $17.95

THE ORIGIN OF CONTINENTS AND OCEANS, Alfred Wegener. One of the most influential, most controversial books in science, the classic statement for continental drift. Full 1966 translation of Wegener's final (1929) version. 64 illustrations. 246pp. 5⅜ x 8½. 61708-4 Pa. $4.50

THE PRINCIPLES OF PSYCHOLOGY, William James. Famous long course complete, unabridged. Stream of thought, time perception, memory, experimental methods; great work decades ahead of its time. Still valid, useful; read in many classes. 94 figures. Total of 1391pp. 5⅜ x 8½.
20381-6, 20382-4 Pa., Two-vol. set $13.00

THE SENSE OF BEAUTY, George Santayana. Masterfully written discussion of nature of beauty, materials of beauty, form, expression; art, literature, social sciences all involved. 168pp. 5⅜ x 8½.   20238-0 Pa. $2.50

ON THE IMPROVEMENT OF THE UNDERSTANDING, Benedict Spinoza. Also contains *Ethics, Correspondence,* all in excellent R. Elwes translation. Basic works on entry to philosophy, pantheism, exchange of ideas with great contemporaries. 402pp. 5⅜ x 8½.   20250-X Pa. $4.50

THE TRAGIC SENSE OF LIFE, Miguel de Unamuno. Acknowledged masterpiece of existential literature, one of most important books of 20th century. Introduction by Madariaga. 367pp. 5⅜ x 8½.
20257-7 Pa. $4.50

THE GUIDE FOR THE PERPLEXED, Moses Maimonides. Great classic of medieval Judaism attempts to reconcile revealed religion (Pentateuch, commentaries) with Aristotelian philosophy. Important historically, still relevant in problems. Unabridged Friedlander translation. Total of 473pp. 5⅜ x 8½.   20351-4 Pa. $6.00

THE I CHING (THE BOOK OF CHANGES), translated by James Legge. Complete translation of basic text plus appendices by Confucius, and Chinese commentary of most penetrating divination manual ever prepared. Indispensable to study of early Oriental civilizations, to modern inquiring reader. 448pp. 5⅜ x 8½.   21062-6 Pa. $4.00

THE EGYPTIAN BOOK OF THE DEAD, E. A. Wallis Budge. Complete reproduction of Ani's papyrus, finest ever found. Full hieroglyphic text, interlinear transliteration, word for word translation, smooth translation. Basic work, for Egyptology, for modern study of psychic matters. Total of 533pp. 6½ x 9¼. (Available in U.S. only)   21866-X Pa. $5.95

THE GODS OF THE EGYPTIANS, E. A. Wallis Budge. Never excelled for richness, fullness: all gods, goddesses, demons, mythical figures of Ancient Egypt; their legends, rites, incarnations, variations, powers, etc. Many hieroglyphic texts cited. Over 225 illustrations, plus 6 color plates. Total of 988pp. 6⅛ x 9¼. (Available in U.S. only)
22055-9, 22056-7 Pa., Two-vol. set $12.00

THE ENGLISH AND SCOTTISH POPULAR BALLADS, Francis J. Child. Monumental, still unsuperseded; all known variants of Child ballads, commentary on origins, literary references, Continental parallels, other features. Added: papers by G. L. Kittredge, W. M. Hart. Total of 2761pp. 6½ x 9¼.
21409-5, 21410-9, 21411-7, 21412-5, 21413-3 Pa., Five-vol. set $37.50

CORAL GARDENS AND THEIR MAGIC, Bronsilaw Malinowski. Classic study of the methods of tilling the soil and of agricultural rites in the Trobriand Islands of Melanesia. Author is one of the most important figures in the field of modern social anthropology. 143 illustrations. Indexes. Total of 911pp. of text. 5⅝ x 8¼. (Available in U.S. only)
23597-1 Pa. $12.95

THE COMPLETE BOOK OF DOLL MAKING AND COLLECTING, Catherine Christopher. Instructions, patterns for dozens of dolls, from rag doll on up to elaborate, historically accurate figures. Mould faces, sew clothing, make doll houses, etc. Also collecting information. Many illustrations. 288pp. 6 x 9. 22066-4 Pa. $4.50

THE DAGUERREOTYPE IN AMERICA, Beaumont Newhall. Wonderful portraits, 1850's townscapes, landscapes; full text plus 104 photographs. The basic book. Enlarged 1976 edition. 272pp. 8¼ x 11¼. 23322-7 Pa. $7.95

CRAFTSMAN HOMES, Gustav Stickley. 296 architectural drawings, floor plans, and photographs illustrate 40 different kinds of "Mission-style" homes from *The Craftsman* (1901-16), voice of American style of simplicity and organic harmony. Thorough coverage of Craftsman idea in text and picture, now collector's item. 224pp. 8⅛ x 11. 23791-5 Pa. $6.00

PEWTER-WORKING: INSTRUCTIONS AND PROJECTS, Burl N. Osborn. & Gordon O. Wilber. Introduction to pewter-working for amateur craftsman. History and characteristics of pewter; tools, materials, step-by-step instructions. Photos, line drawings, diagrams. Total of 160pp. 7⅞ x 10¾. 23786-9 Pa. $3.50

THE GREAT CHICAGO FIRE, edited by David Lowe. 10 dramatic, eyewitness accounts of the 1871 disaster, including one of the aftermath and rebuilding, plus 70 contemporary photographs and illustrations of the ruins—courthouse, Palmer House, Great Central Depot, etc. Introduction by David Lowe. 87pp. 8¼ x 11. 23771-0 Pa. $4.00

SILHOUETTES: A PICTORIAL ARCHIVE OF VARIED ILLUSTRATIONS, edited by Carol Belanger Grafton. Over 600 silhouettes from the 18th to 20th centuries include profiles and full figures of men and women, children, birds and animals, groups and scenes, nature, ships, an alphabet. Dozens of uses for commercial artists and craftspeople. 144pp. 8⅜ x 11¼. 23781-8 Pa. $4.00

ANIMALS: 1,419 COPYRIGHT-FREE ILLUSTRATIONS OF MAMMALS, BIRDS, FISH, INSECTS, ETC., edited by Jim Harter. Clear wood engravings present, in extremely lifelike poses, over 1,000 species of animals. One of the most extensive copyright-free pictorial sourcebooks of its kind. Captions. Index. 284pp. 9 x 12. 23766-4 Pa. $7.95

INDIAN DESIGNS FROM ANCIENT ECUADOR, Frederick W. Shaffer. 282 original designs by pre-Columbian Indians of Ecuador (500-1500 A.D.). Designs include people, mammals, birds, reptiles, fish, plants, heads, geometric designs. Use as is or alter for advertising, textiles, leathercraft, etc. Introduction. 95pp. 8¾ x 11¼. 23764-8 Pa. $3.50

SZIGETI ON THE VIOLIN, Joseph Szigeti. Genial, loosely structured tour by premier violinist, featuring a pleasant mixture of reminiscenes, insights into great music and musicians, innumerable tips for practicing violinists. 385 musical passages. 256pp. 5⅝ x 8¼. 23763-X Pa. $3.50

TONE POEMS, SERIES II: TILL EULENSPIEGELS LUSTIGE STREICHE, ALSO SPRACH ZARATHUSTRA, AND EIN HELDEN-LEBEN, Richard Strauss. Three important orchestral works, including very popular *Till Eulenspiegel's Marry Pranks,* reproduced in full score from original editions. Study score. 315pp. 9⅜ x 12¼. (Available in U.S. only)
23755-9 Pa. $7.50

TONE POEMS, SERIES I: DON JUAN, TOD UND VERKLARUNG AND DON QUIXOTE, Richard Strauss. Three of the most often performed and recorded works in entire orchestral repertoire, reproduced in full score from original editions. Study score. 286pp. 9⅜ x 12¼. (Available in U.S. only)
23754-0 Pa. $7.50

11 LATE STRING QUARTETS, Franz Joseph Haydn. The form which Haydn defined and "brought to perfection." *(Grove's).* 11 string quartets in complete score, his last and his best. The first in a projected series of the complete Haydn string quartets. Reliable modern Eulenberg edition, otherwise difficult to obtain. 320pp. 8⅜ x 11¼. (Available in U.S. only)
23753-2 Pa. $6.95

FOURTH, FIFTH AND SIXTH SYMPHONIES IN FULL SCORE, Peter Ilyitch Tchaikovsky. Complete orchestral scores of Symphony No. 4 in F Minor, Op. 36; Symphony No. 5 in E Minor, Op. 64; Symphony No. 6 in B Minor, "Pathetique," Op. 74. Bretikopf & Hartel eds. Study score. 480pp. 9⅜ x 12¼.
23861-X Pa. $10.95

THE MARRIAGE OF FIGARO: COMPLETE SCORE, Wolfgang A. Mozart. Finest comic opera ever written. Full score, not to be confused with piano renderings. Peters edition. Study score. 448pp. 9⅜ x 12¼. (Available in U.S. only)
23751-6 Pa. $11.95

"IMAGE" ON THE ART AND EVOLUTION OF THE FILM, edited by Marshall Deutelbaum. Pioneering book brings together for first time 38 groundbreaking articles on early silent films from *Image* and 263 illustrations newly shot from rare prints in the collection of the International Museum of Photography. A landmark work. Index. 256pp. 8¼ x 11.
23777-X Pa. $8.95

AROUND-THE-WORLD COOKY BOOK, Lois Lintner Sumption and Marguerite Lintner Ashbrook. 373 cooky and frosting recipes from 28 countries (America, Austria, China, Russia, Italy, etc.) include Viennese kisses, rice wafers, London strips, lady fingers, hony, sugar spice, maple cookies, etc. Clear instructions. All tested. 38 drawings. 182pp. 5⅜ x 8.
23802-4 Pa. $2.50

THE ART NOUVEAU STYLE, edited by Roberta Waddell. 579 rare photographs, not available elsewhere, of works in jewelry, metalwork, glass, ceramics, textiles, architecture and furniture by 175 artists—Mucha, Seguy, Lalique, Tiffany, Gaudin, Hohlwein, Saarinen, and many others. 288pp. 8⅜ x 11¼.
23515-7 Pa. $6.95

PRINCIPLES OF ORCHESTRATION, Nikolay Rimsky-Korsakov. Great classical orchestrator provides fundamentals of tonal resonance, progression of parts, voice and orchestra, tutti effects, much else in major document. 330pp. of musical excerpts. 489pp. 6½ x 9¼.   21266-1 Pa. $6.00

TRISTAN UND ISOLDE, Richard Wagner. Full orchestral score with complete instrumentation. Do not confuse with piano reduction. Commentary by Felix Mottl, great Wagnerian conductor and scholar. Study score. 655pp. 8⅛ x 11.   22915-7 Pa. $12.50

REQUIEM IN FULL SCORE, Giuseppe Verdi. Immensely popular with choral groups and music lovers. Republication of edition published by C. F. Peters, Leipzig, n. d. German frontmaker in English translation. Glossary. Text in Latin. Study score. 204pp. 9⅜ x 12¼.
23682-X Pa. $6.00

COMPLETE CHAMBER MUSIC FOR STRINGS, Felix Mendelssohn. All of Mendelssohn's chamber music: Octet, 2 Quintets, 6 Quartets, and Four Pieces for String Quartet. (Nothing with piano is included). Complete works· edition (1874-7). Study score. 283 pp. 9⅜ x 12¼.
23679-X Pa. $6.95

POPULAR SONGS OF NINETEENTH-CENTURY AMERICA, edited by Richard Jackson. 64 most important songs: "Old Oaken Bucket," "Arkansas Traveler," "Yellow Rose of Texas," etc. Authentic original sheet music, full introduction and commentaries. 290pp. 9 x 12.   23270-0 Pa. $6.00

COLLECTED PIANO WORKS, Scott Joplin. Edited by Vera Brodsky Lawrence. Practically all of Joplin's piano works—rags, two-steps, marches, waltzes, etc., 51 works in all. Extensive introduction by Rudi Blesh. Total of 345pp. 9 x 12.   23106-2 Pa. $14.95

BASIC PRINCIPLES OF CLASSICAL BALLET, Agrippina Vaganova. Great Russian theoretician, teacher explains methods for teaching classical ballet; incorporates best from French, Italian, Russian schools. 118 illustrations. 175pp. 5⅜ x 8½.   22036-2 Pa. $2.50

CHINESE CHARACTERS, L. Wieger. Rich analysis of 2300 characters according to traditional systems into primitives. Historical-semantic analysis to phonetics (Classical Mandarin) and radicals. 820pp. 6⅛ x 9¼.
21321-8 Pa. $10.00

EGYPTIAN LANGUAGE: EASY LESSONS IN EGYPTIAN HIERO-GLYPHICS, E. A. Wallis Budge. Foremost Egyptologist offers Egyptian grammar, explanation of hieroglyphics, many reading texts, dictionary of symbols. 246pp. 5 x 7½. (Available in U.S. only)
21394-3 Clothbd. $7.50

AN ETYMOLOGICAL DICTIONARY OF MODERN ENGLISH, Ernest Weekley. Richest, fullest work, by foremost British lexicographer. Detailed word histories. Inexhaustible. Do not confuse this with Concise Etymological Dictionary, which is abridged. Total of 856pp. 6½ x 9¼.
21873-2, 21874-0 Pa., Two-vol. set $12.00

HISTORY OF BACTERIOLOGY, William Bulloch. The only comprehensive history of bacteriology from the beginnings through the 19th century. Special emphasis is given to biography-Leeuwenhoek, etc. Brief accounts of 350 bacteriologists form a separate section. No clearer, fuller study, suitable to scientists and general readers, has yet been written. 52 illustrations. 448pp. 5⅝ x 8¼.   23761-3 Pa. $6.50

THE COMPLETE NONSENSE OF EDWARD LEAR, Edward Lear. All nonsense limericks, zany alphabets, Owl and Pussycat, songs, nonsense botany, etc., illustrated by Lear. Total of 321pp. 5⅜ x 8½. (Available in U.S. only)   20167-8 Pa. $3.00

INGENIOUS MATHEMATICAL PROBLEMS AND METHODS, Louis A. Graham. Sophisticated material from Graham Dial, applied and pure; stresses solution methods. Logic, number theory, networks, inversions, etc. 237pp. 5⅜ x 8½.   20545-2 Pa. $3.50

BEST MATHEMATICAL PUZZLES OF SAM LOYD, edited by Martin Gardner. Bizarre, original, whimsical puzzles by America's greatest puzzler. From fabulously rare Cyclopedia, including famous 14-15 puzzles, the Horse of a Different Color, 115 more. Elementary math. 150 illustrations. 167pp. 5⅜ x 8½.   20498-7 Pa. $2.75

THE BASIS OF COMBINATION IN CHESS, J. du Mont. Easy-to-follow, instructive book on elements of combination play, with chapters on each piece and every powerful combination team—two knights, bishop and knight, rook and bishop, etc. 250 diagrams. 218pp. 5⅜ x 8½. (Available in U.S. only)   23644-7 Pa. $3.50

MODERN CHESS STRATEGY, Ludek Pachman. The use of the queen, the active king, exchanges, pawn play, the center, weak squares, etc. Section on rook alone worth price of the book. Stress on the moderns. Often considered the most important book on strategy. 314pp. 5⅜ x 8½.
                    20290-9 Pa. $4.50

LASKER'S MANUAL OF CHESS, Dr. Emanuel Lasker. Great world champion offers very thorough coverage of all aspects of chess. Combinations, position play, openings, end game, aesthetics of chess, philosophy of struggle, much more. Filled with analyzed games. 390pp. 5⅜ x 8½.
                    20640-8 Pa. $5.00

500 MASTER GAMES OF CHESS, S. Tartakower, J. du Mont. Vast collection of great chess games from 1798-1938, with much material nowhere else readily available. Fully annotated, arranged by opening for easier study. 664pp. 5⅜ x 8½.   23208-5 Pa. $7.50

A GUIDE TO CHESS ENDINGS, Dr. Max Euwe, David Hooper. One of the finest modern works on chess endings. Thorough analysis of the most frequently encountered endings by former world champion. 331 examples, each with diagram. 248pp. 5⅜ x 8½.   23332-4 Pa. $3.50

THE EARLY WORK OF AUBREY BEARDSLEY, Aubrey Beardsley. 157 plates, 2 in color: *Manon Lescaut, Madame Bovary, Morte Darthur, Salome,* other. Introduction by H. Marillier. 182pp. 8⅛ x 11. 21816-3 Pa. $4.50

THE LATER WORK OF AUBREY BEARDSLEY, Aubrey Beardsley. Exotic masterpieces of full maturity: *Venus and Tannhauser, Lysistrata, Rape of the Lock, Volpone,* Savoy material, etc. 174 plates, 2 in color. 186pp. 8⅛ x 11. 21817-1 Pa. $4.50

THOMAS NAST'S CHRISTMAS DRAWINGS, Thomas Nast. Almost all Christmas drawings by creator of image of Santa Claus as we know it, and one of America's foremost illustrators and political cartoonists. 66 illustrations. 3 illustrations in color on covers. 96pp. 8⅜ x 11¼. 23660-9 Pa. $3.50

THE DORÉ ILLUSTRATIONS FOR DANTE'S DIVINE COMEDY, Gustave Doré. All 135 plates from Inferno, Purgatory, Paradise; fantastic tortures, infernal landscapes, celestial wonders. Each plate with appropriate (translated) verses. 141pp. 9 x 12. 23231-X Pa. $4.50

DORÉ'S ILLUSTRATIONS FOR RABELAIS, Gustave Doré. 252 striking illustrations of *Gargantua and Pantagruel* books by foremost 19th-century illustrator. Including 60 plates, 192 delightful smaller illustrations. 153pp. 9 x 12. 23656-0 Pa. $5.00

LONDON: A PILGRIMAGE, Gustave Doré, Blanchard Jerrold. Squalor, riches, misery, beauty of mid-Victorian metropolis; 55 wonderful plates, 125 other illustrations, full social, cultural text by Jerrold. 191pp. of text. 9⅜ x 12¼. 22306-X Pa. $6.00

THE RIME OF THE ANCIENT MARINER, Gustave Doré, S. T. Coleridge. Dore's finest work, 34 plates capture moods, subtleties of poem. Full text. Introduction by Millicent Rose. 77pp. 9¼ x 12. 22305-1 Pa. $3.50

THE DORE BIBLE ILLUSTRATIONS, Gustave Doré. All wonderful, detailed plates: Adam and Eve, Flood, Babylon, Life of Jesus, etc. Brief King James text with each plate. Introduction by Millicent Rose. 241 plates. 241pp. 9 x 12. 23004-X Pa. $6.00

THE COMPLETE ENGRAVINGS, ETCHINGS AND DRYPOINTS OF ALBRECHT DURER. "Knight, Death and Devil"; "Melencolia," and more—all Dürer's known works in all three media, including 6 works formerly attributed to him. 120 plates. 235pp. 8⅜ x 11¼. 22851-7 Pa. $6.50

MAXIMILIAN'S TRIUMPHAL ARCH, Albrecht Dürer and others. Incredible monument of woodcut art: 8 foot high elaborate arch—heraldic figures, humans, battle scenes, fantastic elements—that you can assemble yourself. Printed on one side, layout for assembly. 143pp. 11 x 16. 21451-6 Pa. $5.00

THE COMPLETE WOODCUTS OF ALBRECHT DURER, edited by Dr. W. Kurth. 346 in all: "Old Testament," "St. Jerome," "Passion," "Life of Virgin," Apocalypse," many others. Introduction by Campbell Dodgson. 285pp. 8½ x 12¼. 21097-9 Pa. $7.50

DRAWINGS OF ALBRECHT DURER, edited by Heinrich Wolfflin. 81 plates show development from youth to full style. Many favorites; many new. Introduction by Alfred Werner. 96pp. 8⅛ x 11. 22352-3 Pa. $5.00

THE HUMAN FIGURE, Albrecht Dürer. Experiments in various techniques—stereometric, progressive proportional, and others. Also life studies that rank among finest ever done. Complete reprinting of *Dresden Sketchbook.* 170 plates. 355pp. 8⅜ x 11¼. 21042-1 Pa. $7.95

OF THE JUST SHAPING OF LETTERS, Albrecht Dürer. Renaissance artist explains design of Roman majuscules by geometry, also Gothic lower and capitals. Grolier Club edition. 43pp. 7⅞ x 10¾ 21306-4 Pa. $8.00

TEN BOOKS ON ARCHITECTURE, Vitruvius. The most important book ever written on architecture. Early Roman aesthetics, technology, classical orders, site selection, all other aspects. Stands behind everything since. Morgan translation. 331pp. 5⅜ x 8½. 20645-9 Pa. $4.00

THE FOUR BOOKS OF ARCHITECTURE, Andrea Palladio. 16th-century classic responsible for Palladian movement and style. Covers classical architectural remains, Renaissance revivals, classical orders, etc. 1738 Ware English edition. Introduction by A. Placzek. 216 plates. 110pp. of text. 9½ x 12¾. 21308-0 Pa. $8.95

HORIZONS, Norman Bel Geddes. Great industrialist stage designer, "father of streamlining," on application of aesthetics to transportation, amusement, architecture, etc. 1932 prophetic account; function, theory, specific projects. 222 illustrations. 312pp. 7⅞ x 10¾. 23514-9 Pa. $6.95

FRANK LLOYD WRIGHT'S FALLINGWATER, Donald Hoffmann. Full, illustrated story of conception and building of Wright's masterwork at Bear Run, Pa. 100 photographs of site, construction, and details of completed structure. 112pp. 9¼ x 10. 23671-4 Pa. $5.50

THE ELEMENTS OF DRAWING, John Ruskin. Timeless classic by great Viltorian; starts with basic ideas, works through more difficult. Many practical exercises. 48 illustrations. Introduction by Lawrence Campbell. 228pp. 5⅜ x 8½. 22730-8 Pa. $2.75

GIST OF ART, John Sloan. Greatest modern American teacher, Art Students League, offers innumerable hints, instructions, guided comments to help you in painting. Not a formal course. 46 illustrations. Introduction by Helen Sloan. 200pp. 5⅜ x 8½. 23435-5 Pa. $4.00

"OSCAR" OF THE WALDORF'S COOKBOOK, Oscar Tschirky. Famous American chef reveals 3455 recipes that made Waldorf great; cream of French, German, American cooking, in all categories. Full instructions, easy home use. 1896 edition. 907pp. 6⅝ x 9⅜. 20790-0 Clothbd. $15.00

COOKING WITH BEER, Carole Fahy. Beer has as superb an effect on food as wine, and at fraction of cost. Over 250 recipes for appetizers, soups, main dishes, desserts, breads, etc. Index. 144pp. 5⅜ x 8½. (Available in U.S. only) 23661-7 Pa. $2.50

STEWS AND RAGOUTS, Kay Shaw Nelson. This international cookbook offers wide range of 108 recipes perfect for everyday, special occasions, meals-in-themselves, main dishes. Economical, nutritious, easy-to-prepare: goulash, Irish stew, boeuf bourguignon, etc. Index. 134pp. 5⅜ x 8½. 23662-5 Pa. $2.50

DELICIOUS MAIN COURSE DISHES, Marian Tracy. Main courses are the most important part of any meal. These 200 nutritious, economical recipes from around the world make every meal a delight. "I . . . have found it so useful in my own household,"—N.Y. Times. Index. 219pp. 5⅜ x 8½. 23664-1 Pa. $3.00

FIVE ACRES AND INDEPENDENCE, Maurice G. Kains. Great back-to-the-land classic explains basics of self-sufficient farming: economics, plants, crops, animals, orchards, soils, land selection, host of other necessary things. Do not confuse with skimpy faddist literature; Kains was one of America's greatest agriculturalists. 397pp. 5⅜ x 8½. 20974-1 Pa. $3.95

A PRACTICAL GUIDE FOR THE BEGINNING FARMER, Herbert Jacobs. Basic, extremely useful first book for anyone thinking about moving to the country and starting a farm. Simpler than Kains, with greater emphasis on country living in general. 246pp. 5⅜ x 8½. 23675-7 Pa. $3.50

A GARDEN OF PLEASANT FLOWERS (PARADISI IN SOLE: PARADISUS TERRESTRIS), John Parkinson. Complete, unabridged reprint of first (1629) edition of earliest great English book on gardens and gardening. More than 1000 plants & flowers of Elizabethan, Jacobean garden fully described, most with woodcut illustrations. Botanically very reliable, a "speaking garden" of exceeding charm. 812 illustrations. 628pp. 8½ x 12¼. 23392-8 Clothbd. $25.00

ACKERMANN'S COSTUME PLATES, Rudolph Ackermann. Selection of 96 plates from the Repository of Arts, best published source of costume for English fashion during the early 19th century. 12 plates also in color. Captions, glossary and introduction by editor Stella Blum. Total of 120pp. 8⅜ x 11¼. 23690-0 Pa. $4.50

UNCLE SILAS, J. Sheridan LeFanu. Victorian Gothic mystery novel, considered by many best of period, even better than Collins or Dickens. Wonderful psychological terror. Introduction by Frederick Shroyer. 436pp. 5⅜ x 8½.   21715-9 Pa. $6.00

JURGEN, James Branch Cabell. The great erotic fantasy of the 1920's that delighted thousands, shocked thousands more. Full final text, Lane edition with 13 plates by Frank Pape. 346pp. 5⅜ x 8½.
                                                          23507-6 Pa. $4.50

THE CLAVERINGS, Anthony Trollope. Major novel, chronicling aspects of British Victorian society, personalities. Reprint of Cornhill serialization, 16 plates by M. Edwards; first reprint of full text. Introduction by Norman Donaldson. 412pp. 5⅜ x 8½.   23464-9 Pa. $5.00

KEPT IN THE DARK, Anthony Trollope. Unusual short novel about Victorian morality and abnormal psychology by the great English author. Probably the first American publication. Frontispiece by Sir John Millais. 92pp. 6½ x 9¼.   23609-9 Pa. $2.50

RALPH THE HEIR, Anthony Trollope. Forgotten tale of illegitimacy, inheritance. Master novel of Trollope's later years. Victorian country estates, clubs, Parliament, fox hunting, world of fully realized characters. Reprint of 1871 edition. 12 illustrations by F. A. Faser. 434pp. of text. 5⅜ x 8½.   23642-0 Pa. $5.00

YEKL and THE IMPORTED BRIDEGROOM AND OTHER STORIES OF THE NEW YORK GHETTO, Abraham Cahan. Film *Hester Street* based on *Yekl* (1896). Novel, other stories among first about Jewish immigrants of N.Y.'s East Side. Highly praised by W. D. Howells—Cahan "a new star of realism." New introduction by Bernard G. Richards. 240pp. 5⅜ x 8½.   22427-9 Pa. $3.50

THE HIGH PLACE, James Branch Cabell. Great fantasy writer's enchanting comedy of disenchantment set in 18th-century France. Considered by some critics to be even better than his famous *Jurgen*. 10 illustrations and numerous vignettes by noted fantasy artist Frank C. Pape. 320pp. 5⅜ x 8½.   23670-6 Pa. $4.00

ALICE'S ADVENTURES UNDER GROUND, Lewis Carroll. Facsimile of ms. Carroll gave Alice Liddell in 1864. Different in many ways from final Alice. Handlettered, illustrated by Carroll. Introduction by Martin Gardner. 128pp. 5⅜ x 8½.   21482-6 Pa. $2.00

FAVORITE ANDREW LANG FAIRY TALE BOOKS IN MANY COLORS, Andrew Lang. The four Lang favorites in a boxed set—the complete *Red, Green, Yellow* and *Blue* Fairy Books. 164 stories; 439 illustrations by Lancelot Speed, Henry Ford and G. P. Jacomb Hood. Total of about 1500pp. 5⅜ x 8½.   23407-X Boxed set, Pa. $14.95

THE AMERICAN SENATOR, Anthony Trollope. Little known, long unavailable Trollope novel on a grand scale. Here are humorous comment on American vs. English culture, and stunning portrayal of a heroine/villainess. Superb evocation of Victorian village life. 561pp. 5⅜ x 8½.
23801-6 Pa. $6.00

WAS IT MURDER? James Hilton. The author of *Lost Horizon* and *Goodbye, Mr. Chips* wrote one detective novel (under a pen-name) which was quickly forgotten and virtually lost, even at the height of Hilton's fame. This edition brings it back—a finely crafted public school puzzle resplendent with Hilton's stylish atmosphere. A thoroughly English thriller by the creator of Shangri-la. 252pp. 5⅜ x 8. (Available in U.S. only)
23774-5 Pa. $3.00

CENTRAL PARK: A PHOTOGRAPHIC GUIDE, Victor Laredo and Henry Hope Reed. 121 superb photographs show dramatic views of Central Park: Bethesda Fountain, Cleopatra's Needle, Sheep Meadow, the Blockhouse, plus people engaged in many park activities: ice skating, bike riding, etc. Captions by former Curator of Central Park, Henry Hope Reed, provide historical view, changes, etc. Also photos of N.Y. landmarks on park's periphery. 96pp. 8½ x 11. 23750-8 Pa. $4.50

NANTUCKET IN THE NINETEENTH CENTURY, Clay Lancaster. 180 rare photographs, stereographs, maps, drawings and floor plans recreate unique American island society. Authentic scenes of shipwreck, lighthouses, streets, homes are arranged in geographic sequence to provide walking-tour guide to old Nantucket existing today. Introduction, captions. 160pp. 8⅞ x 11¾. 23747-8 Pa. $6.95

STONE AND MAN: A PHOTOGRAPHIC EXPLORATION, Andreas Feininger. 106 photographs by *Life* photographer Feininger portray man's deep passion for stone through the ages. Stonehenge-like megaliths, fortified towns, sculpted marble and crumbling tenements show textures, beauties, fascination. 128pp. 9¼ x 10¾. 23756-7 Pa. $5.95

CIRCLES, A MATHEMATICAL VIEW, D. Pedoe. Fundamental aspects of college geometry, non-Euclidean geometry, and other branches of mathematics: representing circle by point. Poincare model, isoperimetric property, etc. Stimulating recreational reading. 66 figures. 96pp. 5⅝ x 8¼.
63698-4 Pa. $2.75

THE DISCOVERY OF NEPTUNE, Morton Grosser. Dramatic scientific history of the investigations leading up to the actual discovery of the eighth planet of our solar system. Lucid, well-researched book by well-known historian of science. 172pp. 5⅜ x 8½. 23726-5 Pa. $3.00

THE DEVIL'S DICTIONARY. Ambrose Bierce. Barbed, bitter, brilliant witticisms in the form of a dictionary. Best, most ferocious satire America has produced. 145pp. 5⅜ x 8½. 20487-1 Pa. $2.00

THE PHILOSOPHY OF HISTORY, Georg W. Hegel. Great classic of Western thought develops concept that history is not chance but a rational process, the evolution of freedom. 457pp. 5⅜ x 8½.   20112-0 Pa. $4.50

LANGUAGE, TRUTH AND LOGIC, Alfred J. Ayer. Famous, clear introduction to Vienna, Cambridge schools of Logical Positivism. Role of philosophy, elimination of metaphysics, nature of analysis, etc. 160pp. 5⅜ x 8½. (Available in U.S. only)   20010-8 Pa. $2.00

A PREFACE TO LOGIC, Morris R. Cohen. Great City College teacher in renowned, easily followed exposition of formal logic, probability, values, logic and world order and similar topics; no previous background needed. 209pp. 5⅜ x 8½.   23517-3 Pa. $3.50

REASON AND NATURE, Morris R. Cohen. Brilliant analysis of reason and its multitudinous ramifications by charismatic teacher. Interdisciplinary, synthesizing work widely praised when it first appeared in 1931. Second (1953) edition. Indexes. 496pp. 5⅜ x 8½.   23633-1 Pa. $6.50

AN ESSAY CONCERNING HUMAN UNDERSTANDING, John Locke. The only complete edition of enormously important classic, with authoritative editorial material by A. C. Fraser. Total of 1176pp. 5⅜ x 8½.
20530-4, 20531-2 Pa., Two-vol. set $14.00

HANDBOOK OF MATHEMATICAL FUNCTIONS WITH FORMULAS, GRAPHS, AND MATHEMATICAL TABLES, edited by Milton Abramowitz and Irene A. Stegun. Vast compendium: 29 sets of tables, some to as high as 20 places. 1,046pp. 8 x 10½.   61272-4 Pa. $14.95

MATHEMATICS FOR THE PHYSICAL SCIENCES, Herbert S. Wilf. Highly acclaimed work offers clear presentations of vector spaces and matrices, orthogonal functions, roots of polynomial equations, conformal mapping, calculus of variations, etc. Knowledge of theory of functions of real and complex variables is assumed. Exercises and solutions. Index. 284pp. 5⅝ x 8¼.   63635-6 Pa. $5.00

THE PRINCIPLE OF RELATIVITY, Albert Einstein et al. Eleven most important original papers on special and general theories. Seven by Einstein, two by Lorentz, one each by Minkowski and Weyl. All translated, unabridged. 216pp. 5⅜ x 8½.   60081-5 Pa. $3.00

THERMODYNAMICS, Enrico Fermi. A classic of modern science. Clear, organized treatment of systems, first and second laws, entropy, thermodynamic potentials, gaseous reactions, dilute solutions, entropy constant. No math beyond calculus required. Problems. 160pp. 5⅜ x 8½.
60361-X Pa. $3.00

ELEMENTARY MECHANICS OF FLUIDS, Hunter Rouse. Classic undergraduate text widely considered to be far better than many later books. Ranges from fluid velocity and acceleration to role of compressibility in fluid motion. Numerous examples, questions, problems. 224 illustrations. 376pp. 5⅝ x 8¼.   63699-2 Pa. $5.00

HOUSEHOLD STORIES BY THE BROTHERS GRIMM. All the great Grimm stories: "Rumpelstiltskin," "Snow White," "Hansel and Gretel," etc., with 114 illustrations by Walter Crane. 269pp. 5⅜ x 8½.
21080-4 Pa. $3.00

SLEEPING BEAUTY, illustrated by Arthur Rackham. Perhaps the fullest, most delightful version ever, told by C. S. Evans. Rackham's best work. 49 illustrations. 110pp. 7⅞ x 10¾. 22756-1 Pa. $2.50

AMERICAN FAIRY TALES, L. Frank Baum. Young cowboy lassoes Father Time; dummy in Mr. Floman's department store window comes to life; and 10 other fairy tales. 41 illustrations by N. P. Hall, Harry Kennedy, Ike Morgan, and Ralph Gardner. 209pp. 5⅜ x 8½. 23643-9 Pa. $3.00

THE WONDERFUL WIZARD OF OZ, L. Frank Baum. Facsimile in full color of America's finest children's classic. Introduction by Martin Gardner. 143 illustrations by W. W. Denslow. 267pp. 5⅜ x 8½.
20691-2 Pa. $3.50

THE TALE OF PETER RABBIT, Beatrix Potter. The inimitable Peter's terrifying adventure in Mr. McGregor's garden, with all 27 wonderful, full-color Potter illustrations. 55pp. 4¼ x 5½. (Available in U.S. only)
22827-4 Pa. $1.25

THE STORY OF KING ARTHUR AND HIS KNIGHTS, Howard Pyle. Finest children's version of life of King Arthur. 48 illustrations by Pyle. 131pp. 6⅛ x 9¼. 21445-1 Pa. $4.95

CARUSO'S CARICATURES, Enrico Caruso. Great tenor's remarkable caricatures of self, fellow musicians, composers, others. Toscanini, Puccini, Farrar, etc. Impish, cutting, insightful. 473 illustrations. Preface by M. Sisca. 217pp. 8⅜ x 11¼. 23528-9 Pa. $6.95

PERSONAL NARRATIVE OF A PILGRIMAGE TO ALMADINAH AND MECCAH, Richard Burton. Great travel classic by remarkably colorful personality. Burton, disguised as a Moroccan, visited sacred shrines of Islam, narrowly escaping death. Wonderful observations of Islamic life, customs, personalities. 47 illustrations. Total of 959pp. 5⅜ x 8½.
21217-3, 21218-1 Pa., Two-vol. set $12.00

INCIDENTS OF TRAVEL IN YUCATAN, John L. Stephens. Classic (1843) exploration of jungles of Yucatan, looking for evidences of Maya civilization. Travel adventures, Mexican and Indian culture, etc. Total of 669pp. 5⅜ x 8½. 20926-1, 20927-X Pa., Two-vol. set $7.90

AMERICAN LITERARY AUTOGRAPHS FROM WASHINGTON IRVING TO HENRY JAMES, Herbert Cahoon, et al. Letters, poems, manuscripts of Hawthorne, Thoreau, Twain, Alcott, Whitman, 67 other prominent American authors. Reproductions, full transcripts and commentary. Plus checklist of all American Literary Autographs in The Pierpont Morgan Library. Printed on exceptionally high-quality paper. 136 illustrations. 212pp. 9⅛ x 12¼. 23548-3 Pa. $7.95

AMERICAN ANTIQUE FURNITURE, Edgar G. Miller, Jr. The basic coverage of all American furniture before 1840: chapters per item chronologically cover all types of furniture, with more than 2100 photos. Total of 1106pp. 7⅞ x 10¾.   21599-7, 21600-4 Pa., Two-vol. set $17.90

ILLUSTRATED GUIDE TO SHAKER FURNITURE, Robert Meader. Director, Shaker Museum, Old Chatham, presents up-to-date coverage of all furniture and appurtenances, with much on local styles not available elsewhere. 235 photos. 146pp. 9 x 12.   22819-3 Pa. $5.00

ORIENTAL RUGS, ANTIQUE AND MODERN, Walter A. Hawley. Persia, Turkey, Caucasus, Central Asia, China, other traditions. Best general survey of all aspects: styles and periods, manufacture, uses, symbols and their interpretation, and identification. 96 illustrations, 11 in color. 320pp. 6⅛ x 9¼.   22366-3 Pa. $6.95

CHINESE POTTERY AND PORCELAIN, R. L. Hobson. Detailed descriptions and analyses by former Keeper of the Department of Oriental Antiquities and Ethnography at the British Museum. Covers hundreds of pieces from primitive times to 1915. Still the standard text for most periods. 136 plates, 40 in full color. Total of 750pp. 5⅜ x 8½.
23253-0 Pa. $10.00

THE WARES OF THE MING DYNASTY, R. L. Hobson. Foremost scholar examines and illustrates many varieties of Ming (1368-1644). Famous blue and white, polychrome, lesser-known styles and shapes. 117 illustrations, 9 full color, of outstanding pieces. Total of 263pp. 6⅛ x 9¼. (Available in U.S. only)
23652-8 Pa. $6.00

Prices subject to change without notice.

Available at your book dealer or write for free catalogue to Dept. GI, Dover Publications, Inc., 180 Varick St., N.Y., N.Y. 10014. Dover publishes more than 175 books each year on science, elementary and advanced mathematics, biology, music, art, literary history, social sciences and other areas.